RESEARCH DESIGN

Also Available

Handbook of Emergent Methods
Edited by Sharlene Nagy Hesse-Biber and Patricia Leavy

Method Meets Art, Second Edition:
Arts-Based Research Practice
Patricia Leavy

Forthcoming

Handbook of Arts-Based Research
Edited by Patricia Leavy

Research Design

Quantitative,
Qualitative, Mixed Methods,
Arts-Based, and Community-Based
Participatory Research Approaches

PATRICIA LEAVY

THE GUILFORD PRESS
New York   London

Copyright © 2017 The Guilford Press
A Division of Guilford Publications, Inc.
370 Seventh Avenue, Suite 1200, New York, NY 10001
www.guilford.com

Printed in the United States of America

This book is printed on acid-free paper.

Last digit is print number: 9   8   7   6   5

Library of Congress Cataloging-in-Publication Data is available from
the publisher.

ISBN 978-1-4625-1438-0 (paper) – ISBN 978-1-4625-2999-5 (hard)

To Mark Robins,
the best spouse and friend anyone could have

Thank you for your unfailing support, wisdom,
and encouragement during the long process
of writing this book.

PREFACE

I think of research design as building a structure or plan for your research. Just as architects work with many different general types of structure—single-family homes, multifamily homes, nonresidential buildings, and so forth—social researchers have five primary structures with which they work: **quantitative, qualitative, mixed methods, arts-based,** and **community-based participatory.** We call these **approaches to research design,** and the one we select for a given research project depends on considerations including our topic and purpose. The selected approach provides only the general purpose and structure for the research project, just as an architect with an assignment to design a single-family home still has many choices with respect to the style, layout, and size of the building.

Within each of the five major design approaches, there are innumerable possibilities for how research might proceed. We have to consider two questions: What do we want to achieve? and How do we execute that goal? This is the process of building a **methodology,** which is a plan for how the research will be carried out. There are many tools at our disposal—methods, theories, and so forth—that we use to build a research plan. The philosophical point of view, professional experience, ethical standpoint, and practical skill set we, as individual researchers, bring to the table also influence how we design a project. We put our own stamp on our research projects the same way an architect might through unique stylistic features.

In addition to reviewing these five approaches to design, this book is unique because of its attention to ethical practice, emphasis on writing a research proposal (and how this proposal differs across approaches to design), modeling of the use of appropriate language for each of the five designs, and the extensive pedagogical features employed to make this text user-friendly for students, professors, and researchers.

Special Features of This Book

A Focus on Ethics

Often research design texts present a chapter on ethics in research or, in some cases, just a section of a chapter. However, ethics are intertwined with all phases of the research design process. Therefore, in addition to including a robust chapter devoted to ethics, the five chapters that address methods each feature "Ethics in Practice" flags, highlighting some moments in the research process in which ethics have a bearing on decision making.

Writing a Proposal

Most students of research methods and novice researchers alike need assistance in learning how to write a solid research proposal. Therefore, at the beginning of each of the design approach chapters (Chapters 4–8), I present a template for a research proposal. The remainder of the chapter elaborates on the elements in the template. So, instead of arbitrarily learning the dos and don'ts of each approach to design, as you learn the nuts and bolts of each approach, you are *simultaneously* learning how to put it all together in a research proposal. As a pedagogical feature, a summary of the proposal template is presented at the end of each chapter as well. It's important to note that the format for writing research proposals bears close similarities to the organization of journal articles. In other words, writing a proposal mirrors the process of a final write-up intended for publication. So for those readers not planning to write a formal research proposal, the structure of the chapters may help you reflect on how to structure your research write-up, in addition to providing the content you need for your work. Finally, because quantitative research and (often) mixed methods research follow "deductive" research models, whereas qualitative arts- and community-based participatory research approaches generally follow "inductive" designs, I have followed those models in the structuring of the five chapters on methods. In the quantitative and mixed methods chapters, the methods instruction occurs *prior* to the use of published research examples. In the qualitative arts- and community-based participatory chapters, the methods instruction occurs *after* published research examples are presented. In these subtle ways, each methods chapter models the tenets of that approach to design.

A Note about Language

The issue of language in how we write research proposals and ultimately represent our research is important and often overlooked in the literature. Researchers using the five different approaches reviewed in this book tend to use different words to describe the components of their work. These words are meaningful and carry implications about what we, as researchers, can know and how we develop that knowledge. Here are some examples of words that may be employed as a result of the approach with which you are working (this is by no means exhaustive):

- *respondent, subject, participant, co-creator, collaborator:* the people on whom our research is focused.
- *discover, generate, unearth, collect:* how knowledge is acquired.
- *method, practice:* the tools used to gather/generate data.

- *findings, results, renderings, outcomes:* the final product of research.
- *data, content:* raw information.
- *research study, inquiry:* our process.

Just taking the first example of the words used to describe the people on whom our research is focused, different approaches lead us to weight words differently. In quantitative research, we often see the word *subject* or *respondent* (although some quantitative researchers have shifted to the word *participant*); in qualitative research, we may see *participant*; in mixed methods research, we may see *respondent, subject,* or *participant*; in arts-based research, we typically see *participant, co-creator,* or *collaborator*; and in community-based participatory research we generally see *co-creator* or *collaborator*. These differences in language are not random but rather speak to deeper issues about the philosophical beliefs and research practices guiding inquiry. In order to highlight the importance of language and model how you might write a research proposal with these five approaches in Chapters 4–8, I employ the terms commonly used in that type of research.

Extensive Pedagogical Features

This text is meant to be very user-friendly. As such, numerous pedagogical features are employed. Key terms and concepts appear in **bold** type, and there are easy-to-read tables and figures throughout the book. Every chapter includes multiple "Review Stops" so that readers can review the information in the preceding sections. Readers are then directed to "Go" to the end of the chapter to check their answers. The "Review Stops" are an opportunity to pause, recap, and make sure the information has been processed before continuing. The end of every chapter also includes a "Further Engagement" section, which provides more advanced writing and research activities designed to put the chapter content into practice. Resources (books, chapters, websites) and suggested journals are also provided for each chapter, as appropriate.

At the end of each methods chapter, there is a summarized version of the research proposal template. I also interviewed leading researchers across the disciplines known for their work with the five approaches reviewed in this text. Some of their top tips appear in "Expert Tip" boxes in Chapters 4–8.

The book also includes a glossary of key terms that follows Chapter 8.

Lastly, PowerPoints are available for instructors who adopt the book for class use. Instructors can email Guilford at info@guilford.com (with subject line "PowerPoints for Research Design") to request the files. Instructors should provide the following information in their email:

- Department
- University
- Name of course and level

- Expected enrollment
- Author/title of previous book used, if applicable

Audience for the Book

This book is appropriate for undergraduate and graduate research methods courses across the social and behavioral sciences. The format of Chapters 4–8, each of which models a research proposal and shows readers how to fill in that proposal, makes the book useful for individual graduate students writing their master's or dissertation research proposals, as well as researchers at any level looking for assistance with this process.

Organization of the Book

Part I provides a detailed discussion of research design in general: what it is, why we do it, what the five approaches are well suited for, ethical practice, and the nuts and bolts of starting to design a project. Part II presents a chapter on each of the five approaches to research design. These chapters can be read independently and out of order (although it's advisable to read the quantitative and qualitative chapters prior to reading the mixed methods chapter). Chapters that aren't of interest can also be skipped.

ACKNOWLEDGMENTS

Books are never the result of one person's work, but rather represent the work and generosity of many.

First and foremost, I am profoundly grateful to my publisher and editor extraordinaire, C. Deborah Laughton. There is no one else like you in this business. When I dreamed of being an author as a kid, you were my fantasy editor. Who knew you were real? This is a much better book because of your careful reading of numerous drafts, vast knowledge of the field, advice and suggestions, and, above all, your belief in the value of this project. You're simply the best. Not only are you an exemplary publisher, but you're a wonderful person and cherished friend.

I extend a spirited thank you to the entire team at The Guilford Press, a class act. I'm truly honored to work with you. In particular, thank you to Seymour Weingarten, Bob Matloff, Katherine Sommer, Anna Brackett, Judith Grauman, Katherine Lieber, Marian Robinson, Margaret Ryan, Paul Gordon, Carly DaSilva, and Andrea Sargent.

Thank you to the formerly anonymous reviewers: Barbara B. Levin, Department of Teacher Education and Higher Education, University of North Carolina at Greensboro; Amanda Byron, Conflict Resolution Program, Portland State University; Mary P. Martinasek, Public Health Program, University of Tampa; and Larry Maucieri, Division of Psychology and Counseling, Governors State University. You provided thoughtful and detailed suggestions that have greatly strengthened this book. Your advice was invaluable and deeply appreciated.

I couldn't do any of this work without my long-time assistant and dear friend, Shalen Lowell. Your assistance with the literature review, creating tables, helping with permissions and rights to republish, keeping me laughing through the long writing process (no small task), and so much more was absolutely instrumental. Furthermore, had you not kept so many other balls in the air, I would not have been able to give this book the attention it demanded. Thank you!

Many generous colleagues have also contributed to this book. Thank you, Gioia Chilton, for your assistance in interviewing the researchers whose "Expert Tips" appear in boxes throughout this book. Thank you kindly to those experts willing to share their insider advice for the betterment of the field. Your wisdom and generosity are deeply appreciated. Marianne Fallon, you're an exemplary colleague. Thank you for sharing your unpublished manuscript with me and offering advice when I needed it.

I'm also appreciative of my friends and colleagues for lending their support during the process. Special thanks to Melissa Anyiwo, Celine Boyle, Pam DeSantis, Sandra Faulkner, Ally Field, Anne Harris, Jessica Smartt Gullion, Monique Robitaille, and Adrienne Trier-Bieniek.

Finally, I'm grateful to my family. Daisy Doodle, my little best friend, I'm so blessed to have all of the daily cuddles, which are a constant source of joy and peacefulness in my life. Madeline, you are my heart. Mark, you are the best spouse anyone could have. Thank you for lending invaluable support and encouragement along the way, as you have with all of my work, for your true partnership, and for picking up take-out and staying in on weekends, when the book needed me.

CONTENTS

PART I
The Nuts and Bolts of Research Design

PART II

Five Approaches to Research Design

PART I

The Nuts and Bolts of Research Design

CHAPTER 1

Introduction to Social Research

Different Ways of Knowing

An event happens that everyone is talking about. Let's take the deeply polarizing verdict in the case against George Zimmerman in the killing of Trayvon Martin. People have strong beliefs about whether racism was at play, the way law enforcement officials handled the tragedy, and "stand your ground"[1] laws. People's ideas are formed by what authorities in the media and criminal justice system report, cultural understandings of race and racism, and individuals' own personal experiences. People may come to very different conclusions about the state of race in the United States and how justice is dispensed based on their personal experiences, the media channels they choose to consume, and their overarching understanding of how race impacts our lives. For example, consider the news we elect to consume. Here are two snippets from different news sources after the Trayvon Martin killing, with diametrically opposed takes on "stand your ground" laws:

> These laws allow people who face serious bodily harm or death to defend themselves without first having to retreat as far as possible.—*Chicago Tribune* (Lott, 2013)

> If you are using the stand your ground law, it actually encourages that person not only to shoot, but to shoot to kill . . . because if you eliminate the only potential other witness, you're much more likely to be able to prevail in a stand your ground hearing.—*MSNBC*, quoting criminal defense attorney Ken Padowitz (Whitaker, 2013)

The news source you happen to choose may have a significant impact on your understanding of this issue. It's no surprise that after the killing and acquittal, some people assuredly stated this was a hate crime based on race and, moreover, had the race of the defendant and victim been reversed, the outcome in the criminal justice system would have been different. Others argued that we live in a postracial society

3

and that legitimate fears for safety were at play. Yet others argued those so-called fears were the result of systemic racism that serves to reinforce stereotypes. In all of the instances, people were likely to state their perspective—their knowledge—as not only valid, but correct. This process is a product of the ways in which we develop a commonsense understanding of the world in daily life.

There are many different ways that we gain knowledge in everyday life. **Authorities or experts** are one source of knowledge. For example, we develop ideas about the world through individuals we know personally such as our parents or guardians, friends, and teachers. We also develop ideas about the world through experts we may or may not know personally, including leaders in major societal institutions such as the news media, religious authorities, the Census Bureau, politicians, health care experts, and others. It is important to bear in mind that each of these authorities has his/her own perspectives and biases. Factors such as religion, political leanings, education, and status characteristics, including race, class, gender, and sexuality, may influence authorities' ideas as well as our own.

Cultural beliefs are another common source of knowledge. For example, our ideas about race and racism have changed over time as our culture has changed. In order to understand how biased our cultural understandings can be, consider norms regarding race before the civil rights movement. At that time, strongly held ideas about race, which most people would find racist today, were taken for granted.

We also develop knowledge from our **personal and sensory experiences.** We learn about our world based on what we see, hear, smell, taste, and touch. Sometimes these different ways of knowing coalesce to convince us of something. For example, as children, authority figures such as parents may tell us not to touch the stove because it is hot and we will burn ourselves. Then, if we do accidentally touch the stove and it hurts, our personal sensory experience confirms for us what we were told. In a more complex example, if we personally experience or witness racial profiling or stereotyping, we may be more apt to believe that others experience the same.

Although we do learn through daily life experiences, as already noted, there are considerable limitations with these sources of "knowledge." When using personal experiences, people have a tendency to overgeneralize, make inaccurate observations, perceive things selectively, and close off inquiry as soon as they have developed an idea. In some cases, authorities, cultural beliefs, and personal experiences can confirm each other in ways that are misleading, serving to reinforce misinformation and bias. For example, if you're in the dominant racial group, it's likely you haven't personally experienced racism. If your naïveté regarding race is reinforced by your family, friends, and the news you watch, you may come to the conclusion that racism is no longer an issue. Although your sources of daily knowledge confirm this perspective, such confirmation does not make it so. *Beliefs* and *knowledge* are not the same. We may develop personal beliefs that racism is no longer an issue; however, knowledge based on research disconfirms that belief. Research is needed in order to challenge and overcome the biases and limitations inherent in "learning" from experts, culture, and personal experiences.

Social research, the focus of this book, also produces knowledge and helps us come to understand the social world and our place in it. Social research has developed as a way of building knowledge that promotes agreed-upon practices within the research community that help us avoid the limitations and pitfalls of other ways of knowing. The personal beliefs we have developed from the other sources (experts, culture, personal experience) may be the impetus for our interest in a topic for a research project. However, the knowledge produced in this rigorous social scientific manner may support or refute those personal beliefs.

Purposes of Social Research

There are many purposes for conducting social research. Although projects frequently fall into one of the following categories, in some projects there may be more than one of these purposes. Here are the primary purposes for which social research is conducted.

Exploration

When we have a new or relatively underresearched topic, exploratory research is a way of learning about that topic. Exploratory research can help us fill a gap in our knowledge about a new or underresearched topic, or approach the topic from a different perspective to generate new and emerging insights. When you conduct a literature review and come up short, this absence of adequate research is often an indicator that exploratory research is needed. Such research may prompt further investigation, including the development of an appropriate methodological plan. Accordingly, this initial research may point you or other researchers toward certain research questions, methods for data collection, participants, and/or audiences.

Description

When we want to describe individuals, groups, activities, events, or situations, descriptive research is appropriate. Descriptive research aims to generate what Clifford Geertz (1973) referred to as "thick descriptions" of social life (those that provide details, meanings, and context), typically from the perspective of the people living it. Researchers may turn to rigorous observation or related methods of interview in order to document how things are experienced, with respect to the phenomenon under investigation.

Explanation

When we want to explain causes and effects, correlations, or why things are the way they are, explanatory research is appropriate. For example, if we want to know the particular factors that shape people's attitudes about a controversial issue such as fracking, stem cell research, or immigration policies, we may conduct explanatory research. This type of research can also provide evidence for causal relationships, suggesting that A causes B, or that A causes B only under certain circumstances.

Or, we may want to study correlations between A and B, showing, for example, that A is positively associated with B. Explanatory research is useful when we want to explain why things are the way they are, with respect to the phenomenon under investigation. (The different kinds of explanation you might seek are described in Chapter 4 on quantitative research.)

Community Change or Action

When relevant stakeholders have identified the need for community change or action, we may conduct research with the aim of prompting such community change, social action, or community intervention. For instance, if a community is undergoing rapid development and some stakeholders in the community are being excluded from the development process, we may develop a research project with the aim of intervening in that process. Political or social justice concerns underscore this kind of research. In some cases, the goal may be to impact public policy. In order to conduct research with the aim of community change or action, we may also end up conducting descriptive, explanatory, or evaluative research.

Evaluation

When we want to assess the effectiveness or impact of a program or policy, evaluation research provides a means of doing so (Patton, 2015; Scriven, 1998). Evaluation can be considered a type of explanation (Adler & Clark, 2011). Evaluation research is useful in numerous kinds of research projects, from evaluating particular outreach programs, educational programs, to public policies, campaigns of various sorts, and so forth. For instance, evaluation research can help us determine how changes in a policy have impacted successes or failures in a particular program or the effectiveness of a particular awareness campaign.

Evoke, Provoke, or Unsettle

When we want to jar specified audiences (groups of people) into thinking about or seeing something differently, promote new learning, or create an awareness campaign, we may conduct research with the aim of evoking, provoking, or unsettling. This kind of research may aim to disrupt or unsettle stereotypes or "commonsense" ideologies, serve as an intervention, stimulate self-reflection, or generate social awareness. Research conducted with this purpose may follow a generative model whereby the inquiry itself is the research act (elaborated in Chapter 7, on arts-based research). In order to conduct research with the aim of evoking meanings, we may also end up conducting exploratory or descriptive research.

Earlier we saw how we might develop ideas about the killing of Trayvon Martin based on personal experiences, authorities, and cultural beliefs. Let's return to that example to see how we might explore issues related to this tragic event using social research with the aforementioned purposes. (There are countless ways one can develop knowledge about these issues via social research, so these examples are meant for illustrative purposes only).

- *Exploration.* If we want to explore how young people of different racial backgrounds have used social media to learn about or share their ideas about this event, and their motivations for doing so, we might turn to focus group interviews to explore their attitudes (where several participants are interviewed in a group setting).

- *Description.* If we want to describe community response to this event, we might conduct field research in Sanford, Florida (involving observations, participation in local meetings/protests, and informal interviews).

- *Explanation.* If we want to determine the factors that shape people's attitudes about "stand your ground" policies we might conduct survey research, via a questionnaire, to see the extent to which race, gender, age, socioeconomic background, political affiliation, media consumption, and experience with the criminal justice system impact people's viewpoints.

- *Community change or action.* If we want to assist a community to create change in how its "community watch" programs are created and maintained in order to eliminate racial profiling, we might conduct community-based research by involving local stakeholders—residents, community watch members, law enforcement officials—to develop a project with community goals and norms at the center, ultimately to prompt positive community change.

- *Evaluation.* If we want to evaluate the effectiveness of a community watch program and how it operates with respect to race (i.e., if it is being enacted fairly), we might conduct research analyzing documents such as incident reports.

- *Evoke, provoke, or unsettle.* If we want to evoke people's perceptions of race and racism, unsettle stereotypes, and provoke new understandings, we may have racially diverse high school students create visual art responding to the Trayvon Martin killing and aftermath, and then textually or verbally describe their art. The art could later be displayed in school settings, community centers, and/or online.

As you can see, these examples illustrate some ways social research can help us to systematically learn about a range of issues. Further, conducting social research around these issues can result in many different kinds of projects with different goals and action plans for how to achieve those goals. Topic selection, coupled with the research purpose, leads us to specific design strategies and methodological choices. This is ultimately the aim of this book: to show you the five major approaches of designing a research project based on your topic, interests, and abilities, and how those approaches lead you to a range of methodological choices.

REVIEW STOP 1

1. What are the three primary ways people develop beliefs and knowledge in daily life?

2. Social research is a way of building knowledge that uses agreed-upon practices within the research community to help avoid some of the limitations of other ways of knowing. What are the six primary purposes of social research?

3. A researcher is interested in the correlation between gender and attitudes about handgun legislation. He/she conducts research with what primary purpose?

☞ **Go to the end of the chapter to check your answers.**

Now that you have a sense of what distinguishes social research from other ways of knowing, and of some of the major purposes research can serve, let's turn to the specifics regarding available approaches to social research and building a project.

The Five Approaches to Research

Architects design plans to build physical structures. When an architect designs a house or a building, his/her ultimate goal will dictate decision-making. For example, there are many differences between building a house versus a cathedral. Further, building different kinds of homes, located in different geographic areas and serving different purposes, also requires different building strategies. For instance, consider building a beach house on the Maine coast, a colonial-style home in Vermont, a Mediterranean-style home in Florida, and a hillside home in Southern California. Stylistically these homes will require different features in terms of both exterior and interior designs. Although there are some issues that are always at play, such as those related to laying a foundation and creating safe loadbearing walls, due to location and potential weather issues alone, there will be many differences: the need for storm windows or not, whether or not the home has a basement, and so forth. In these examples we are talking about private single-family homes. Now consider multifamily homes, apartment buildings, and nonresidential buildings, including those that will serve the public in some capacity. Next consider differences in nonresidential buildings based on their purposes: for example, medical facilities, schools, houses of worship, retail spaces, and so forth. The type of structure alone will dictate many of the choices an architect makes.

I think of research design as the process of building a structure, or plan, for your research project. Whereas architects have many general structures with which they work—single-family homes, multifamily homes, nonresidential buildings, and the like—social researchers have five primary structures with which they work. In social research we call these *approaches to research design.*

There are five major approaches to research reviewed in this text: quantitative, qualitative, mixed methods research, arts-based research, and community-based participatory research. In actuality, there may be overlaps between these approaches. For example, there are some methods (e.g., narrative inquiry) that are used by qualitative and arts-based researchers.[2] For another example, community-based participatory research may rely on quantitative, qualitative, mixed methods, or arts-based methods. The differences between these approaches will become clearer throughout this book showing that despite overlap, projects can be categorized.

Quantitative research is characterized by deductive approaches to the research process aimed at proving, disproving, or lending credence to existing theories. This type of research involves measuring variables and testing relationships between variables in order to reveal patterns, correlations, or causal relationships. Researchers may employ linear methods of data collection and analysis that result in statistical data. The values underlying quantitative research include neutrality, objectivity, and the acquisition of a sizeable scope of knowledge (e.g., a statistical overview from a large sample). This approach is generally appropriate when your primary purpose is to explain or evaluate.

Qualitative research is generally characterized by inductive approaches to knowledge building aimed at generating meaning (Leavy, 2014). Researchers use this approach to explore; to robustly investigate and learn about social phenomenon; to unpack the meanings people ascribe to activities, situations, events, or artifacts; or to build a depth of understanding about some dimension of social life (Leavy, 2014). The values underlying qualitative research include the importance of people's subjective experiences and meaning-making processes and acquiring a depth of understanding (i.e., detailed information from a small sample). Qualitative research is generally appropriate when your primary purpose is to explore, describe, or explain.

Mixed methods research (MMR) involves collecting, analyzing, and in some way integrating both quantitative and qualitative data in a single project. The phases of a research project are integrated or synergistic, with the quantitative phase influencing the qualitative phase, or vice versa (Hesse-Biber, 2010; Hesse-Biber & Leavy, 2011). MMR may result in a comprehensive understanding of the phenomenon under investigation because of the integration of quantitative and qualitative data. MMR is generally appropriate when your purpose is to describe, explain, or evaluate. MMR is also routinely used in applied social and behavioral science research, including that which seeks to prompt community change or social action.

Arts-based research (ABR) involves adapting the tenets of the creative arts in a social research project. Researchers aim to address social research questions in holistic and engaged ways in which theory and practice are intertwined. Arts-based practices draw on literary writing, music, dance, performance, visual art, film, and other artistic mediums. ABR is a generative approach whose researchers place the inquiry process at the center and value aesthetic understanding, evocation, and provocation. ABR is generally appropriate when your purpose is to explore, describe, or evoke, provoke, or unsettle.

Community-based participatory research (CBPR) involves collaborative partnerships between researchers and nonacademic stakeholders (e.g., community members). Researchers may partner with established community-based organizations (CBOs); however, this is not always the case. CBPR is an attempt by researchers to actively involve the communities they aim to serve in every aspect of the research process, from the identification of a problem to the distribution of research findings. This is a highly collaborative and problem-centered approach to research that requires the sharing of power. CBPR is generally appropriate when your purpose is to promote community change or action.

Each general approach—quantitative, qualitative, mixed methods, arts-based, community-based participatory—is an umbrella term comprising numerous strategies for conducting research. These approaches are all characterized by different philosophical belief systems and rely on different methodological practices. These beliefs and practices are the elements of research.

REVIEW STOP 2

1. Deductive approaches to the research process characterize which of the five approaches to research? _____

   a. These are appropriate when your primary purpose is _____
   _____.

2. Inductive approaches to the research process characterize which of the five approaches to research? _____

   a. These are appropriate when your primary purpose is _____
   _____.

3. A researcher is interested in challenging people's stereotypes about gender and profession. He/she uses an installation of visual images of women in traditionally male jobs, such as construction worker, electrician, and pilot, to provoke viewers into questioning their assumptions. What approach to research is the researcher using?

☛ Go to the end of the chapter to check your answers.

The Elements of Research

The elements of research can be thought of as the building blocks for any research project. These are integral components of any social research project. Together, our decisions regarding these various elements determine which of the five approaches to research to use.

The main elements of research can be organized into three general categories: (1) philosophical, (2) praxis, (3) and ethics (Leavy, 2014). The philosophical substructure of research consists of three elements: paradigm, ontology, and epistemology. At the level of praxis there are four key elements of research: genre/design, methods/practices, theory, and methodology. The ethical component (which combines philosophical and praxis elements) includes values, ethics, and reflexivity (see Table 1.1).

Chapter 2 is devoted to the topic of ethics because of its centrality to all social research practice. The remainder of this chapter reviews the philosophical and praxis elements of research and their relationship to the five major research approaches. Although all of these terms may seem confusing at first, they are really addressing two simple questions:

1. The philosophical elements of research answer the question "What do we believe?"

2. The praxis elements of research answer the question "What do we do?"

Philosophical Elements: What Do We Believe?

What we take for granted is important because it impacts how we think, see, and act. There is a range of beliefs that guide research practice—beliefs about the nature of the social world, what can be known about social life, how research should proceed, who can be a knower, what kind of knowledge is valued, and how we come to know. Together, these beliefs form the **philosophical substructure of research**, informing decisions from topic selection all the way to the final representation and dissemination of the research findings.

A **paradigm** is a worldview or framework through which knowledge is filtered (Kuhn, 1962; Lincoln, Lynham, & Guba, 2011); it is a foundational perspective carrying a set of assumptions that guides the research process. Paradigms are often difficult to see because they are taken for granted (Babbie, 2013). Consider the old

TABLE 1.1. The Elements of Research	
Philosophical	Paradigm *Ontology* *Epistemology*
Praxis	*Genre/design* Methodology *Methods/practices* *Theory*
Ethics (philosophical and praxis)	Values Ethics Reflexivity

Note. Adapted from Leavy (2014, p. 2). Copyright © 2014 Oxford University Press. Adapted by permission.

saying "I don't know who discovered water, but I doubt it was the fish." Paradigms become the lenses through which research is conceived and executed, and thus they are often difficult to see. I think of paradigms as sunglasses, with differently shaped frames and differently colored lenses. When you put on a pair, it influences every-thing you see. Thus, paradigms are important to acknowledge because the beliefs that compose them guide our thinking and actions (Guba, 1990). Ontological and epistemological belief systems are joined in paradigms.

An **ontology** is a philosophical belief system about the nature of the social world (e.g., whether it is patterned and predictable or constantly re-created by humans). Our ontological belief system informs both our sense of the social world and, cor-respondingly, what we can learn about it and how we can do so. Egon Guba and Yvonna Lincoln explained the ontological question as "What is the form and nature of reality and, therefore, what is there that can be known about it?" (1998, p. 201).

An **epistemology** is a philosophical belief system about how research proceeds and what counts as knowledge. Our epistemological position informs how we enact the role of researcher and how we understand the relationship between the researcher and research participants (Guba & Lincoln, 1998; Harding, 1987; Hesse-Biber & Leavy, 2004, 2011). Figure 1.1 visually depicts the components of a paradigm.

There are multiple paradigms or worldviews that guide social research. Differ-ent researchers utilize different ways of grouping and naming paradigms, so note that there is some measure of inconsistency in the literature and you may come across other terms when you conduct a literature review. I suggest the six follow-ing terms as a way of categorizing a multiplicity of paradigms: (1) postpositivism, (2) interpretive/constructivist, (3) critical, (4) transformative, (5) pragmatic, and (6) arts-based/aesthetic intersubjective.

Postpositivism

This philosophical belief system originally developed in the natural sciences and espouses an objective, patterned, and knowable reality. Research involves making and testing claims, including identifying and testing causal relationships, such as A causes B or A causes B under certain conditions (Creswell, 2014; Phillips & Bur-bules, 2000). Researchers aim to support or disprove assertions (Babbie, 2013). To do so, the scientific method is employed. Therefore, this worldview values scientific objectivity, researcher neutrality, and replication (Hesse-Biber & Leavy, 2011).

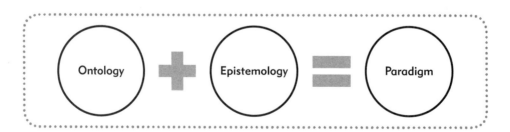

FIGURE 1.1. The components of a paradigm.

Interpretive or Constructivist

This philosophical belief system developed in disciplinary contexts in the social sciences and emphasizes people's subjective experiences, which are grounded in social–historical contexts (Hesse-Biber & Leavy, 2011). This worldview suggests that we are actively engaged in constructing and reconstructing meanings through our daily interactions—often referred to as the *social construction of reality*. Thus, we make and remake the social world through our patterns of interaction and inter-pretive processes, by which we assign meaning to activities, situations, events, ges-tures, and so forth. Researchers therefore value people's subjective interpretation and understanding of their experiences and circumstances. Interpretive or construc-tivist worldviews are overarching categories that include a broad range of perspec-tives (reviewed in the discussion of theory), including symbolic interactionism, dra-maturgy, phenomenology, and ethnomethodology.

Critical

This philosophical belief system developed in interdisciplinary contexts, includ-ing areas studies and other fields forged in critique (e.g., women's studies, Afri-can American studies), and emphasizes power-rich contexts, dominant discourses, and social justice issues (Hesse-Biber & Leavy, 2011; Klein, 2000; Leavy, 2011a). Research is understood as a political enterprise with the ability to empower and emancipate. Researchers aim to prioritize the experiences and perspectives of those forced to the peripheries of a hierarchical social order, and they reject grand theo-ries that disavow or erase differences. Collaborative and participatory approaches (i.e., those in which participants are actively involved in developing the project) are often privileged. Critical worldviews are overarching categories that include a broad range of perspectives (reviewed in the discussion of theory), including femi-nist, critical race, queer, indigenous, postmodernist, and poststructuralist theories.

Transformative

This philosophical belief system, developed in transdisciplinary contexts, draws on critical theory, critical pedagogy, feminist, critical race, and indigenous theo-ries and promotes human rights, social justice, and social-action-oriented perspec-tives (Mertens, 2009). Research should be inclusive, participatory, and democratic, involving nonacademic stakeholders during all parts of the process. Research is understood as an engaged, politically and socially responsible enterprise with the power to transform and emancipate.

Pragmatic

This philosophical belief system, developed at the start of the 20th century out of the work of Charles Sanders Peirce, William James, John Dewey, and George Hebert Mead (Hesse-Biber, 2015; Patton, 2015), holds no allegiance to a particular set of rules or theories but rather suggests that different tools may be useful in different research contexts. Researchers value utility and what works in the context of a particular research question. Pragmatists "focus on the outcomes of action" (Morgan, 2013, p. 28), suggesting that whichever theories are useful in a particular context are thereby valid. Any of the methods and theories reviewed in this text may become a part of a pragmatic design.

Arts-Based or Aesthetic Intersubjective[3]

This philosophical belief system, which developed at the intersection of the arts and sciences, suggests that the arts are able to access that which is otherwise out of reach. Researchers value preverbal ways of knowing, including sensory, emotional, perceptual, kinesthetic, and imaginal knowledge (Chilton, Gerber, & Scotti, 2015; Conrad & Beck, 2015; Cooper, Lamarque, & Sartwell, 1997; Dewey, 1934; Langer, 1953; Harris-Williams, 2010; Whitfield, 2005). Research is understood as a relational, meaning-making activity. The arts-based or aesthetic intersubjective paradigm draws on theories of embodiment and phenomenology and may include a range of additional perspectives such as interpretive/constructivist theories and critical theories.

Praxis: What Do We Do?

How can we conduct research? What tools are available with which to build a project? *Praxis* refers to the doing of research—the *practice* of research. There are various tools that we use to conduct research, including methods and theories. When we combine those tools, we develop a methodology: that is, a plan for how we will execute our research.

The specific methods or tools we use to collect or generate data can be grouped into larger **genres or designs**. These are overarching categories for different ways of approaching research (Saldaña, 2011b). A **research method** is a tool for data collection or generation. It is important to note that sometimes the term **research practice** is used instead of *research method*, particularly in the case of ABR. Research methods are selected because they are the best tools to produce the data sought for a particular project. So, for example, the interview format is a general genre or design. There are numerous specific interview methods that include, but are not limited to, structured interviews, semistructured interviews, in-depth interviews, focus group interviews, and oral history interviews. Each research method is best suited for particular kinds of research questions. As reviewed in later chapters, the selection of research methods should be made in conjunction with the research question(s) and hypothesis or research purpose as well as more pragmatic issues such as access to participants or other data sources, time constraints, and researcher skills.

Methods for data collection/generation also lead to particular methods or strategies for analysis, interpretation, and representation (i.e., what form or shape the research outcome will take). Specific methods for data collection/generation, analysis, interpretation, and representation are discussed in detail in Chapters 4–8, as appropriate to each of the five approaches reviewed in this text. For now, Table 1.2 lists research genres/designs and their corresponding research methods for data collection/generation (this is not an exhaustive list).

A **theory** is an account of social reality that is grounded in data but extends beyond that data (Adler & Clark, 2011). There are two levels of theory: (1) small-scale theories that researchers suggest based on their data (theory with a small *t*) and (2) large-scale theories that are widely legitimated based on prior research and that may be used to predict new data or frame new studies (Theory with a big *T*). For example, beginning with the former, based on your research, you may develop a theory about how children's media consumption impacts their self-esteem. The theory will be directly based on the data you collected for your study; however, it makes assertions beyond those data (perhaps generalizing to a larger population of children). Theories with a big *T* have already been rigorously tested and applied. These theories and theoretical perspectives are available for use in your study. There are numerous theoretical perspectives that may guide the research process, which you may discover during the literature review process (discussed in Chapter 3). Whereas paradigms are overarching worldviews, theories specify paradigms (Babbie, 2013). Guiding paradigms can be difficult to discern, but specific

TABLE 1.2. Genres/Designs and Research Methods/Practices

Genre/design	Research methods/practices
Experiments	Randomized, quasi, single-subject
Survey research	Questionnaires (administered in numerous ways)
Interview	Structured, semistructured, in-depth, oral history, biographical minimalist, focus group
Field research	Participant observation, nonparticipant observation, digital ethnography, visual ethnography
Unobtrusive methods	Content analysis, document analysis, visual analysis, audio analysis, audiovisual analysis, historical–comparative
Case study	Single case, multicase
Self-data	Autoethnography, duoethnography
Mixed methods	Sequential, convergent, nested
Literary practices	Fiction-based research, narrative inquiry, experimental writing, poetic inquiry
Performative practices	Drama, play building, ethnodrama, ethnotheatre, film, video, music, dance, and movement
Visual arts practices	Collage, painting, drawing, photography, photovoice, comics, cartoons, sculpture
Community-based	Participatory-action research, social-action research

theories—tested, applied, or generated during research praxis—are more detailed statements grounded in the project's guiding paradigm.

For now, Table 1.3 presents the six major paradigms with their corresponding theoretical schools of thought/major theories, each of which contains numerous specific disciplinary and interdisciplinary theories (this is not an exhaustive list). Specific disciplinary and interdisciplinary theories are found during literature reviews and are not detailed here.

In research practice, methods and theory combine to create a **methodology,** which is a plan for how research will proceed—how you will combine the different elements of research into a plan that details how the specific research project will be carried out (Figure 1.2). The methodology is what the researcher actually does once he/she has combined the different elements of research. In addition to one's philosophical beliefs and the selection of appropriate methods and theories, ethics also influence how a study is designed and executed (ethics are discussed in depth in the next chapter). Although two studies may use the same research method—for instance, a focus group interview—the researchers' methodologies may be completely different. In other words, how they proceed with the research, based not only on their data collection tool but also on how they conceive of *the use of that tool,* thus structures the study and determines their methodology. For example, the level of moderation and/or control a researcher exhibits during focus group interviews can vary greatly. So, how much the researcher talks, interjects, asks specific

TABLE 1.3. Paradigms and Theoretical Schools of Thought (Big-*T* Theories)	
Paradigm	**Theoretical schools of thought**
Postpositivism	Empiricism
Interpretive/constructivist	Symbolic interactionism Ethnomethodology Dramaturgy Phenomenology
Critical	Postmodernism Poststructuralism Indigenous Critical race Queer Feminism
Transformative	Critical theory Critical pedagogy Indigenous Critical race Feminism
Pragmatic	N/A (any)
Arts-based/aesthetic intersubjective	Embodiment Phenomenology

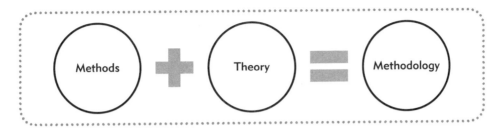

FIGURE 1.2. The components of a methodology.

participants for responses, and so on, changes the nature of the focus group. Specific methodologies lead to variations in methods.

 REVIEW STOP 3

1. The philosophical elements of research answer the question _____
   _____?

2. A researcher is interested in how students in one high school create and maintain their social hierarchy through their daily patterns of interaction: for example, how they reinforce, demonstrate, and/or challenge notions of popularity in their school and social cliques. The researcher would adopt which paradigm to guide their study?

3. A _____ is a plan for how research will actually proceed. It combines _____ and theory.

☛ **Go to the end of the chapter to check your answers.**

Putting It All Together

Table 1.4 puts some of the pieces together, illustrating the elements of research available for each of the five approaches to design. Note that there are always exceptions, but these represent the most commonly used combinations.

Considering the five approaches abstractly only takes us so far. In order to get a better sense of each approach, let's take one research topic and look at how we might design a project within each of the five approaches. Please bear in mind that in each case, I am offering only one of innumerable possibilities for how we might design each study. They are examples. Here is our research topic: students' experiences with drinking on college campuses. For the sake of simplicity, let's assume that each study will occur on your own college campus or one in your community.

TABLE 1.4. The Five Design Approaches with Their Elements

Approach	Paradigm	Theoretical schools	Genres	Methods
Quantitative	Postpositivist	Empiricism	Experiments Survey research	Randomized, quasi, single-subject Questionnaires
Qualitative	Postpositivist Interpretive/constructivist Critical	Empiricism Symbolic interactionism Ethnomethodology Dramaturgy Phenomenology Postmodernism Poststructuralism Indigenous Critical race Queer Feminist	Interview Field research Unobtrusive methods	Structured, semistructured, in-depth, oral history, biographical minimalist, focus group Participant observation, nonparticipant observation, digital ethnography, visual ethnography Content analysis, document analysis, visual analysis, audio analysis, audiovisual analysis, historical–comparative
Mixed methods	Pragmatic	N/A (any)	Mixed methods	Sequential, convergent, nested (integrated uses of any quantitative and qualitative method)
Arts-based	Arts-based/aesthetic intersubjective	Embodiment Phenomenology	Literary practices Performative practices Visual arts practices	Fiction-based research, narrative inquiry, experimental writing, poetic inquiry Drama, play building, ethnodrama, ethnotheatre, film, video, music, dance and movement Collage, painting, drawing, photography, comics, cartoons, sculpture
Community-based participatory	Transformative	Critical theory Critical pedagogy Feminist Critical race Indigenous	Community-based	Participatory action research, social action research (uses of any methods qualitative, quantitative, mixed methods and/or arts-based practices there within)

Quantitative

Working from a *postpositivist paradigm,* design a *survey research project* with a *questionnaire* as the data collection method. The questionnaire could be administered online so that students, who are guaranteed anonymity, feel comfortable responding to questions on sensitive subject matter, including underage drinking. Predetermined questions with a limited range of possible answers, such as those ranging from *strongly agree* to *strongly disagree,* would ask students to self-report on their attitudes and behaviors in relation to drinking on their campus, including their own participation, peer rates of drinking, accessibility of alcohol, behaviors associated with drinking, other relevant aspects of peer culture, and their attitudes about their school's policies regarding drinking on campus. The major advantage of this approach is that you could collect a wide range of data from a large number of students, which would allow you to make determinations about the *prevalence* of drinking on campus and about associated issues. In other words, the study would result in *statistics about each of the major dimensions of drinking on campus* about which you ask the respondents.

Qualitative

Working from an *interpretive paradigm,* design an *interview study* using *focus groups* as your data collection method. You could hold four focus group sessions, each comprised of six students, in a private room adjacent to a student center or other student-friendly part of campus. In a group setting, students may feel more comfortable talking about drinking on their campus, and one student's sharing may prompt others to agree or disagree, and so on. An open-ended focus group would allow the students to talk about the issues they think are important, using their own language and describing their experiences in detail, with stories and examples. With a low level of moderation, you could guide the discussion, asking some key questions, but allowing students the freedom to talk at their discretion. The major advantage of this approach is that you could collect rich *data with descriptions and examples,* and the *participants' language and concerns would be at the forefront.*

Mixed Methods Research

Working from the *pragmatic paradigm,* design a *sequential mixed methods study.* Use a *questionnaire* as your first data collection method in order to learn about the prevalence of drinking on campus, the factors most often at play when drinking occurs, and the like. Then, after analyzing the data statistically, hold *focus groups* to ask a smaller sample of students to talk at greater length about some of the findings, explaining their personal experiences and describing the circumstances of drinking on their campus. By using the questionnaire first, you will learn broadly what students report is happening on their campus. You can then design focus groups specifically to pick up on the major data points to emerge from the survey research, in an effort to unpack the meanings behind the statistics. The focus groups will help you to describe and explain the issues, in language chosen by the participants, at a greater depth so that you understand not only the rates of certain behaviors but the experience, motivation, and context. Whereas the survey research might point to, for instance, the failure of a certain on-campus policy, the interviews might help explain *why* the policy has failed. By using the two methods in an *integrated way,* you can learn *comprehensively* about the *prevalence, context, and individual experience* of drinking on campus.

Arts-Based Research

Working from a *critical paradigm,* design a *participatory visual arts study* using *collage* as your data generation method. A group of student participants could be presented with materials commonly used in *collage making* (magazines, newspapers, colorful selection of paper, drawing tools, pens, scissors, glue, tape, etc.) and asked to create a collage or drawing that represents their perception of the drinking culture on their campus and how it makes them feel. Students also could be asked to provide a textual description of their collage. Both the visual art and their textual descriptions could be analyzed. This approach has the potential to bring forth data that would not emerge with written or verbal communication alone. For example, there may be an emphasis on a certain kind of image that points to something unanticipated. The major advantages of this approach are that the *participatory nature of the design,* with students creating the data, may serve as an empowering experience for them, affording them the opportunity to express themselves without preconceived notions of what is expected or wanted, and *insights that would otherwise be unavailable may emerge.* (The art could potentially be displayed in selected locations on campus as well.)

Community-Based Participatory Research

Working from a *transformative paradigm,* design a CBPR study. First, assemble relevant stakeholders, including students in different class years, resident advisors, campus police, health services staff, administrators, and faculty. Together, develop a project to assess and improve the policies and procedures for dealing with drinking on campus, in ways that identify and meet student needs (e.g., being able to call campus police or health services, without fear, if a student is in trouble) and meet institutional needs (e.g., keeping students safe and not endorsing unlawful behavior). Together, determine the research purpose, questions, and methodology. The major advantage of this approach is that all *relevant stakeholders are equally valued and can collectively identify core issues, problems, and solutions.*

The preceding examples are merely illustrative of the many kinds of studies that can be developed with the different approaches to research and their corresponding methodological tools. Because each approach carries its own set of advantages, research design decisions should be made to best serve your objectives for the particular project.

Conclusion

Regardless of the topic under investigation or the approach selected, above all else research is a human endeavor. Ethics underscores every aspect of social research: the philosophical and praxis levels, what we believe, and what we do. As reviewed in the next chapter, there is a historical legacy of egregious exploitation and abuse of human research subjects, which has informed contemporary ethical standards. As Maya Angelou said, "When you know better, you do better." This is very much the case in the sphere of research ethics.

✓ REVIEW STOP ANSWER KEY

Review Stop 1

1. authorities/experts, cultural beliefs, personal experiences
2. exploration, description, explanation, community change or action, evaluation, evoke/provoke/unsettle
3. explanation

Review Stop 2

1. quantitative
   a. explain or evaluate
2. qualitative
   a. explore, describe, or explain
3. ABR

Review Stop 3

1. What do we believe?
2. interpretive/constructivist
3. methodology, methods

Further Engagement

1. Pick a topic you're interested in studying and write down everything you think you know about it, based on your own life experiences and perceptions (e.g., exposure to the news, what you've learned in school, family and peer opinions, personal experiences) (one page maximum). Then get one article from a peer-reviewed journal in your discipline that presents a study on some aspect of your topic. Read the article and write a short response (one paragraph). What new information have you learned? What, if anything, in the article surprised you? Did the article give you any new language or new ways to understand the topic?

2. Pick a current or controversial event. Select two newspaper articles written on the topic from different newspapers in different geographic regions. Write a short compare-and-contrast response (one page maximum). How do the two articles represent the same set of facts or circumstances? What kinds of language do the two articles use to set their tone? Could readers develop a different perspective based on which news source they read?

3. A team of researchers is interested in how prisoners experience their time being incarcerated. The primary research purpose is to describe prison life from the perspective of prisoners. The researchers conduct a qualitative study on prisoners' experience of incarceration in a minimum security facility using focus groups. They hold four focus groups with six prisoners in each session and ask questions about daily routines, the dynamics of fear and power, relationships that form in prison, their perception of the guards, and other aspects of daily life. Now imagine that the research team changes its primary purpose. Instead of seeking to describe prisoners' experiences, they aim to identity problems in the prison experience in order to facilitate change within prisons. Now the researchers want to collectively create a project investigating prisoners' experiences of incarceration in order to lobby policy officials for improved conditions and outcomes for prisoners, also accounting for the demands placed on prison guards and how their roles might be improved. The researchers' reimagined purpose leads them to design a CBPR project. How might their CBPR project proceed? What are the first steps?

Resources

Lemert, C. (2013). *Social theory: The multicultural, global, and classic readings* (5th ed.). Boulder, CO: Westview Press.

Mertens, D. M. (2011). *Transformative research and evaluation.* New York: Guilford Press.

Trier-Bieniek, A. (2015). *Feminist theory and pop culture.* Rotterdam, The Netherlands: Sense Publishers.

Notes

1. "Stand your ground" laws permit an individual to defend him/herself against an imminent or perceived threat that would result in bodily harm or death. There is no duty to retreat from the situation (as there is in the case of "retreat" laws).
2. Some researchers consider arts-based research a genre of qualitative research, creating even more overlap in the literature.
3. Gioia Chilton, Nancy Gerber, and Victoria Scotti (2015) coined the term *aesthetic intersubjective paradigm*.

CHAPTER 2

Ethics in Social Research

In 1971 the Stanford Prison Experiment occurred. Philip Zimbardo, a Stanford University psychology professor, led a team of researchers in a study about the psychology of imprisonment (Haney, Banks, & Zimbardo, 1973). They created a simulation of a prison in the basement of a Stanford building, including prison cells, solitary confinement quarters, and other common features of a prison. Twenty-four male students, from primarily middle-class backgrounds and deemed stable, were recruited for what was supposed to be a 2-week experiment. Half were assigned the role of prison guard and half the role of prisoner. Zimbardo assumed the role of superintendent, and a research assistant was assigned the role of warden. Guards and prisoners were given clothing to match their roles as well as props to simulate prison life. Guards worked in shifts, and prisoners were left in their cells 24 hours a day. The guards were instructed not to physically harm prisoners but to give them a negative, disempowering experience (e.g., by calling them by numbers, not names; denying them privacy; giving them a sense of having no control or power). Researchers watched the action unfold from video monitors.

The participants internalized their roles and acted upon them far beyond what the researchers had predicted. By the second day, mayhem began to ensue. The prisoners began to resist their conditions, and the guards decided to up the ante by psychologically controlling them. The guards employed various measures of psychological abuse and torture, demeaning and degrading the prisoners. Some prisoners had their mattresses taken away and were forced to sleep on the floor, and some had their clothing taken away to cause humiliation. The treatment of the prisoners continued to worsen. Two prisoners left the experiment. On the sixth day, to the dismay of many of the guards, Zimbardo stopped the experiment. He later noted that more than 50 people observed the experiment, and only one raised ethical concerns.

Imagine if you were a participant in this experiment. If you were assigned the role of prisoner, how might you feel, knowing that the researchers had put you in a situation in which you were mistreated? What might be some of the consequences of being dehumanized in these ways, such as being stripped naked to maintain your submission? Would you be able to comfortably return to school with the others from the study? If you were in the role of a guard, how might you feel outside of the constructed experimental environment, knowing that you had participated in these behaviors? Might you feel guilty or ashamed? What if something violent or hateful was stirred up in you? How might that kind of experience impact you or others in your life? Parts of the experiment were filmed and are publicly available. How might it make you feel if others witnessed you being psychologically abused or causing such abuse?

Now imagine that you were a researcher. What would you do if you were in this situation? Once you observed psychological abuse, would you allow the study to continue? How would you protect the welfare of all of the research participants? What if the information you were learning was really interesting? Would you be enticed to let the experiment continue? How would you know if you were doing the *right* thing?

The Stanford Prison Experiment is one of the most infamous experiments in modern U.S. history, likely made more shocking because it occurred at a prestigious university. It has even been the subject of stories and films, including a 2015 film. In the research community, the experiment is most frequently cited in discussions about ethics in social research.

The word **ethics** comes from the Greek word *ethos*, which means *character*. Ethics involve morality, integrity, fairness, and truthfulness. *Morality* is about knowing what is right and wrong, and *integrity* is about acting on that knowledge. Ethics are central to social research. Because we are human beings engaged in understanding other human beings—social realities—ethics are of the utmost importance so that our research is not harmful.

There is an **ethical substructure** that impacts every aspect of the research process (Hesse-Biber & Leavy, 2011; Leavy, 2011a). Right from the beginning, as we select a topic to study, ethical considerations come into play. Topic selection is informed by our values, our understanding of which problems are in need of research, and the potential impact of the research. Every aspect of dealing with the "who" of our study—the people involved—is an ethical decision. For example, from how we decide which group of people to study or build projects with, how we identify potential participants for our study, the manner in which we interact with the people involved in the study, our research relationships, to how we disseminate our research findings to interested parties and therefore who gets to "know" and benefit from the research, are all examples of research components that require ethical considerations in decision making and practice. These are just the tip of the iceberg. In short, embedded within every aspect of the research endeavor are ethical considerations.

The ethical substructure of research contains dimensions on three levels: philosophical, praxis, and reflexivity.

1. The **philosophical dimension** of ethics is based on your **values system** and addresses the question "What do you believe?"
2. The **praxis dimension** of ethics addresses the question "What do you do?"
3. Finally, the **reflexivity dimension** of ethics, which combines the philosophical and praxis, addresses the question "How does power come to bear?"

The remainder of the chapter is divided into three sections: values system, ethical praxis, and reflexivity. Please note that although many of the issues reviewed in this chapter apply, in some way or another, to research regardless of approach, there are some issues that are heightened or unique to particular research designs or methods used within those designs. These are noted and expounded on, as appropriate, in Chapters 4–8.

Values System

As noted, this dimension of ethics addresses the question "What do you believe?" Each of us brings our own moral compass into our research experiences. We each have beliefs, attitudes, and ideas about the world. The values we bring to the research experience shape every decision we make; they shape what we think and therefore how we act. Our beliefs don't just develop in our own minds; rather, they develop in a social context. Let's take an example from everyday life. Your religious beliefs, whether regarding a specific religion, a nonreligious form of spirituality, agnosticism, or atheism, impact your worldview. These beliefs did not develop in a vacuum but were likely a part of your socialization. For example, if you are religious, you may have learned religious values in your childhood home. Your beliefs impact your behaviors. For example, if you are religious, you may attend religious services, engage in regular prayer or meditation, follow dietary restrictions, and so forth.

The values and sense of morality that we bring to the research experience don't just come from our personal lives. Specific social–historical events have impacted the values system researchers bring to their work. Although numerous historical events have influenced the research community's understanding of ethics, there are two major events (each a series of events) that are considered landmarks in understanding how our communal values system has emerged.

First, a legacy of historical ethical atrocities in social research, and second, the social justice movements, have impacted the values of research fields that include human subjects.

Historical Abuses

Sadly, there is a long history of biomedical abuses and the exploitation of human research subjects. For example, there were horrid abuses during World War II, including brutal experiments in concentration camps and related war crimes. As a result, the **Nuremberg Code** (1949) was established, outlining rules for experiments with human beings, such as voluntary participation. Although not formalized into law, this was the first major effort at getting the medical community to regulate itself. Later, the **Declaration of Helsinki** (1964) was developed and, together with the Nuremberg Code, they are the basis for federal codes regarding the treatment of human beings in medical research.

Biomedical abuses are not particular to times of war, nor are they foreign to those in the United States. The **Tuskegee Syphilis Experiment,** which occurred from 1932 to 1972, is perhaps the most infamous case of unethical biomedical research ever conducted in North America. In 1932 The U.S. Public Health Service began working with the Tuskegee Institute. They recruited 600 impoverished African American men in Alabama, 399 who had syphilis prior to enrollment and 201 who did not. What makes this experiment unconscionable is that the men did not know they had syphilis and were not treated for it. They were instead told that they had "bad blood" and were being treated for that. By 1947 penicillin was the legitimized treatment for syphilis, but the researchers still withheld it from the unknowing research subjects. Many of the men in the study died of syphilis and related complications, many infected their wives, and some had children born with congenital syphilis. The experiment was only stopped in 1972 when the truth was leaked to the press. Although only made known publicly in recent years, from 1946 to 1948 the U.S. Public Health Service conducted even more unethical experiments in Guatemala on prisoners and patients in mental health facilities. They purposely infected 696 men and women with syphilis and, in some instances, gonorrhea, and then treated them with antibiotics.

Racism, and more specifically, stereotypes about African American men as sexually promiscuous, permeated Tuskegee. The men in the study were not regarded as medical patients, or even as human beings, thus absolving the doctors involved of treating them to the best of their abilities. They were deemed research "subjects," available for the exploitation of the researchers. Imagine a modern-day version of this. What if prisoners were unknowingly put it an experiment to see if torture, such as "waterboarding," caused prisoners to reveal accurate information about their criminal activities? What if Muslim prisoners were targeted for this experiment? Without regulations, what would stop this kind of research?

As a result of the Tuskegee undertaking, the research community developed a new set of principles or values regarding the rights of human participants in research studies. Participants began to be viewed as people first, with the right to know the nature of the study they are participating in, including possible **risks and benefits,** and to **voluntarily** choose whether or not to participate. Further, over time a **principle of mutuality,** in which the research benefits both the researchers and the participants (Loftin, Barnett, Bunn, & Sullivan, 2005), has become important to many practitioners (particularly those working with qualitative and CBPR approaches). In this regard, an important question to ask regarding any project is "Whose interests are being served?"

These core values were put into ethical praxis with the development of various codes and regulations regarding research. The Tuskegee Syphilis Experiment precipitated the **Belmont Report** (1979), which led to the development of the **National Commission for the Protection of Human Subjects.** The three primary guiding principles identified in the Belmont Report are (1) respect for person, (2) beneficence, and (3) justice. These principles are enacted via informed consent, analysis of risks and benefits, and the selection of participants. Here is a YouTube link where you can learn more about the Belmont Report: *www.youtube.com/watch?v=W7sfIA1dIGQ.* The Tuskegee Syphilis Experiment also led to federal laws regarding **institutional review boards** and the protection of human subjects in research. Institutional review boards are discussed in the section on ethical praxis.

The Social Justice Movements

The **social justice movements of the 1960s and 1970s—the civil rights movement, the women's movement, the gay rights movement, the labor movement—**reflected and created major shifts in our cultural values. The justice movements sought equality on the basis of **status characteristics,** including sex, race, sexual orientation, and economic class, and the eradication of sexism, racism, homophobia, and classism. In various arenas of social life, from education to employment to home life to legal protection in the private and public spheres, inequalities were exposed and change demanded. Although many social injustices persist, the 1960s and 1970s were decades of great change. Increased attention to issues of gender, race, and sexuality and efforts to rectify historical inequities impacted the values guiding social research. A common effect from the justice movements was a thorough reexamination of **power** within the social research enterprise, in order to avoid creating knowledge that continued to collude in the oppression of minority groups (the issue of power is expanded in the section on reflexivity.)

Social Justice and Subjugated Voices

The cumulative effects these movements have had on the research community include reconsiderations of why we undertake research, what we believe about who should be included in research, what topics are valuable to study, and the uses to which social research might be put. All researchers are impacted by these ideas, but they shape individual researchers' values systems differently.

Values to emerge from the justice movements include, but are not limited to, inclusivity in the research process; addressing inequalities and injustices; societal improvement (making the world better); and anti-sexist, anti-racist, anti-homophobic, and anti-classist agendas. Social research became an important vehicle for **identity politics**[1] and **social change and for influencing public policy.**

Because historically marginalized groups had been rendered invisible in social research or included in ways that reinforced stereotypes, populations comprised of women, people of color, or lesbian/gay/bisexual/transgender (LGBT) individuals were sought out for meaningful inclusion. This effort was an attempt to include **underrepresented groups** in research. Sometimes researchers talk about including *subjugated voices* and *marginalized perspectives,* the perspectives of those typically forced to the peripheries of society. Researchers working from the five approaches may have different perspectives and practices with respect to **inclusivity.**

For example, in quantitative research, attempts at inclusivity often center on including persons from marginalized groups in research samples. For instance, whereas prior to the women's movement, an experiment may have included only male research subjects, an effect of the women's movement in the research arena has been to design experiments around women as well men. In qualitative research, increased value may be placed on allowing participants to use their own language to describe their experiences as a way of including differences based on gender and other status characteristics. In mixed methods projects, the approaches to inclusivity fostered in both quantitative and qualitative traditions come to bear. In arts-based research (ABR), there may be an effort to use an art form to include formerly marginalized perspectives in ways that jar people into thinking differently about commonly accepted stereotypes. In community-based participatory research (CBPR), there may be an effort to develop the project from the outset with people from different groups so that, for example, the perspectives of people across gender, race, class, or sexual orientation, or people who share a stigmatized characteristic such as schizophrenia or HIV-positive status, help build the project from the ground up. These are just a few examples to show how the changing beliefs that emerged from the previous social justice movements have influenced researchers: the beliefs that people/groups with different status characteristics should be included in research. However, researchers adapt differently to those changing beliefs in accord with the principles of the specific research design. Inclusivity can be understood and internalized as a part of our values system in numerous ways. How we think about and put into practice the value of inclusivity invariably affects the selection of participants for our project. Who do we identify as *stakeholders* (i.e., those groups with a vested interest in the research topic)? Around whose experiences and perspectives do we build the study? Whom do we choose to include?

By changing the populations researchers were interested in studying, research topics and purposes changed as well. As a result of the social justice movements, researchers have been able to ask new groups old research questions, and to ask entirely new questions. Let's take the example of studying parenting. Whereas historically, research would have focused exclusively on the nuclear family ideal, as a result of the social justice movements there has been a wealth of new research on parenting that has included single parents, gay and lesbian parents, interracial parents, families with stay-at-home dads, and families with two heterosexual working parents. This new body of research has greatly broadened our understanding of parenting in numerous ways. As a result of including previously neglected groups, we have also been able to ask entirely new research questions based on varying perspectives and experiences, including conducting comparative research. So, for example, we may conduct a study comparing parenting and family issues in households with heterosexual or homosexual parents. The findings from this kind of research can potentially be used to combat stereotypes and lobby for related policy changes.

Our values concerning inclusivity also come to bear during the process of data collection or generation. **Language** is a central issue. From the outset, we need to think about how we employ language both in written and verbal communication. With respect to the written word, as we develop our topic, create the instrumentation for the project (such as a questionnaire or interview guide), and choose how to represent our research to audiences, our use of language must be considered. Likewise, we need to carefully consider the language we use in our interactions with the research participants so that we don't offend anyone. It is important to use **politically and culturally sensitive terminology** with respect to status characteristics. Think about how often an actor, actress, or politician makes a public apology because he/she used an outdated or otherwise offensive racial term, for instance. It is important to be **culturally competent** and employ **cultural sensitivity** in all dealings with research participants and collaborators (Leavy, 2011a; Loftin et al., 2005) and in the documentation of the process and findings. This means, when you are conducting research on or with individuals with whom you share social or cultural differences, such as race, ethnicity, religion, social class, or education, it is important to be mindful of these differences, including different cultural understandings or experiences and commonly used expressions and other ways of communicating. It is vital to use nonoffensive and mutually understandable language. Some strategies for discovering what language is appropriate with your participants include:

- Conducting literature reviews
- Conducting pilot studies
- Initially immersing yourself in the setting/field
- Creating and consulting with community advisory boards

As a result of the historical atrocities reviewed earlier, as well as the values that emerged from the social justice movements, some researchers achieve cultural sensitivity by engaging their research participants as full collaborators in the process, which is commonplace in CBPR (reviewed in Chapter 8). *Full collaboration* means that participants help design all aspects of the research project, beginning with identifying a worthwhile topic.

As noted earlier, due to the social justice movements, social research became an important vehicle for **identity politics** and **social change and for influencing public policy.** Therefore, our values system impacts how we think about issues related to the **audience** for our research. The audience for our research may include a range of stakeholders.

You can see social justice values reflected in the following questions:

- Whom do we include in our research? How do we identify relevant stakeholders?
- What do we choose to study?
- How do we come up with topics, write purpose statements and hypotheses, and frame research questions?

- What measures have we taken to ensure that our language is appropriate and respectful and reflects sensitivity to cultural differences?
- How do we write up or otherwise represent our research?
- How will we think about issues such as authorship and ownership of the research findings/output?
- How will we identify relevant audiences? How do we take status characteristics into account as we identify relevant audiences?
- How will we distribute our findings to relevant audiences?
- Will we contribute to public scholarship, and if so, how?
- Do we intend to apply our research to a particular group or setting in pursuit of social change?
- Will we attempt to impact public policy, and if so, how?
- What is our political or social agenda?

Bear in mind that the preceding questions may not be paramount in every project, but they serve as examples of the different ways in which the values that emerged from the social justice movements have infiltrated the research process.

The research community has composed the moral principles that should underscore all research in response to the jarring historical atrocities reviewed earlier as well as the cumulative and continued progress made by the social justice movements. Our community responded to these events by continually reevaluating our values and ethical standards. This constant renegotiation of the important role of values in our work has moved research practice forward. Ultimately, our values impact our goals and what we do, including the treatment of those who participate in research, the kinds of people and topics we choose to include, and the uses to which we put our research.

 REVIEW STOP 1

1. The ethical substructure impacts every aspect of the research process and consists of three dimensions: _____, _____, and _____.

2. How was the Tuskegee Syphilis Experiment unethical?

   a. Tuskegee spurred new codes and regulations about the protection of human research participants, including the 1979 _____.

3. The language that researchers use should be sensitive and culturally competent. What are the four strategies for discovering what language is appropriate with your participants?

☛ **Go to the end of the chapter to check your answers.**

Ethical Praxis

This dimension of ethics addresses the question "What do you do?" What we actually do in terms of designing and executing our research agendas is greatly influenced by our beliefs. Carolyn Ellis (2007) notes there are three subcategories of ethics at the praxis stage: *procedural ethics, situational ethics,* and *relational ethics.* There is a historical context for guidelines and regulations (discussed earlier), but as you will see in this section, regulations only take us so far, and we must also rely on our own moral compasses. This section is divided into the issues that arise during three phases of research: research design (setup), data collection or content generation, and representation and dissemination.

Research Design/Setup

This phase involves preparing and designing your project. There are two main ethical issues applicable to this part of research design. First, ethical considerations emerge during the development of your research topic. Second, you need to consider the protection of the research participants and seek necessary approvals before you can begin working with human subjects.

Ethical Considerations as You Develop Your Topic

There are many considerations that go into the selection of a research topic, as reviewed in the next chapter; your moral compass comes into play as you select and develop a topic. Ethically, you must ask first yourself, "What is the **potential value or significance** of research on the proposed topic?" The value or significance of a research topic is determined by who will benefit from new knowledge on the topic, if the research will address an identified social need, and its potential to promote new learning or social change. Second, you must ensure there are no potential **conflicts of interest.** For instance, if your research is funded, make sure that your funder's agenda does not compete with your own. There should be no pressure or monetary gain for deriving certain outcomes or research findings.

You can reflect on these questions as you develop your topic:

- Who will benefit from research on this topic?
- Will research on this topic promote new learning, social justice, or social change?
- Is there a moral basis for conducting research on this topic (e.g., are you correcting a historical bias by focusing on a minority group or seeking to destigmatize a disenfranchised group)?
- Are you aware of any conflicts of interest?

As you continue to develop your topic, you will also identify potential populations of interest (those people or groups you are interested in, from whom you will seek participants for the study). During this time additional ethical questions come to bear:

- Does your research involve underrepresented persons or groups?

- Will the research participants benefit from their participation in the project?

- Will the distribution of burdens and benefits to the participants be fair (Adams, Holman Jones, & Ellis, 2015)?

The Protection of Research Participants

First, do no harm is the primary principle governing the protection of research participants. Adapted from the biomedical community, this principle states that no harm should come to research participants. This protection is extended to the settings in which research occurs (in cases when you are conducting research in real-world environments such as the participants' community).

Once you have selected a research topic, you will need to develop a research proposal that includes your intentions regarding the protection of your research participants (research proposals are discussed in depth in Chapters 4–8). Every discipline has a professional association with an established **code of ethics** that outlines discipline-specific ethical considerations (see the select list provided in the resource section at the end of this chapter). As you develop your research proposal, or plan for how the research will proceed, you can consult the codes of ethics in your discipline (Creswell, 2014). You will then need to seek appropriate approvals from your **institutional review board (IRB)**.

IRBs are established in universities to ensure that ethical standards are applied. Although there are variations at different kinds of institutions, IRBs have a minimum of five members and must include at least one scientist and one nonscientist. In addition to being diverse in terms of disciplinary backgrounds, IRBs should be diverse in terms of gender and race, although this is not always the case. The composition of an IRB can have serious consequences for how proposals are understood and evaluated. Prior to contacting potential research participants or beginning any data collection, you must seek permission from your IRB. IRBs are primarily in place to ensure the protection of human subjects. They dictate **procedural ethics** (Ellis, 2007). Your proposal to the IRB will include information such as the purpose of the study, the benefits of doing this research, the intended outcomes of the study, the population you are interested in, the proposed sampling strategy (how you will select participants), the possible risks to participants (which may include any possible physical, psychological, or emotional harm), benefits to participants, and your plan to garner informed consent. Consult your university's website for their particular requirements; typically there is a sample proposal you can use as a template or that you can download.

Once you have received IRB approval, you need to obtain informed consent from the research participants. At this early stage, there may be two phases of obtaining informed consent. First, you may provide your potential participants with an **invitation letter** or a **recruitment letter**. Although you don't want to inundate people at first contact, the letter should outline the basics of the study. After first identifying yourself as the researcher, providing your qualifications, and describing your interest in the topic (if there is more than one researcher, each one should be identified), describe the following (Leavy, 2011b, p. 35):

- The purpose of the study
- Why or how he/she has been selected as a potential participant
- What his/her participation would entail, including the time commitment
- Information about how and when follow-up to this letter will occur
- Contact information for the principle investigator or whomever they should contact if they have questions or concerns

Here is a sample invitation/recruitment letter[2]:

Dear Jane Smith,

My name is Patricia Leavy, and I am a sociology professor at Stonehill College, where I have taught for 7 years. I am writing to you because I am conducting an oral history interview study about the experience of divorce for stay-at-home mothers. Through my recruitment process, your name was mentioned as someone who might be interested in participating.

Should you choose to participate, your participation is completely voluntary and you are free to change your mind and stop your participation at any time. Your identity will be kept strictly confidential. It is my hope to publish this study as an academic journal article; however, I will not use your name or any other identifying information.

Your participation would mean that I would set up two or three interview sessions with you, lasting 60–90 minutes each. I would work around your schedule. The interviews could be held in my office, your home, or another quiet location of your choosing. I will provide light refreshments and reimburse you for any travel expenses.

I am very interested in the issues women face regarding marriage, parenting, and work. I think you have valuable knowledge to share that could benefit others. It is my hope that the interview experience would be personally rewarding for you, as well.

I can be reached at (phone) or (e-mail) to answer any questions you may have. I will follow up in 1–2 weeks with a phone call to see if you're interested in learning more (unless, of course, I hear from you first). Thank you.

Sincerely,

Patricia Leavy, PhD

Second, you will need to obtain written **informed consent** from the participants. Check your academic institution's website for their guidelines and the samples they may provide. There are also many discipline-specific examples available online. Generally, your written informed consent request should include the following (Leavy, 2011b, pp. 36–37):

- Title of the research project
- Identification of the principal investigator (and any other researchers) with contact information
- Basic information, including the purpose of the project and the research methods/procedures
- The intended outcomes of the project (including plans for publication)
- Details about what the individual's participation will entail, including the time commitment
- Possible risks of participation
- Possible benefits of participation
- The voluntary nature of participation, including the right to withdraw at any time
- The right of all participants to ask questions
- The steps that will be taken to ensure confidentiality and privacy
- Compensation for participation (even if there is none, this should be stated)
- Contact information for the principle investigator or whomever they should contact if they have questions or concerns
- A space should be provided for the principal investigator and participant's signatures with dates

Here is a sample informed consent letter[3]:

Informed Consent

Title: Oral History Project on Divorce for Stay-at-Home Mothers

Principal Investigator and Contact Information: Dr. Patricia Leavy (contact info.)

Purpose of the Study: The purpose of this study is to learn about the experience of divorce for stay-at-home-mothers from their own perspective. The study aims to produce new knowledge about how divorce impacts the identity of stay-at-home-mothers, practical matters such as daily routine, financial issues, and any other points of interest to the participants.

Intended Outcomes of the Study: The study is intended to contribute to our understanding of the lives of stay-at-home-mothers and the impact of divorce on those women. The knowledge gained from the study will contribute to the literature on marriage and family, gender, and identity in the social sciences. The results of the study will be published as an article in a peer-reviewed academic journal, shared in professional conference presentations, and may be published in other forms (such as a book chapter in an edited volume).

Procedures and What Participation Entails: This study relies on the method of oral history interview, which is a highly in-depth form of interview in which participants can share their experiences and stories. You will be asked to set up an initial interview expected to last 60–90 minutes. The interview will be scheduled around your scheduling needs. You can elect to have the interview conducted in the principal investigator's office located at (address), in your home, or in another quiet location of your choosing. You may bring a family photo album or any other pictures or objects you wish to share and discuss. During the interview, you will be asked a series of open-ended questions about your marriage, divorce, and your life as a stay-at-home mother before and after your divorce. You will be able to speak for as long as you like, and there aren't right or wrong responses. The goal is to share your experience. With your permission, the interview session will be audiotaped so that it can later be transcribed accurately. You will be provided with light refreshments during your interview. After the initial interview there will be an e-mail follow-up within 2 weeks, and you will be asked to schedule a second interview (same location and procedure as already described). The second interview is an opportunity to elaborate or explain previous comments and answer new questions that have arisen as a result of your first interview. A third interview session may be requested within 2 weeks after your second interview, if clarifications are needed.

Confidentiality: Your participation is strictly confidential; your identity will be kept anonymous and you will be assigned a pseudonym (a fictitious name) in any resulting publications or presentations. The audiotapes will be destroyed after they are transcribed and the interview transcripts will bear only your assigned pseudonym. Likewise, any people you mention in your interview will also be assigned pseudonyms. Details that are so specific they might alert readers to your identity will not be used.

Participant Rights and Compensation: Your participation in this study is strictly voluntary and can be withdrawn at any time without consequence. You also have the right to ask questions at any point during the study. Your time and experiences are greatly valued. Although you will not be compensated for your participation, you will be reimbursed for any travel expenses. Please be aware that possible risks of your participation include emotional or psychological distress from talking about your divorce, your children, and your identity. Should you experience any distress, please let the principal investigator know. Please be aware that possible benefits you may experience as a result of your participation include having your voice heard and valued and feeling empowered by sharing your experience with the knowledge that it may help others.

If you have any questions or concerns about participating in this study, please contact Dr. Patricia Leavy at (e-mail) or (phone).

If you agree to participate in the study, please sign and date this form below and return it to (include information). Once I have received your signed informed consent letter, I will e-mail you to set up an interview time. Thank you.

_____   _____

Participant signature   Date

Both the invitation and informed consent letters are generally hand delivered, mailed, or e-mailed. Obtaining written consent is an important measure of protection not only for participants but also for researchers, and in this age of technology, information about the project can also be communicated via video chatting (Skype, Facetime, and the like), social media, websites, blogs, and other technologically enabled means.

One additional issue emerges for minors. In studies involving participants who are minors and not legally able to give informed consent, but are old enough to understand the basics of the study and what their participation entails, assent is required. **Assent** means a minor understands and agrees to participate in a study. Once assent is acquired, informed consent must be given by the minor's legal guardian.

The Messiness of Informed Consent in Practice

Although it is important to obtain informed consent, which is a real and valid measure for the protection of research participants, it would be a mistake to gloss over the complexity and messiness of informed consent in practice. This is an area in which procedural ethics bumps up against situational and relational ethical issues, which come to bear after you have begun the research process. **Situational ethics** refers to "ethics in practice" (Ellis, 2007, p. 4). **Relational ethics** refers to an "ethics of care" (Ellis, 2007, p. 4). This set of ethical issues centers on the interpersonal relationships between the researcher and participants (Ellis, 2007). (Situational and relational ethics are discussed further in the section on data collection and working with the research participants.)

The procedural aspect of obtaining informed consent is straightforward. However, once that informed consent has been obtained, there are two additional issues to be aware of: process consent and unanticipated experiences.

Informed consent must be obtained prior to beginning research in order to satisfy your IRB. In addition, in a project for which participation extends over a period of time, it is appropriate to **process consent** at multiple stages (Adams et al., 2015). This means that you designate times to check in with research participants and review consent issues, including the voluntary nature of the study and their right to withdraw. This effort also provides an opportunity to see how participants are doing, to learn if they are experiencing any discomfort, stress, or unanticipated burden, from their participation. Likewise this is also a time during which you may hear about the positive benefits of their participation. In a short-term study such as a quantitative survey project or a qualitative in-depth interview project where data are collected at one designated time, or in an experiment conducted over a short period of time, you will only need to obtain informed consent once. However, in a long-term qualitative field research study or community-based project, for example, it is ethically sound to process consent at multiple stages.

A part of obtaining informed consent is detailing all of the possible risks and benefits of participation in the research project. However, despite your best efforts at imagining the likely risks and benefits, no one can anticipate every possible way a participant might be affected, nor could you entirely anticipate every way in which you, as the researcher, might be affected. Therefore, it is important to acknowledge that despite your best efforts to foreshadow how the process will unfold, a participant might have **unanticipated experiences.** Joanna Zylinksa (2005) explains that there is a "surprise element" in social research. R. S. Parker (1990) writes that ethical uncertainty "does not indicate a failure of rule-and-principle-based reasoning; rather, it is a reminder of its limits (p. 36, as quoted in Adams, 2008, p. 178). Tony Adams (2008) summarizes these issues beautifully:

> Working with ethics involves realizing that we do not know how others will respond to and/or interpret our work. It's acknowledging that we can never definitively know who we harm or help with our communicative practices. And ethics involves the simultaneous welcoming and valuing of endless questions, never knowing whether our decisions are "right" or "wrong." (p. 179)

These issues of ethical messiness and how to deal with them are revisited later in the section on reflexivity.

✋ REVIEW STOP 2

1. A researcher secures funding from the state to study patient care at a state psychiatric facility. The funder wants the researcher to find that patient care is excellent so they retain federal funding. Should the researcher proceed?

   a. Why or why not?

2. IRBs are established in universities for what purpose?

3. Beyond the basics, including the title of the project, information about the principal investigator and compensation, what information is provided to participants in order to obtain informed consent?

   a. In a project that occurs over a long period of time, it is appropriate to

_____ consent at multiple stages, which means you review consent issues and participants' right to withdraw.

☞ **Go to the end of the chapter to check your answers.**

Data Collection/Generation/Content Creation

Ethics come to bear during data collection or generation as you work with the participants. The amount of contact you have with the research participants as well as the nature of that contact are largely based on the research design approach you are working with, as well as specifics about the study.

"Objectivity" and "Strong Objectivity"

In Chapter 1, I discussed the philosophical elements of research. The **paradigm or worldview** you are working within influences your perspective on your role in the research process. Your **epistemological position** is a belief system about how to embody the role of researcher and the nature of the relationship between the researcher and research participants (Guba & Lincoln, 1998; Harding, 1987; Hesse-Biber & Leavy, 2004, 2011). Whereas there are numerous epistemological positions one might adopt, there are two major perspectives: objectivity and strong objectivity.

Researchers holding a **positivist or postpositivist worldview** (generally those in quantitative research and sometimes in mixed methods research) practice **objectivity** in the data collection process. Social scientific objectivity was modeled after practices in the physical sciences. When practicing objectivity, researchers adopt a position of **neutrality**, which means they table their personal biases and feelings. For example, we expect doctors to treat patients the same way regardless of each patient's race, gender, or other attributes. They are trained to practice neutrality. The same holds true in postpositivist research.

Researchers holding an **interpretive, constructivist, critical, or transformative worldview** (generally those in qualitative, arts-based, or community-based participatory research) reject the social scientific model of objectivity. Instead, they may practice **strong objectivity** (Harding, 1993), which involves actively acknowledging and accounting for one's biases, values, and attitudes (see Table 2.1). These researchers contend that neutrality and pure objectivity can never be reached because researchers, like all people, have life experiences, attitudes, and beliefs that impact how they see, think, and act. Further, those working from critical worldviews, in

TABLE 2.1. "Objectivity" and "Strong Objectivity"	
Objectivity	Researcher tables personal biases and feelings
Strong objectivity	Researcher acknowledges and even uses personal biases and feelings

particular, may find objectivity not only impossible but also undesirable as they actively seek to advance social or political agendas, which are necessarily **value-laden.** For example, we might expect a gun control advocate who lost her child to gun violence, to speak from her personal position as a grieving parent, acknowledging and using her experiences and political beliefs. The same is true in some interpretive, constructivist, critical, and transformative research.

Researcher–Researched Relationships

The kinds of interactions you have with your research participants depend on what is appropriate per the research design approach and corresponding worldview you are employing. In quantitative research, such as experiments or surveys, direct contact with participants may be limited. For instance, in an online experiment, all of your communication may be in written form online. Generally speaking, due to the values of objectivity, you don't develop relationships with your research subjects or respondents. The main ethical issues during data collection in a quantitative approach include **acting respectfully, avoiding coercion, and enacting the agreed-upon informed consent points.**

In qualitative research, arts-based research, and community-based participatory research, relationships may constitute the cornerstone of the research endeavor. Depending on the type of research project, the extent to which the following issues are relevant will vary; however, interactions and relationships between the researcher and research participant come to bear on ethical practice. If you are conducting research in a natural setting, such as in qualitative field research or community-based research, you begin building relationships with participants as you seek access into the community. However, if you are conducting in-depth interview research in an artificial setting—meaning a setting the participant would not normally be in, such as your office—issues of access are not relevant. This topic is discussed in more detail in Chapter 5 on qualitative research. For now, the takeaway is that you begin to form relationships from the moment of each participant's involvement in the project.

When you're using a research approach that requires you to work closely with participants to unearth or generate data, key ethical issues include **building trust, developing rapport, and setting expectations.** Ways of building trust and developing rapport may include showing an active interest in participants' experiences and stories; using appropriate body language and facial expressions; demonstrating that you care about the project and the participants' experiences; and sharing things about yourself, including your personal interest in the topic. It is important to demonstrate an **ethic of honesty, integrity, and caring.** Be mindful that you are truthfully representing yourself and the project, and use **nonjudgmental and nondenigrating language** (there are some rare instances in which a field researcher must use deception because of the dangerous nature of the topic; this issue is addressed in brief shortly). In field research, and sometimes in CBPR or collaborative arts-based research, you may engage in the activities of the participants in order to build trust and demonstrate your interest and caring. For example, Patti Lather (2000) is a well-known qualitative researcher who infamously got into a hot tub with her research participants in order to bond with them and facilitate the research project. There are many qualitative researchers who advocate "friendship as a method" to garner data and "acknowledge our interpersonal bonds to others" (Adams et al., 2015, pp. 60–61).

As we develop relationships with the research participants, we must attend to **relational ethics** (Adams et al., 2015; Ellis, 2007). Ellis defines relational ethics as follows:

> Relational ethics recognizes and values mutual respect, dignity, and connectedness between the researcher and research, and between researchers and the communities in which they live and work. . . . Act from our hearts and minds, to acknowledge our interpersonal bonds to others. . . . (2007, p. 4)

It becomes our responsibility to nurture our relationships with the research participants, change our patterns of interaction if they don't serve our participants or cause conflicts, and be mindful of how the research process is affecting our participants (Adams et al., 2015).

Setting appropriate **expectations** is a vital part of ethical practice. The informed consent letter contains a description of what participation in the study entails, and at the start of data collection you should expand on your discussion of expectations in two regards. First, it is important to set expectations about the **time commitment** you anticipate and how that time will be spent. Depending on the kind of project, you may set these expectations and then review them with the participants, making adjustments as they deem needed, or you may develop expectations with your participants or collaborators. For example, in the case of CBPR, it is typical to develop these expectations as a team so that academic and nonacademic stakeholders have an opportunity to state their needs and expectations and to shape the process together. In CBPR or any group research project it is important to plan the **division of labor** so that each person knows what is expected of him/her. It is also vital that everybody has input in this process and that no one is overburdened. For example, as is discussed in Chapter 8, co-researchers working in a community-based organization may have different scheduling demands and needs then an academic researcher. It is essential to balance everyone's needs as you set expectations.

Second, it is also important to set expectations regarding the nature of your relationship with the research participants. You may want to set some **boundaries** and allow participants the opportunity to do the same. It is also advisable to set expectations regarding what happens to your relationship at the end of the project. Will you continue to have contact? Are friendships sustainable outside of the context of research? What, if any, help do the participants anticipate receiving from you? These issues are elaborated in appropriate chapters.

Completion of Data Collection or Generation

Your ethical responsibilities toward your participants do not end once you have collected the data for your study. Always remember, these are people whose lives you have disrupted to some extent in order to garner valuable information for your research agenda. Depending on the nature of your research project, you may build a **debriefing** phase into the research design (Babbie, 2013). Debriefing provides an opportunity to elicit feedback from the participants about their experiences. Depending on the nature of the project, you might present participants with a brief questionnaire, conduct a small focus group, or have private in-person conversations. In some instances, what you learn during this debriefing phase may cause you to make modifications to the project moving forward or to report on areas you would suggest changing in future research. The debriefing phase is particularly important when the study has investigated sensitive subject matter or presented the research in a form likely to cause an emotional response. For example, if participants in arts-based research are involved in a performance piece such as a play, or serve as audience members for a play, that medium is likely to engage a visceral and emotional response, and you want to check back and gauge how people are handling that aspect of the project

It is important to be armed with **resources** for the participants, if appropriate to the topic. For example, if the study focuses on eating disorders or body image issues, you may want to provide participants with a list of online resources, information about support groups, therapists, nutritionists, and other professionals in their community who specialize in this area.

It is also courteous to send participants a letter or e-mail thanking them for their participation. This act demonstrates that you value their time and knowledge and may also provide closure for your interactions with them. As noted earlier, there are cases in which your relationships with participants continue after data collection. For example, they may be assisting with the analysis, interpretation, and/or representation of the research findings. Further, you may have developed friendships that will extend beyond the research. Nevertheless, at either the completion of data collection or the completion of their formal participation in the project (e.g., assisting with representing the research findings), it is customary to send a thank-you letter. Here is a sample letter illustrating the bare bones of what you might include; obviously, if this has been highly relational research, such as a long-term life history project, you would probably send a more personalized and detailed letter.

Dear X,

Thank you for your participation in this study (title). Your participation was vital to learning about (topic). I greatly appreciate your time. I will be in touch to pass on my final report on the research study, which I hope to have published in (X amount of time). If you have any follow-up questions or concerns, please contact me at (phone) or (e-mail). Thank you again for your participation.

Sincerely,

Patricia Leavy, PhD

Note that regardless of whether or not you have any personal relationship with the participants, it is ethical practice to share your research findings with them. This issue is discussed shortly in the section on dissemination.

Before moving on to the topics of representation and dissemination, it is important to acknowledge that although the discussion of ethics during data collection or data generation is focused on working with the research participants, ethical issues still apply in studies involving the collection and analysis of nonliving data such as statistical data, census data, historical or archival data, and other forms of document/textual/visual/audiovisual data. The issues specific to nonliving data are discussed at greater length in appropriate chapters; for now, here are some of the ethical issues you need to consider during practice:

- Verify the origin of the data.

- Pay attention to any biases or problems with how the data were collected or archived.

- Pay attention to your procedure of dealing with the data.

- Pay attention to anomalies or discrepancies in the data and make sure to report on them accurately.

- Do not omit data that refute your hypothesis or assumptions.

 **REVIEW STOP 3**

1. Regardless of your epistemological position, what are the main ethical issues during data collection?

2. A researcher is conducting a study in a community setting needs to show an active interest in participants' stories and demonstrate caring in order to build trust and develop _____.

3. It's important to set expectations with participants around which two areas so that they know what is expected of them and what they can expect from you?

☞ **Go to the end of the chapter to check your answers.**

Representation and Dissemination

Ethics comes to bear during the final phases of representing and sharing research findings. We need to consider how to condense, format, shape, and ultimately distribute what we have learned.

Representation

As you represent the research findings, you will have several ethical considerations. The primary considerations involve disclosure of the methodology, the format of the representation, and how you shape the information you present.

Disclosing the methodology involves answering the questions "What did you aim to do and how did you do it?" (Leavy, 2011b, p. 70) Disclosing the methodology is sometimes referred to as providing the **context of justification.** This is where you explain and justify your research design procedures and the methods you employed. Methodological **transparency** is generally considered important so that those who are exposed to your research can understand the process by which you formed your conclusions. However, as is discussed in Chapters 4–8, there are methods-specific considerations in terms of what is normative to disclose with respect to methodology. For example, in some genres of arts-based research, full transparency is not a norm.

Research may be represented in many different **formats.** Historically, research findings were almost exclusively represented as research articles, reports, or books. Most research studies still result in published peer-reviewed journal articles. However, given the emergence of CBPR practices, arts-based research practices, and innovations in quantitative and qualitative research, many researchers now represent their projects in other formats. In some instances, one research project is represented in **multiple formats** in an attempt to reach different stakeholders or to emphasize different dimensions of the data. The format you select inevitably impacts who has access to the research findings—and that alone makes it an ethical decision. In other words, the format of the research representation is inextricably bound to issues of **audience and dissemination.** Here are some of the ways researchers represent their projects:

- Peer-reviewed journal articles
- Research reports
- Conference presentations
- Books
- Brochures/informational pamphlets
- Popular media, including op-eds and blogs
- Websites
- Artistic forms (in all mediums)

It is important to note although it is fine to publish a study as a journal article and also in popular forms (e.g., op-eds or blogs) to reach different audiences, it is generally not acceptable to publish the same data in multiple peer-reviewed publications. This is particularly frowned upon in the social sciences and viewed as unethical.

Finally, and perhaps most importantly, is the **content** that you share and how you shape that content. Obviously the form in which you represent the findings will impact certain considerations. Specific considerations based on which of the five approaches to research you are employing as well as methods-specific considerations are noted in Chapters 4–8. What follows are some general considerations.

Above all, be **honest and truthful.** With that said, you have a lot of latitude. You will need to consider **what data are included** and, what data, if any, are omitted. As a part of this consideration, you will need to make ethical decisions about how to deal with unexpected findings, outliers, or anomalies. Sometimes there is a wealth of data and you simply aren't able to include or reference it all. For example, if you have conducted focus group interviews with a total of 30 people, you may only quote the exact words of a few people in your research write-up. How do you select which quotes to use? Are they representatives of the wealth of data you have collected? How will you contextualize the quotes you selected?

Another issue to consider when representing the research in a written format is the formality with which you will write and the **narrator point of view.** In quantitative and mixed methods research, third-person narration is typically employed. However, when using qualitative, arts-based, or community-based approaches, it is common to see third- or first-person accounts. The narrator point of view we impose shapes the way that audiences will receive the work. In other words, it impacts the experience of reading the text. Jonathan Wyatt (2006) notes, "the general ethical principle at stake . . . is how close we choose to position our readers" (p. 814).

In this regard pay careful attention to **language,** choosing your words carefully. Use forthright, simple, and clear language whenever possible. Try to avoid unnecessary jargon, and if discipline-specific jargon is needed, define terms so that someone outside of your discipline could follow your meaning. Naturally, also avoid any disrespectful or degrading language and show attentiveness to cultural differences as appropriate to your topic. Soliciting feedback on drafts of the write-up from participants, members of the audiences we aim to reach, peers, and/or colleagues may be helpful for gauging our use of clear language.

When working with human participants, attempt to **sensitively portray people and their situations** (Cole & Knowles, 2001). Avoid reifying stereotypes. These issues don't come to bear only when employing the written format. For example, in arts-based research you may be representing your project through visual art, which also has the power to reinforce or dislodge stereotypes. There is a range of choices you will make that are bound to ethical practice. For example, in a field research or interview study, you may quote excerpts from the participants' interview transcripts in your final write-up. When people speak, they may stutter, trip over their words, say things like "um" or "uh" or "like," repeat words, and so forth. You'll need to decide how to best represent what the participants have told you. Sometimes researchers "beautify" transcript excerpts, which means that they clean up some of the language to put the participant in the best light. In other cases the researchers do not beautify the transcript excerpts because they may feel it misrepresents or homogenizes the voices of their participants (making them all sound alike). These issues are particularly pronounced when cultural differences are at play. For example, if you are talking with people from a lower socioeconomic or educational background, is it ethical to correct their grammar in quoted transcripts? There are no hard-and-fast rules on any of these issues, but they are important decisions and will influence how others read and perceive your research findings.

Dissemination

Dissemination refers to **sharing or distributing** the research. As the famous saying goes, "The candle is not there to illuminate itself" (Nowab Jan-Fishan Khan, 19th century). When we conduct social research, there is an ethical mandate to share the research with others. It is important to get the work out so that others have access to the knowledge you have generated.

The first major question to answer is "With whom do I plan to share the research findings?" The second major question to ask yourself is "How can I reach my intended audience(s)?"

First, in most cases you should **share your research findings with your research participants.** Historically, social scientists conducted research with human subjects and often did not share the results of that research with those individuals. For example, there are countless stories of anthropologists going into communities and villages in the global South, living with people for months or years as a part of their field research, and then leaving and publishing their research as a monograph (a research book) and never even bothering to send a copy to the local library in the community in which they were enmeshed. Sharing research wasn't customary practice and likely an unfortunate oversight.

Even researchers with the best of intentions can fall into thinking that justifies a failure to share the products of research with the research participants. For example, Ellis, who is now one of the qualitative research community's most vocal advocates of ethics in research practice, writes candidly about mistakes she made in the beginning of her career. As a part of her undergraduate and then later her graduate research, she conducted a study called "Fisher Folk: Two Communities on Chesapeake Bay," comparing two isolated fishing communities. Among the choices she winces at now, her social class biases about those in her study fostered the idea that she could write whatever she wished because the participants would never see it. She writes:

> It embarrasses me now; however, at the time I sometimes found myself thinking that because most of the people with whom I interacted couldn't read, they would never see what I had written anyway and, if they did, they wouldn't understand the sociological and theoretical story I was trying to tell" (Ellis, 2007, p. 8).

It is important to consider how to share the research findings with the participants. When you engage in this process, you inevitably also think about the *content* of the representations, which facilitates the process of sensitively portraying people and their circumstances. I suggest setting expectations upfront with your participants about how the findings will be made available. For example, this issue could be covered in the invitation letter and/or in the informed consent document.

Despite the typically strong ethical mandate to share findings with the research participants, there are cases in which doing so isn't appropriate or isn't an appropriate personal decision. For example, there are rare instances in which a researcher needs to conduct **covert research** and employ **deception**, in order to access a hard-to-reach group or subculture engaged in illicit activities. For example, there are instances when a qualitative field researcher deceptively conducts research within a criminal organization such as a gang or the mafia. It is very unlikely you will ever conduct this type of research. There are also situations in which you may make a **personal decision** not to share your research findings. For example, in qualitative autoethnographic research, you use your own experiences as data (discussed in Chapter 5). None of us lives in a vacuum. It is likely that others are complicit in any story we may write about our own lives (Ellis, 2011; Wyatt, 2006). The question is, do we then share what we have written with those in our lives? For example, Ellis (2011) wrote about her mother before her death and did not feel comfortable sharing the story with her. In the spirit of sustained ethical practice, this was a considered decision that she seriously reflected on at the time, and again, after the fact.

Second, social researchers typically share their research findings with their **academic research community or communities.** It is important that other researchers interested in the subject matter or methodology have access to the research findings. By sharing the research findings within our academic communities, we are able to build a repository of knowledge on a topic. Other researchers are able to cite your work in their literature reviews, replicate your study, expand on your study by going in a new direction or replicating the study with a different population, or adapt the methodology. Typically, researchers publish their studies in peer-reviewed journals and present their research at appropriate conferences. You will need to make decisions about the academic audiences you wish to reach. Ask yourself the following:

- "Do I wish to reach a discipline-specific audience?" If so, identify the discipline and look for appropriate journals and conferences.
- "Do I wish to reach an interdisciplinary audience?" If so, identify the disciplines or area of study and look for appropriate journals and conferences.
- "In funded research, do I wish to reach my funding organization or institute?" If so, find out what their procedures are (in many cases there is a required format for writing a grant report, which was stipulated upon receipt of your award).
- "Do I wish to reach the methodology community in order to share the unique design of my study?" If so, identify the approach you used (quantitative, qualitative, mixed methods, arts-based, community-based) and look for appropriate research methods related journals and conferences.

Third, social researchers need to decide if they will try to share their research findings with other **relevant stakeholders outside of the research academy.** In recent years there has been more pressure to share research findings beyond the academy, making research relevant in the real world. In some institutions, particularly in the United Kingdom and Australia, academic researchers are assessed, in part, based on the impact of their research. This shift represents a push toward **public scholarship.** You will need to make decisions about the audiences you aim to reach and the best way of doing so. Ask yourself the following:

- Who are the relevant nonacademic stakeholders? In other words, which populations are impacted by the subject matter covered in my research?
- What issues of difference, such as social class, education, or cultural differences, should I be aware of as I attempt to reach the stakeholders? For example, should I avoid jargon and other highly academic language?
- What is my goal in reaching the nonacademic stakeholders I have identified? Do I aim to accomplish any of the following: raise awareness about a topic or issue, educate people with new information about a topic or issue, or challenge commonly held beliefs/assumptions/stereotypes?
- Do my research objectives include either of the following: influencing public policy or creating community change?

Once you have identified the stakeholders you wish to reach and your goal in doing so, you can determine the best course of action. You may do any of the following (which is, by no means, an exhaustive list):

- Produce popular writings such as op-eds or blogs.
- Create a website (which may or may not have an interactive feature for those who log on).
- Appear on local radio or television.
- Create and distribute flyers or pamphlets in relevant community spaces.
- Offer public lectures in community-accessible spaces.
- Share art in venues stakeholders are able to reach (whether it is visual art displayed in a gallery space or library; or a performance given in community theaters; or relevant spaces per the topic, ranging from hospitals to schools).

Finally, in some kinds of projects it is also appropriate to **archive** the raw data and/or final research representation. For example, it is common practice in the qualitative method of oral history interview to deposit the oral history interview transcripts in an appropriate repository. This is another way of making the research available to others.

Reflexivity

This ethical dimension of reflexivity in research addresses the question "How does power come to bear?" The key issues are how power comes to bear on the process and how we reflect on our own position as researchers. Earlier I discussed the context of justification, which is the disclosure and justification of our methodology. Another issue is the **context of discovery**, which is where we account for our own role in the research process. This issue involves personal accountability and an awareness of the role of power in research practice. In other words, the context of discovery is not only about "*what* we have discovered, but *how* we have discovered it" (Etherington, 2007, p. 601). Reflexivity is an area where values and praxis intersect.

Power

In order to understand reflexivity in research practice today, it is important to consider the historical context in which reflexivity emerged as a cornerstone of ethical practice. The social justice movements highlighted historical inequities in research that served to exclude minorities from the research process and reinforce dominant ideologies and stereotypes. As noted earlier, one common effect from the social justice movements was a thorough reexamination of **power** within the social research enterprise in order to avoid creating knowledge that continued to collude with factors/powers that oppressed women and other minority groups. Over the years, as qualitative practices and then later arts-based and community-based research practices developed, as well as interpretive and critical approaches to research, the focus on reflexivity increased.

Being reflexive in our research practice means paying attention to how power influences our attitudes and behaviors, and our own role in shaping the research experience. Some of the issues that qualitative researchers, in particular, consider are the planes of **hierarchy and authority** on which researchers and participants operate. Many qualitative researchers reject a hierarchical relationship between researchers and participants. This is a classic example of how values and praxis intersect in discussions of reflexivity. Let's say you are entering into an in-depth interview study. Given that you value nonhierarchical research relationships and respect your participants as authorities over their own knowledge, there are numerous actions you might take to *enact* your reflexivity. For example, you could offer your participants opportunities to check their interview transcripts and expand, revise, explain, or omit aspects of them. You might engage them in the analysis and interpretive process, even as coauthors. You could also keep a record of your own attitudes and beliefs throughout the project, analyzing your role in shaping the process. Your stance on reflexive practice may also impact the use of a particular theoretical framework. For example, you might employ a constructivist or critical worldview. If so, there is a range of power-sensitive or power-attentive approaches (Haraway, 1991; Pfohl, 2007). These are just examples of how you might proceed.

Although the term *reflexivity* most often appears in the literature on qualitative practice, the idea of reflexivity, or something like it, is relevant in quantitative practice as well. The term **Hawthorne effect** in quantitative research refers to how participation in a research study may, inevitably, impact subjects' responses. From 1924 to 1932, experiments were conducted in The Hawthorne Works, an electric factory near Chicago. The researchers studied whether improving worker conditions, for example, through better lighting, would increase productivity. They found that better lighting did improve productivity; however, when they lowered the lighting, they also found increased productivity. When the research ended, the productivity decreased. It seemed productivity had increased because of the study itself, not the lighting. As a result, quantitative researchers have developed measures to account for the effect of the study. **Control groups** are used in experiments in order to mitigate against the effect of the experiment itself. A control group is similar to the experimental group in all relevant factors, but the subjects do not receive the experimental intervention. In some instances, more than one experimental or control group may be needed (discussed in Chapter 4).

Voice

Another way that we engage in reflexive practice is to be attentive to issues of **voice**. This term is typically used to talk about the **ability to speak and be heard** and is implicitly **political** (Hertz, 1997; Matzafi-Haller, 1997; Wyatt, 2006). Who is seen as an authority? Who has the right to speak on behalf of others? The issue of speaking for those with whom we share differences or who may be members of marginalized or oppressed groups—often referred to as "others" in the social science literature—is an ethical quagmire. As we have learned from the social justice movements, it is important to seek out the perspectives of those who historically have been marginalized for active inclusion in the knowledge-building process. However, when doing so we must be very mindful of the ways in which we attempt to speak for others or represent the experiences and perspectives of others. In our attempts to be inclusive, we don't want to inadvertently colonize the stories and experiences of others. In this regard, it is important to be cognizant of these issues and to carefully reflect on how we position ourselves and others in representations of our research.

Putting Reflexivity into Practice across the Five Approaches

Enacting reflexivity will look different across the different approaches to research. For example, in quantitative research neutrality and objectivity are paramount. Therefore, reflexivity may involve self-awareness of one's attempt to remain impartial throughout the process. In qualitative research, on the other hand, the researcher's emotions may be a valuable part of the process that he/she attempts to be in tune with and document. Neither strategy for the researcher's accounting for his/her role in shaping the research experience is better or worse; rather, they are better suited to different kinds of research projects. So, what can we do as we attempt to engage in reflexive practice?

- In quantitative research, we could conduct small-scale pilot studies to gauge the appropriateness of our language, assumptions, and research instruments (e.g., a questionnaire or experimental intervention). We might also rely on peer review as a step toward attaining validity and ensuring that our biases are not coloring the research design.

- In qualitative research, we could engage in a process of writing reflexive memo notes throughout data collection and analysis in order to document and account for our position within the process. We might also pay particular attention to our relationships with our participants, demonstrating "an ethics of caring" during all phases (Ellis, 2007).

- In MMR, we could combine strategies used in both quantitative and qualitative research in order to maximize reflexivity.

- In ABR, we could make a concerted effort to listen to our hearts (Pelias, 2004); pay attention to the emotional tenor of our work, including how it may impact audiences; and be cognizant that we are presenting people in multidimensional ways that do not reinforce stereotypes.

- In CBPR, we could engage cultural insiders as we develop and refine our assumptions, appropriate language to employ, our strategies moving forward, and our goals.

There are many different ways of bringing others into the research process and/or documenting the project ourselves, including our location in it. The preceding list is intended only as an introduction to this topic; a range of appropriate strategies is reviewed in Chapters 4–8.

✋ REVIEW STOP 4

1. Research is typically represented in research articles, reports, or books. What are some other formats for representing research?

   a. In some instances, a project is represented in multiple formats to reach different stakeholders. Is it generally acceptable to publish the same data in two journal articles?

2. Research findings should be shared with whom?

3. _____ centers on how power comes to bear on the research process and how we reflect on our own role as researchers.

👉 **Go to the end of the chapter to check your answers.**

Conclusion

Bear in mind that some of the ethical issues that have been discussed are more pronounced in different approaches, and these will be noted accordingly in Chapters 4–8.

For example, the nature of the relationships formed in quasi-experimental research versus those in qualitative ethnography differs entirely, and even within the genre of ethnography, for example, there is a continuum. What is important is that you are using strategies that are in line with your values and methodology. What constitutes ethical practice in some areas, such as "First do no harm" and obtain informed consent, are uniform. However, what constitutes ethical practice is radically different in other ways (objectivity vs. strong objectivity).

As the issue of ethics comes to bear throughout the practice of each of the five approaches to research, ethical decision making is highlighted throughout Chapters 4–8.

✓ REVIEW STOP ANSWER KEY

Review Stop 1

1. philosophical, praxis, reflexivity
2. Participants were not told they had syphilis and were not treated for it.
   a. Belmont Report
3. conducting literature reviews, conducting pilot studies, initially immersing myself in the field/setting, and creating and consulting with community advisory boards.

Review Stop 2

1. no
   a. conflict of interest
2. to protect human subjects in research
3. purpose of the project and methods, intended outcomes, what participation entails, possible risks and benefits, voluntary, confidential, right to ask questions
   a. process

Review Stop 3

1. acting respectfully, avoiding coercion, enacting the agreed-upon informed consent points
2. rapport
3. time commitment and boundaries (relationship expectations)

Review Stop 4

1. conference presentations, brochures/informational pamphlets, popular media (op-eds and blogs), websites, artistic forms
   a. no
2. the research participants, the academic research community, and in some cases, relevant stakeholders outside of the academy
3. reflexivity

Further Engagement

1. The 1971 Stanford Prison Experiment is frequently used as a case study to discuss ethics in research. Locate another well-known study used to stimulate thinking around research ethics. Examples include Laud Humphrey's 1970 study of homosexual encounters in public places, Stanley Milgram's 1963 study on obeying instruction even if harming another person, John Darlye and Bibb Latane's 1968 study on the bystander effect, and Elliot Liebow's 1967 study on Black "street corner" men. Select one of these or one of the countless other examples you can find online or through your research library. Read the study and write a response that addresses (a) the central ethical issues that emerged and (b) how the study could be redesigned more ethically (one page maximum).

2. Consult your university website's IRB page and download their informed consent requirements. Write a sample informed consent letter for a project you are interested in conducting. If you do not have a project in mind, use one of the five examples given at the end of Chapter 1 on the topic of drinking on college campuses.

3. Here are brief summaries of three different research projects. What are the primary ethical issues the researcher needs to consider?

   a. *Hypothetical research scenario 1:* A researcher conducts survey research in a private Catholic college in order to understand how the identity of the college impacts life in that organization for students and employees.

   b. *Hypothetical research scenario 2:* A researcher moves into an apartment building in a urban working-class neighborhood that has been selected by developers for a development project. The researcher's goal is to understand the impact of the development process on the community and help the community participate in its own development process. The researcher discloses his/her identity and conducts field research, interview research, and document analysis.

   c. *Hypothetical research scenario 3:* A researcher poses as a homeless person in order to conduct field research on what it means to live as a homeless person—how he/she gets food, money, shelter, build relationships, and so forth. The researcher intends to create a performance piece out of the research findings.

Resources

Traianou, A. (2014). The centrality of ethics in qualitative research. In P. Leavy (Ed.), *The Oxford handbook of qualitative research* (pp. 62–77). New York: Oxford University Press.

Emery, B., McQuarrie, C., Friedman, L., Bratman, L., Lauder, K., & Little, G. (Producers), & Alvarez, K. P. (Director). (2015). *The Stanford prison experiment* [Motion Picture]. United States: Coup d'Etat Films.

Suggested Journals

AMA Journal of Ethics (American Medical Association)
http://journalofethics.ama-assn.org

Ethical Theory and Moral Practice (Springer)
www.springer.com/social+sciences/applied+ethics/journal/10677

Ethics & Behavior (Routledge)
*www.tandfonline.com/action/journalInformation?show=aimsScope&journalCode=h
    ebh20#.Vmb6c5UgmM8*

Journal of Empirical Research on Human Research Ethics (SAGE)
http://jre.sagepub.com

Research Ethics (Sage)
http://rea.sagepub.com

Professional Associations with Online Codes of Ethics (not an exhaustive list)

Academy of Criminal Justice Sciences (ACJS)
American Anthropological Association (AAA)
American Counseling Association (ACA)
American Educational Research Association (AERA)
American Evaluation Association (AEA)
American Folklore Society (AFS)
American Nurses Association (ANA)
American Political Science Association (APSA)
American Psychological Association (APA)
American Sociological Association (ASA)
National Association of Social Workers (NASW)
National Women's Studies Association (NWSA)

Notes

1. *Identity politics* refers to groups with shared status negotiating for their common interests.
2. Reprinted from Leavy (2011b, pp. 35–36). Copyright © 2011 Oxford University Press. Reprinted by permission.
3. Based on Leavy (2011b, pp. 35–37).

CHAPTER 3

Getting Started Designing a Project

Selecting a Topic

How do you find a topic to study? Typically you begin with a broad, general interest and then move to a **research topic.** I initially began conducting interview research with women about their body image as a result of personal interests I cultivated during the many years I took ballet and theatre arts classes, during which I witnessed many people struggling with body image issues. Later, when I was in graduate school, a professor who studied body image and eating disorders presented me with opportunities to conduct research in this area. My current interview research with women about their relationships and identities—a topic I have long been interested in and investigating—developed as a result of those early research experiences coupled with my personal experiences. As you can see from my own example, researchers initially come to a topic because of their **personal interests, experiences and values, previous research experience,** and/or opportunities in the form of **funding or collaborations.**

Table 3.1 presents several examples of research topics, which at this stage are extremely broad. I present three columns of research topics: The first is the broadest and most general, which may be where you begin; the second is more specific in terms of the population or setting you are interested in; and the third is the most specific.

Note that even in the second and third columns, the topics remain fairly general. These examples are meant to show you how broad your initial idea is likely to be and how you may begin focusing on one aspect of that topic or narrowing down the particular group in which you are interested. If you begin with a very broad topic such as "music" and are having trouble finding a more specific direction, I suggest conducting a quick keyword search in an online library database to see what kinds of topics come up. Or talk to your peers to see what they suggest. By describing your topic in the manner shown in the second and third columns, you are identifying the focus of your study.

TABLE 3.1. Narrowing Down Initial Research Topics

Bullying	→	Bullying in the workplace	→	Bullying between peers in the workplace
Homelessness	→	Homelessness among women and children	→	Homeless shelters and safety for women and their children
Athleticism	→	Athleticism in college	→	Division 1 college athletes balancing athletics and school
Body image	→	Body image among college athletes	→	Comparing body image among female and male college athletes
Gender identity	→	Gender identity among school-age children	→	Gender identity and self-esteem among middle school-age children
Sexual assault	→	Sexual assault on college campuses	→	Sexual assault on college campuses with fraternities and sororities
Race/racism	→	Race in the criminal justice system	→	The effect of race in sentencing in nonviolent crimes
Music	→	Music in education	→	Music and multiculturalism programs in public secondary schools

After you have identified a general topic, you will need to make sure it is **researchable**. In other words, is it feasible to conduct research on this topic? This is a pragmatic question. At this early stage, consider issues such as whether or not you'll have access to the participants or data needed to investigate the topic. For example, if you are interested in studying people's behaviors at private country clubs, but you are neither a member nor have a close contact who is, this may be an impractical research topic. Beyond access, you will eventually need to consider other pragmatic issues such as funding, the time commitment, and your emotional readiness for the project. However, it is likely that you won't consider those barriers until you have further defined your topic, developing a specific research purpose and hypothesis or research questions.

In addition to pragmatic issues, consider the **significance, value, or worth** of the project. This is where your ethical compass comes to bear. To begin, does this topic align with your values system, sense of morality, or political orientation? Is there a social justice imperative to learning more about this topic? Is it important, in relative terms, to learn more about this topic? The value of the topic is also connected to timeliness. Do current events or "the current political, economic, and social climates" make it important to study this topic at this time (Adler & Clark, 2011, p. 81)? Is there a need for researchers to learn more about this topic? Can the research be applied in some real-world setting?

It's also important to take a **personal inventory to determine personal preparedness**. Beyond considering what your interests and resources are, think about your capabilities as a researcher. Although the specific skill sets you will need to carry out your research aren't determined until you have developed a specific research purpose and research questions and designed the project, there are psychological and emotional dimensions to consider as well. Is the topic something you have personally experienced, and if so, how will that personal component impact the research? Is this a sensitive topic for you, and if so, do you feel emotionally capable of carrying out the research? It's important to get real with yourself and do an honest "gut check" about your relationship to the topic and the potential emotional aspects of delving deeper into it. Remember, even at the earliest stage of selecting a general research topic to begin to explore, it is important to consider the personal motivations that have brought you to the topic as well as any obvious emotional or psychological challenges. These considerations are a part of ethical practice.

Finally, consider the **existing research on the topic**. Being interested in and well suited to study a worthy topic is not enough. Research is intended to contribute to a shortage of research on a topic, fill a gap in the literature, or offer an alternative view to existing research.

To recap, here is a checklist to help you select an initial research topic:

- Select a general topic about which you are interested in learning more.
- Summarize your topic in no more than a few words.
- Consider the feasibility of researching your topic.
- Consider if it is a worthwhile project (how the research will benefit others).
- Consider your emotional connection to the topic.
- Determine if research on the topic is needed.

To further determine the value of studying the proposed topic, what direction to take, and how to move from a general research topic to a specific research purpose and research questions, you need to conduct a literature review.

Literature Reviews

A **literature review** is both a process and product. In other words, it is something you do and then it is something you create. A literature review is "the process of searching for, reading, summarizing, and synthesizing existing work on a topic or the resulting written summary of the search" (Adler & Clark, 2011, p. 89). It results in a "comprehensive overview of the previous research" on a topic as related to your research question (Wilder, Bertrand Jones, & Osborne-Lampkin, in press).

A literature review is relevant at various stages of the research project. In the beginning, you conduct a literature review in order to **learn more about your topic**. At this stage the literature review can help you determine if research on the topic is needed and worthwhile, narrow down the topic so that you are moving from a general idea to a researchable topic, and determine the direction for the research so that you are building on previous work or filling a gap in the literature. Ultimately, the literature review will help you determine your research purpose, hypotheses (if applicable), and research questions.

Later in the process the literature is used in your proposal and ultimately in the final representation of the research findings. There are numerous ways you might use the literature depending on the research topic and which of the five approaches you are using. I elaborate on this point after explaining the process of conducting a literature review.

When you are conducting your literature review, enter **keywords** into relevant databases to search for and filter through the existing literature on your topic (if you need help finding appropriate databases, consult with a research librarian in your university library). Keywords typically come from the phrase you have used to describe the topic. For illustrative purposes, consider the examples in Table 3.1. If your topic is "bullying between peers in the workplace," then your keyword search will include the words *bullying, peers,* and *workplace.* If those search words don't yield the results you're hoping for, you could try changing one or more of the words. For example, replace the word *peers* with the word *coworkers* or *colleagues* and see what comes up. You may need to play around with the keywords, trying synonyms until you get the right combination of words.

It is important to locate **recent research** on the topic so that your literature review is up to date. However, a good literature review also considers **pioneering or landmark studies** on the topic. A *landmark study* is research that is considered pivotal in the field. To locate landmark studies, search for seminal or foundational authors, those who are most well known for writing on the topic. Search *Google Scholar Citations* to find those authors most frequently cited, or, if you run across authors mentioned in an abundance of your literature, search for their articles (Wilder et al., in press). After determining who the seminal authors are, see if they have developed any theories related to your topic that might help frame your thinking (Wilder et al., in press). When you locate a landmark study, don't rely simply on others' recounting of the study. Get your own copy to include in the literature review. Peer-reviewed articles and books may become a part of your literature review. To help frame your thinking about the topic, you can use newspaper articles, essays, blogs, or other forms of conceptual or popular literature, but they should *not* be the primary component of your literature review (Creswell, 2014). The majority of the literature review should consist of scholarly work.

Typically, there will be an abundance of literature on your topic. In the case of exploratory research on an underresearched topic, you can likely still find a wealth of literature on related topics that will be vital as you think through your project and then later situate the project within the larger research landscape. Here's an example. Let's say you're interested in researching teen bullying on image-heavy forms of social media such as Instagram and Snapchat. You conduct a literature review using the keywords *teens, bullying, social media, Instagram,* and *Snapchat,* and you come up short. You can't find any articles that deal specifically with bullying among teens on those forms of social media, or you find one or two articles, but not enough for a literature review. You may need to broaden your search. So, are there studies about teen bullying on Facebook or other social media forums? If so, do any of those focus on pictures/images? What about studies on the Internet and bullying among teens more broadly? Use the literature that is closest to your topic, and if there aren't any studies or many studies specifically on your topic, you can make a case that your research will fill a gap in the literature. If you are studying a new topic, you are probably conducting exploratory research, which later can be used by other researchers aiming to build knowledge in this area.

As you search the literature, you will need to engage in a **sorting process.** You won't be able to use everything you find. For example, if you pick a widely studied topic such as *body image among athletes,* you will likely find thousands of possible sources. You will need to continue narrowing down your keyword search and the disciplinary repositories in which you search. Establish a set of priorities for the areas about which you want to find literature (Ling Pan, 2008), knowing that you may need to modify the areas based on what is available. You will need to quickly evaluate the relevance of articles/books for your project. To do so, read the **abstracts.** Good abstracts provide an overview of the research objectives, methodology, relevant theories or bodies of scholarship, and major findings. You can usually tell from the abstract how relevant the study is for your project. If it's unclear from the abstract, scan the article. As you evaluate possible sources, JeffriAnne Wilder and colleagues suggest asking:

- Is the source relevant to the project?

- Does the source add value to the project (does it add value to what you've already compiled)?

Once you have selected the literature you plan to use, **read and annotate each source** in full. This process involves careful notetaking. I recommend circling keywords, underlining or highlighting key passages or examples, and writing notes in the margins whether you are reading paper or e-copies. After reading the literature, **summarize** each source. A summary includes the full citation information and basic information about the source, including (as applicable):

- Main theory and its definition

- Primary concept and its definition

- Basics of the study (participants and method/s)

- Main findings

- How the source relates to your project

It is vital to keep a record of all citations with their full publication information so that later you are able to properly attribute credit (Ling Pan, 2008), which is referred to as **cataloguing the literature** (Wilder et al., in press). You could type the summaries in a Word or Excel document, use a citation management software program, or write them by hand in a notebook (in which case, I highly recommend scanning and backing them up electronically).

Finally, you will **synthesize and write up** the literature. Whereas *summarizing* involves documenting the major features of each individual source, *synthesizing* involves connecting and integrating the different sources you have compiled. The following is an example from a (2010) study I worked on with Lisa Hastings, titled "Body Image and Sexual Identity: An Interview Study with Lesbian, Bisexual, and Heterosexual College-Age Women."

Sample Summary

Citation information: Beren, S. E., Hayden, H. A., Wilfley, D. E., & Grilo, C. M. (1996). The influence of sexual orientation on body image in adult men and women. *International Journal of Eating Disorders, 20*(2), 135–141.

Purpose: To compare body dissatisfaction for heterosexual and homosexual men, and for heterosexual and homosexual women. The researchers hypothesized that homosexual men's affiliation with gay subculture would increase their body dissatisfaction, whereas affiliation with lesbian subculture may protect against body dissatisfaction.

Method and participants: Beren, Hayden, Wilfley, and Grilo (1996) administered self-report tests to 257 participants: 72 heterosexual women, 69 homosexual women, 58 heterosexual men, and 58 homosexual men. The tests focused on these dimensions: Body Dissatisfaction, Psychosocial Factors, and Affiliation with the Gay/Lesbian Community.

Findings: The Body Dissatisfaction test scores were not significantly different between heterosexual and homosexual women, and the psychosocial factors, such as dieting and weight concern, also were similar. The Body Dissatisfaction test scores were significantly higher for homosexual men than for the heterosexual men. The homosexual men reported significantly more body dissatisfaction and more distress in many of the psychosocial areas related to body dissatisfaction. Homosexual men's affiliation with gay subculture did increase their body dissatisfaction. Homosexual women's affiliation with lesbian subculture was not related positively or negatively to body dissatisfaction.

Sample Synthesis

Beren, Hayden, Wilfley, and Grilo (1996) administered tests to 72 heterosexual and 69 homosexual women that explored Body Dissatisfaction, Psychosocial Factors, and Affiliation with the Gay/Lesbian Community. The Body Dissatisfaction test scores were not significantly different between heterosexual and homosexual women, and the psychosocial factors, such as dieting and weight concern, also were similar. These findings are replicated in other recent research (Cogan, 2001; Epel, Spanakos, Kasl-Godley, & Brownell, 1996; Pitman, 2000; Share & Mintz, 2002). Researchers have hypothesized that heterosexual and homosexual women may be prone to different types of eating disorders and for different reasons (Cogan, 2001; Lakkis, Ricciardelli, & Williams, 1999; Siever, 1994). This is because lesbians, moreso than heterosexual women, are affected by and vulnerable to different relevant social factors that influence the development of eating disorders (French, Story, Remafedi, Resnick, & Blum, 1996; Lakkis et al, 1999; Lancelot & Kaslow, 1994; Pitman, 2000; Siever, 1994; Striegel-Moore, Tucker, & Hsu, 1990). A meta-analytic review of the literature on sexual orientation and body image suggests that, overall, lesbians have higher body satisfaction but comparable levels of awareness of societal standards, which lesbians do not reject outright (Morrison, Morrison, & Sager, 2004).

Think of a synthesis as creating an overview of the forest that is comprised of particular trees. What is the big picture and what are the details that create that big picture?

The process of synthesizing the literature involves providing an overview of the research on your topic and drawing connections between the different pieces of research. For example, group the studies that make a particular claim, noting similarities and differences. Look for synergies or dissonances across the literature. You may also look at the literature chronologically to narrate the historical development of perspectives on the topic over time (Wilder et al., in press). One method for fleshing out these connections between sources is to create a visual representation, such as a **literature map** (Creswell, 2014) or **concept map** (Hunter, Lusardi, Zucker, Jacelon, & Chandler, 2002; Manders & Chilton, 2013; Wheeldon & Ahlberg, 2012). These visual mapping strategies illustrate how all of the literature is connected. You begin with your topic or a central term, concept, or idea from the study and you visually show how the different pieces of literature relate to the primary topic or concept. Different relationships can be denoted by linking words or with lines or arrows or by overlapping circles (Ahloranta & Ahlberg, 2004; Umoquit, Tso, Varga-Atkins, O'Brien, & Wheeldon, 2013). Figure 3.1 offers a brief example.

For a more concrete example at an advanced stage in the literature review process, consider Figure 3.2. In this figure, I returned to the same literature on heterosexual and homosexual women's body image discussed in the sample synthesis. Figure 3.2 illustrates how you can visually connect your literature.

Whether you begin with a visual representation or move straight from your written summaries to a synthesized write-up of the literature, think about the kind of literature review you intend to create when beginning your first draft. You might write a review designed to demonstrate how your research will fill a gap in the literature and thus why your research is warranted. Or, you may organize your review thematically or based around key terms, concepts, and/or theories (Creswell, 2014). Alternatively, you could write a review that is designed to present theoretical perspectives on your topic. Perhaps most commonly for beginning researchers, you will write a review that provides a general overview about the research and thinking related to your topic (Adler & Clark, 2011).

The literature review generally appears as one section within your proposal, at times with subheadings. In the final representation the review may appear as one section, or the literature may be referred to throughout the write-up. The focus

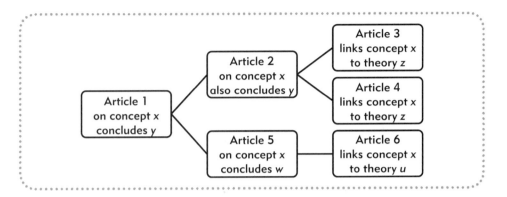

FIGURE 3.1. A literature map (in abstract). This figure depicts what your literature review says about concept *x*. Read the figure from left to right. Begin at article 1 (concept *x* concludes *y*). Start at the top trajectory. From article 1, move to the right top for a *similar* piece of literature and continue moving right for *elaboration*. Now look at the bottom trajectory. Begin again at article 1 (concept *x* concludes *y*) and move to the right for a *dissimilar* piece of literature and continue moving right for *elaboration*. The figure, as a whole, tells you what the literature says about concept *x*.

of your review and where it is placed in your research proposal, and eventually in the final write-up, depend partly on which of the five research approaches you are using. Specifics about how to structure your literature review with examples are given in Chapters 4–8.

To summarize, the process of conducting a literature review involves:

- Searching for literature on your topic using keywords, locating both recent research and landmark studies.
- Establishing priorities for reducing and focusing the review.
- Sorting through the literature by reading abstracts and scanning articles.

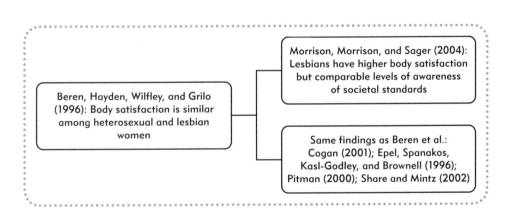

FIGURE 3.2. A concrete example of a literature map.

- Reading the literature and taking careful notes with citation information.
- Summarizing each piece of literature and producing a catalogue of these summaries.
- Synthesizing and structuring the literature.

✋ REVIEW STOP 1

1. After identifying a topic of interest, researchers consider what factors when selecting a research topic?

2. When compiling a literature review, how does a researcher identify and locate landmark studies?

3. What is the difference between summarizing and synthesizing?

☞ **Go to the end of the chapter to check your answers.**

Once the literature review is complete, you are ready to determine the project objectives by constructing the research purpose and hypothesis statement(s) (if appropriate).

Research Purpose Statements, Hypotheses, and Research Questions

Research Purpose Statements

Now that you have refined the research topic, the next step is to construct a research purpose statement. A **research purpose statement** specifically states the purpose or objective of the research project. A strong research purpose statement generally includes information about the research topic or problem, the participants or data, the setting, and the methodology (may reference which of the five approaches to research design is being employed as well as methods of data collection/generation and/or guiding theories). These statements may range from a sentence to a paragraph in length.

There are variations in research purpose statements based on which of the five approaches is employed. The next sections present examples of research purpose statements from published studies using the five different approaches to research design. I have selected statements from studies all centered around one topic to highlight the differences in relation to the approach being used. I've chosen studies on bullying because it is topic studied from a range of disciplinary perspectives. Of course, bullying is a very general topic, and so these studies all consider different dimensions of the subject.

Quantitative Research Purpose Statement

The following research purpose statement is taken from a study examining workplace bullying (WPB) among athletic trainers (ATs) in college environments.

> Our overall objective for this research was to examine the prevalence of WPB among ATs working in the collegiate setting and to identify the personnel involved with the bullying acts. We also sought to investigate the influence of sex on the occurrence of WPB. (Weuve, Pitney, Martin, & Mazerolle, 2014, p. 697)

Let's break down this research purpose statement by underlining the key information and circling the central phenomenon:

> Our <u>overall objective</u> for this research was to examine the <u>prevalence of WPB among ATs</u> working in the <u>collegiate setting and</u> to <u>identify the personnel involved</u> with the bullying acts. We also sought to investigate the <u>influence of sex on the occurrence</u> of WPB. (Weuve et al., 2014, p. 697)

The information conveyed in the purpose statement includes:

- Objectives and phenomenon: Examine the prevalence of WPB among ATs and to identify the personnel involved in the bullying acts
- The population of interest: ATs
- The setting: collegiate setting
- Variable relationship being tested: influence of sex on the occurrence of WPB

Qualitative Research Purpose Statement

The following research purpose statement is taken from a qualitative study about how gay–straight alliances (GSAs) do and do not impact school climates.

> The focus of this study is on the benefits and shortcomings of GSAs in Progress County School District by exploring three key school practices—silence and passive resistance; safe spaces; and breaking the silence and barriers to breaking the silence. We argue that. . . . We also argue that. . . . (Mayberry, Chenneville, & Currie, 2013, p. 311)

Let's break down this research purpose statement:

> The <u>focus of this study</u> is on the <u>benefits and shortcomings of GSAs</u> in <u>Progress County School District</u> by <u>exploring three key school practices—silence and passive resistance; safe spaces; and breaking the silence and barriers to breaking the silence</u>. <u>We argue</u> that. . . . We also argue that. . . . (Mayberry et al., 2013, p. 311)

The information conveyed in the purpose statement includes:

- Focus and phenomenon: The focus of this study is on the benefits and short-comings of GSAs.

- The setting: Progress County School District

- Dimensions of the phenomenon explored: silence and passive resistance; safe spaces; and breaking the silence and barriers to breaking the silence

- Arguments based on research: the phenomenon under investigation

Mixed Methods Research Purpose Statement

The following research purpose statement is taken from a mixed methods study that combined survey research and semistructured interviews to evaluate a bullying prevention intervention in middle schools.

> The primary objective of this article is to describe the strength-based program and to evaluate this program utilizing a mixed methods approach. The rationale for the program was to use a strength-based approach to address the complex needs of students within an inner-city school that had a high proportion of Aboriginal students. It was expected that. . . . (Rawana, Norwood, & Whitley, 2011, p. 287)

Let's break down this research purpose statement.:

> The <u>primary objective</u> of this article is to <u>describe the</u> strength-based program and to <u>evaluate this program</u> utilizing a <u>mixed methods approach. The rationale for the program</u> was to use a strength-based approach to <u>address the complex needs of students</u> within an <u>inner-city school</u> that had a <u>high proportion of Aboriginal students</u>. <u>It was expected that</u>. . . . (Rawana et al., 2011, p. 287)

The information conveyed in the purpose statement includes:

- Objectives and phenomenon: The primary objective is to describe and evaluate the strength-based program.

- Rationale for program under investigation: address the complex needs of students (in target population)

- Research approach: mixed methods

- The population of interest: inner-city school that had a high proportion of Aboriginal students

- Expectations: It was expected that . . .

Arts-Based Research Purpose Statement

The following research purpose statement is taken from an arts-based project designed to explore the stigmatizing of school-age children by using techniques from "theatre of the oppressed" (TO).

One primary goal of the study was to explore how young people at the upper-elementary school levels responded to session content with Boal's Games, Image Theatre, and Forum Theatre—techniques often described in print for adult participants but rarely for youth. The most important goal of the project, however, was to provide children opportunities through TO to explore how their personal oppressions, such as victimization from bullying, could be recognized and dealt with in the classroom and on the playground. (Saldaña, 2010, p. 45)

Let's break down this research purpose statement:

One primary goal of the study was to <u>explore how young people at the upper-elementary school levels responded to session content with</u> Boal's Games, Image Theatre, and Forum Theatre—techniques often described in print for adult participants but <u>rarely for youth</u>. The most important goal of the project, however, was to <u>provide children opportunities through</u> TO <u>to explore how their personal oppressions</u>, such as <u>victimization from bullying</u> could be recognized and dealt with in the <u>classroom and on the playground</u>. (Saldaña, 2010, p. 45)

The information conveyed in the purpose statement includes:

- Objectives and phenomenon: Explore how young people responded to session content with TO. Provide children with opportunities to explore how their personal oppressions, such as victimization from bullying, could be recognized and dealt with in the classroom and on the playground.

- Reasons for study: gap in the literature for kids

- Research approach: arts-based, using tools from Theatre of the Oppressed, specifically Boal's Games, Image Theatre, and Forum Theatre

- Population of interest: kids in upper-elementary school levels

Community-Based Participatory Research Purpose Statement

The following research purpose statement is taken from a community-based participatory research (CBPR) project that developed, implemented, and evaluated an intervention to combat bullying in the workplace.

Our research projects started from a bottom-up perspective in which the objective was to develop and implement, in collaboration with the workplace personnel, an intervention program aimed at preventing and combating bullying; and to subsequently evaluate the implementation from the perspective of health-promoting work settings. To our knowledge, there is not much intervention-based research in collaboration with personnel, in the field of workplace bullying; therefore, the aim of our study was to describe and analyze the process of the intervention and the outcome of its implementation. (Strandmark & Rahm, 2014, p. 67)

Let's break down this research purpose statement:

Our research project started from a <u>bottom-up perspective</u> in which the <u>objective was to develop and implement, in collaboration with the workplace personnel, an intervention program</u> aimed at <u>preventing and combating bullying</u>; and to subsequently <u>evaluate the implementation</u> from the perspective of health-promoting work settings. To our knowledge, there is <u>not much intervention-based research in collaboration with personnel</u>, in the field of workplace bullying; therefore, <u>the aim of our study</u> was to <u>describe</u> and <u>analyze</u> the <u>process</u> of the intervention and the <u>outcome</u> of its implementation. (Strandmark & Rahm, 2014, p. 67)

The information conveyed in the purpose statement includes:

- Objectives and phenomenon: The objective was to develop and implement, in collaboration with the workplace personnel, an intervention program aimed at preventing and combating bullying; the aim of the study was to describe and analyze the process and the outcome.
- Reason for study: (gap in literature) not much intervention-based research in collaboration with personnel
- Research approach: bottom-up perspective in collaboration with the workplace personnel
- Setting: workplace
- Collaborators: the workplace personnel

Considering the preceding examples, we can start to see some variation in how purpose statements are constructed based on the approach used. There are often subtle differences in language as well choices about what information is shared. It's important to realize that there is some discretion about what is included in a research purpose statement. However, we can see from these examples that statements always include:

- The major objectives/goals/focus

Additionally, they generally include some combination of the following (as applicable):

- Phenomenon under investigation
- Variables that are being tested
- Population of interest
- Research participants or collaborators
- Setting
- Research approach

- Reason for research (e.g., identifies a gap in the literature)
- Arguments, predictions, or assumptions (sometimes a research purpose statement leads directly into hypotheses, as reviewed in the next section)

Additional information may be given, such as whether the research seeks to explore, describe, explain, evaluate, promote action, or evoke a response and/or which research methods are used in the study.

Measurement and Variables

Before explaining what hypotheses statements are, it is important to review variables, because hypotheses statements are constructed in terms of variables. In quantitative or mixed methods research, it is common to test or measure variables. A **variable** is a characteristic that can be different from one element to another, or can change over time. For example, sexuality is a variable that can differ across individuals.

From a *statistical perspective*, variables can be classified in two ways: categorical and continuous (Fallon, 2016). **Categorical variables** (also called *discrete variables*) are variables whose categories have names and distinguish among classes. Categorical variables include (Fallon, 2016, pp. 15–16):

- Binary distinctions (e.g., enrolled/not enrolled)
- Multiple options, with none being better or worse (e.g., religion, race, favorite *Star Wars* character)
- Rank-ordered (e.g., class year, Olympic medals)

Continuous variables are variables whose differences steadily progress and "preserve the magnitude of difference between values" (e.g., age, income, precise time running a race) (Fallon, 2016, p. 16).

Let's take the example of income to show how, depending on your word choice and definition, you can create a categorical or continuous variable. If you use the term *socioeconomic status* and then use the following categories, you are working with a categorical variable: working class, middle class, upper class. However, if you use the term *income* and then use precise dollar/cents amounts (e.g., $25,000 . . . $25,437 . . .) income becomes a continuous variable. It is also possible to use the term *income* instead of *socioeconomic status* and still create a categorical variable with subcategories such as low income, middle-class income, upper-class income.

It is important to understand which kind of variables you are working with because it will influence how you're able to analyze your data. At this stage, in order to explore the role of variables in hypotheses, let's first define independent and dependent variables.

An **independent variable** is one that likely affects or influences another variable. Researchers manipulate independent variables (Gravetter & Wallnau, 2013).

A **dependent variable** is a variable that is affected or influenced by another variable. Researchers observe dependent variables to determine the effect of their intervention (manipulation) (Gravetter & Wallnau, 2013). An **intervening variable** (also called a *moderator* or *mediator*) is a variable that can mediate the effect of the independent variable on the dependent variable. Here is an example:

Independent variable   Dependent variable
↓   ↓
(Zero-tolerance bullying policies) in school reduce (the rate of bullying incidents.)

In the preceding statement, *zero-tolerance bullying polices* comprise the independent variable and the *rate of bullying incidents* is the dependent variable (which can change over time). The independent variable affects the dependent variable. The presence of zero-tolerance bullying policies *affects* the rate of bullying incidents.

In research practice, one must also be cognizant of **extraneous variables** that are not under investigation but may impact the data. You can attempt to account for some extraneous variables; for example, the impact of the survey administrators on respondents can be nullified by training them to behave and dress similarly. There are also those you can't account for, such as a respondent rushing through a survey because he/she has a stomachache. Finally, in some studies you may also have **covariates,** which are variables for which you control. For example, if you are conducting research to compare the performance of public high school and private high school students on their SATS, you would also need to control for race and gender, which we know impact these scores.

Because in quantitative research it is typical to measure variables, you need to create an **operational definition** for each variable in your study. Let's say you're conducting a study on "body image among middle-aged women." You begin with the abstract concept *body image.* You then break it down into two categories— variables—"positive body image" and "negative body image," based on previous literature. Using previous research to determine what is known, you create an operational definition for both "positive body image" and "negative body image." What exactly do those variables mean in your study? How, precisely, are you defining the terms? What are the dimensions of "negative body image"? For example, previous literature may indicate the following dimensions of "negative body image":

- Dissatisfaction with weight
- Dissatisfaction with facial features
- Dissatisfaction with overall physical appearance
- Preoccupation with physical appearance

You then construct questions to assess each dimension of "negative body image." Those questions are your **indicators.** Let's say questions 5–10 measure "dissatisfaction with weight" (one dimension of "negative body image," according to your operational definition). If a respondent gets a combines score of x or higher on those questions, it indicates the presence of that dimension of "negative body image."

 REVIEW STOP 2

1. A research purpose statement specifically states the _____ _____.

    a. Research purpose statements generally include some combination of what (each as applicable)?

2. The research purpose statement "Our primary purpose is to work collaboratively with nurses, doctors, nutritionists, and people with diabetes and their loved ones to develop, implement, and evaluate a food management and at-home health program that addresses the needs and concerns of all stakeholders" is likely from a project involving which of the five approaches to research?

3. An independent variable is one that _____.

4. In the following statement, identify the independent variable and the dependent variable? "Safe sex educational programs in secondary school reduce the rate of unplanned pregnancy."

☛ **Go to the end of the chapter to check your answers.**

Hypotheses

A **hypothesis** is a statement predicting how variables relate to each other and that can be tested through research. Hypotheses are typically used in **experimental and quasi-experimental designs and survey research.** Let's say that the independent variable is *A*, the dependent variable is *B*, and if at play, the intervening variable is *C*. In abstract terms, then, a hypothesis might state that *A* causes *B*, or *A* is related to *B*, or *A* causes changes in *B* when *C* is present, or *A* causes no change in *B*. A hypothesis is therefore designed to **test or measure the relationship between variables.**

Let's take this example out of abstractions such as *A*, *B*, and *C* and return to the bullying example earlier.

- Zero-tolerance policies is the independent variable.
- The rate of bullying is the dependent variable.
- Increased teacher presence is the intervening variable.

Here are a couple of hypotheses one could investigate in the same study:

- *Hypothesis 1:* Zero-tolerance bullying policies in school reduce the rate of bullying incidents.
- *Hypothesis 2:* Zero-tolerance bullying policies in school reduce the rate of bullying incidents when there is also increased presence of teachers in hallways, cafeterias, and playgrounds as a part of enforcing the policy.

There are two primary kinds of hypothesis statements—null and alternative (Fallon, 2016)—and there are two kinds of alternative hypotheses—nondirectional and directional. Therefore, in total there are really three primary kinds of hypotheses (see Table 3.2).

A **null hypothesis** predicts that there is no significant difference between two groups with respect to the variable being tested. You write a null hypothesis as follows:

There is no significant difference between group 1 and group 2
with respect to X.

A **directional hypothesis** relies on prior research to make a prediction that there is a specific difference between two groups with respect to the variable being tested. You write a directional hypothesis as follows:

Group 1 experiences higher rates of X than group 2.

Finally, a **nondirectional hypothesis** predicts a difference between two groups with respect to the variable being tested but does not predict what that specific difference will be. You write a nondirectional hypothesis as follows:

There is a difference between group 1 and group 2 with respect to X.

Here is an example from a published study. Weuve et al. (2014) conducted a cross-sectional online survey to study workplace bullying (WPB) among athletic trainers (ATs) in college settings. They state their first two hypotheses as follows (p. 697):

"H1: Female ATs experience more WPB than male ATs."
"H2: Male bullies will be more common than female bullies."

TABLE 3.2. Kinds of Hypotheses

Null hypothesis	Predicts no significant difference between two groups with respect to the variable being tested
Directional hypothesis	Predicts a specific difference between two groups with respect to the variable being tested
Nondirectional hypothesis	Predicts a difference between two groups with respect to the variable being tested but not what the difference will be

These are examples of directional hypotheses. Let's take the first hypothesis and reconstruct it to illustrate the three kinds of hypotheses:

- *Null hypothesis:* There is no significant difference in how much WPB female ATs and male ATs experience.

- *Directional hypothesis:* Female ATs experience more WPB than male ATs.

- *Nondirectional hypothesis:* There is a difference in how much WPB female ATs and male ATs experience.

Remember, not all research projects include a hypothesis. Typically, a research project will have a research purpose statement and a hypothesis *or* a research purpose statement and research questions.

Research Questions

Research questions are the central questions that guide a research project. They are the questions you seek to answer or explore. Once you have developed your research purpose statement, which details your objectives, you can develop questions that will help you achieve those objectives. The questions must be **research-able**. In other words, these are questions that can be directly answered through research. You will ultimately design a project that is well suited for addressing the research purpose and answering the research questions.

There is no set rule for how many research questions you can ask in a study. Typically, there are anywhere from one to three primary research questions. There may be additional more focused, secondary questions attached to the primary questions, aimed at narrowing down the focus. Primary questions are the main questions the research seeks to answer, and secondary questions may address components of those primary questions. Here's an example:

- *Research Question 1 (primary question):* How do students describe the impact of the zero-tolerance bullying policy in their school?

- *Research Question 1a (secondary):* Do students feel safer because of the policy?

- *Research Question 1b (secondary):* Are students more likely to report bullying they experience or witness?

The preceding example shows the primary aim of the study is for students to describe the impact of these policies, and the secondary questions are aimed at assisting that primary goal. You want to avoid creating such a long laundry list of questions that the study becomes unmanageable, and instead create a focused set of central questions.

Your approach to research design impacts question construction. What you are able to ask and the language used to write the research questions are dependent on whether the study is quantitative, qualitative, mixed methods, arts-based, or community-based participatory.

Quantitative Research Questions

In quantitative research you might be using hypotheses instead of research questions (although even when hypotheses are used, they are often preceded by a primary research question). If you are creating research questions, they contain the same components as a hypothesis statement would. However, instead of creating a statement that predicts a certain relationship among variables that you will test, you create a question or series of questions to answer. Quantitative research questions are generally **deductive.** They focus on the variables under investigation and how they relate to each other, how they affect different groups, or how they might be defined. Quantitative questions rely on **directional language.** They often use words such as *cause, effect, determine, influence, relate, associate,* and *correlate.*

Qualitative Research Questions

Qualitative research questions are generally **inductive,** which means they are open-ended. As researchers typically seek to build understanding about the phenomenon under inquiry without a firm set of predictions in place, research questions allow for a great deal of latitude. Accordingly, qualitative research questions often begin with words such as *what* or *how.* Qualitative questions rely on **nondirectional language.** They often use words and phrases such as *explore, describe, illuminate, unearth, unpack, generate, build meaning,* and *seek to understand.*

Mixed Methods Research Questions

Mixed method studies involve three kinds of questions: quantitative, qualitative, and mixed methods. In this research approach, it is vital to present an **integrated set of research questions** (Brannen & O'Connell, 2015; Yin, 2006). First, there should be some combination of quantitative and qualitative hypotheses and/or questions. A mixed methods study may have one or more hypotheses, which are quantitative in nature, as well as one or more qualitative research questions. Or, a mixed methods study may have one or more quantitative questions and one or more qualitative questions. Additionally, it is advisable to also include at least one mixed methods question. Consult the preceding sections for how to write the quantitative and qualitative research questions. The mixed methods research question directly addresses the mixed methods nature of the study. The mixed methods research question may ask something about what is learned by combining the quantitative and qualitative data, or it may ask something about how the mixed methods design aided the research project. To summarize, mixed methods questions may look like the following (which shows only a bare minimum, as there may be more than one of any kind of question):

Quantitative question, qualitative question, mixed methods question

Or

Quantitative hypothesis, qualitative question, mixed methods question

Mixed methods questions rely on **relational language.** They often use words and phrases such as s*ynergistic, integration, connection, comprehensive, fuller understanding,* and *better understanding.*

Arts-Based Research Questions

ABR questions are generally **inductive, emergent, and generative,** which means they are open to the process itself. Arts-based questions often emphasize experiential knowledge, artistic practice or expression, and an emergent inquiry process. They typically use words and phrases such as *explore, create, play, emerge, express, trouble, subvert, generate, inquiry, stimulate, illuminate, unearth, yield,* and *seek to understand.*

Community-Based Participatory Research Questions

CBPR projects may use any combination of quantitative, qualitative, mixed methods, and arts-based practices. Therefore, the design of specific questions is linked to the approach employed within a particular study. With that said, CBPR questions are generally **inductive, change oriented, and inclusive.** This means that they are open-ended, with an aim toward social action, and they account for the perspectives of multiple stakeholders. Due to their inductive nature, research questions often begin with words such as *what* or *how* (but this is not always the case). Further, these approaches are participatory and power sensitive. Research questions often use words and phrases such as *co-create, collaborate, participatory, empower, emancipate, promote, foster, describe,* and *seek to understand from the perspective of various stakeholders.*

Putting It Together

Let's take the topic of bullying that was used as an example throughout this chapter to start putting the pieces together. Let's say you're interested in studying anti-bullying programming in middle school (we'll call it anti-bullying program *x*). Here are some examples of how you might develop your purpose statement and hypotheses or research questions from each of the five approaches. Take note of the kind of language used as well as the focus of each study. Keywords are circled in each research purpose statement in order to highlight language differences.

EXAMPLE 1: QUANTITATIVE

The purpose of this study is to examine the prevalence of bullying in middle school with and without anti-bullying program x in order to determine the effect of program x on the rates of bullying in middle school.

- *Hypothesis 1:* The rates of bullying in middle school will be lower in middle schools that implement anti-bullying program x.
- *Hypothesis 2:* Students will be more likely to report bullying they experience or witness after participating in program x.

EXAMPLE 2: QUALITATIVE

The aim of this study is to understand and describe middle school students' perspectives on anti-bullying program x.

- *Research question 1:* What kinds of bullying did students experience or witness before program x?
- *Research question 2:* What did students think of program x and why?
- *Research question 3:* How, if at all, do students think program x has affected bullying in their school?

EXAMPLE 3: MIXED METHODS

The purpose of this study is to describe and evaluate the effect of anti-bullying program x on bullying in middle school using a mixed methods approach.

- *Quantitative research question:* What effect does anti-bullying program x have on the prevalence of bullying in middle school?
- *Qualitative research question:* How do students describe their experiences with bullying before and after anti-bullying program x?
- *Mixed methods research question:* How does the mixed methods design of the study contribute to our understanding of the effect of anti-bullying program x and the nature of that effect?

EXAMPLE 4: ARTS-BASED

The goal of this inquiry is to unearth how middle school students explore bullying at their school and their experience with anti-bullying program x through the techniques of play building and students' creation of performance vignettes that express their experiences.

- *Research question 1:* How do students use the tools of play building to illustrate their experiences with bullying and with anti-bullying program x?
- *Research question 2:* What themes emerge in the student-created vignettes?
- *Research question 3:* How do students describe their experience with the play building practice? Are there positive outcomes, such as feelings of empowerment?

EXAMPLE 5: COMMUNITY-BASED PARTICIPATORY RESEARCH

(The goal) of this (study) is to work (collaboratively) with (relevant stakeholders,) including middle school students, teachers, school personnel, and parents/guardians, to (evaluate) anti-bullying program x, amend the program accordingly based on insights learned, and (implement) the revised program in order to (promote) anti-bullying culture in a middle school.

- *Research question 1:* What strengths and weaknesses of anti-bullying program x do different stakeholders identify?

- *Research question 2:* How can we strengthen anti-bullying program x based on the needs of various stakeholders?

- *Research question 3:* How can we implement the revised anti-bullying program with the necessary buy-in from different stakeholders in order to positively change school culture?

There are advantages associated with each approach, as they allow us to focus on different dimensions of the same topic, garner different kinds of data, and address a host of research questions. Research done from each of these approaches has the potential to contribute to our understanding of this topic. And remember, these are just examples. There are innumerable possibilities for what any of these projects might actually look like.

REVIEW STOP 3

1. A hypothesis is a statement predicting _____.

2. What are the three primary kinds of hypotheses?

3. "Women who work in service industries experience higher rates of sexual harassment than men who work in service industries." The preceding is which kind of hypothesis?

4. Define research questions.

5. Identify the three kinds of questions mixed methods studies include.
   a. The three questions in mixed methods research should be _____.

☛ **Go to the end of the chapter to check your answers.**

Sampling

Sampling addresses the questions "Who or what is in your study? Where are you getting your data or content?" Typically, discussions of sampling center around *who* is in your study—the subjects, respondents, participants, or collaborators;

however, in studies that involve the use of nonliving data (e.g., content analysis of text or images), it is a question of *what* is in your study.

Whether you realize it or not, you have already been exposed to the idea of sampling in daily life. For example, consider the many political polls you have seen on television that say things like 60% of Americans are in favor of some particular social policy, or 60% of Americans support the president and think he is doing a good job, or 60% of voters feel strongly about question 1 on the ballot. Certainly you know they did not poll every single American. It would be impossible. Instead, they came up with a sample of Americans that is intended to *represent* the general population. To do so, they engaged in a process of sampling.

If you are thinking about a research project you might undertake, then you already may be thinking about who will be in your study. For example, if you are interested in studying under-age drinking in college, you won't be able to study every single college student, so you will have to come up with a smaller group to study. You may start by narrowing down your sampling pool to your campus and then find additional ways to narrow the final sample. Likewise, if you are interested in learning about the qualities that draw some college students to social activism, you won't be able to study all college students, so you will need to narrow down your field. You may start by narrowing it down to two local colleges and the students who participate in a particular formal club or activism program at their school. Depending on the nature of your study, you may narrow down the participants even further. I return to these examples in this section.

Sampling is the process by which you select a number of individual cases from a larger population. The first thing you need to do is determine the elements in your study. An **element** is the kind of person, group, or nonliving item in which you are interested (sometimes the word *unit* or *case* is used). Next you have to identify the population. A **population** is a group of elements about which you might later make claims. For example, if you are interested in exploring the qualities that draw some college students to social activism, the element in your study is *individual college students involved in social activism*. The population you might later make claims about is *all college students who engage in social activism*. Once you have identified the element you are interested in and the population, you will need to determine the study population (sometimes called the *sampling frame*). The **study population** is the group of elements from which you actually draw your sample. So if the population you are interested in is "all college students who engage in social activism," clearly it would be impossible to draw a sample from that population, which is not only large but diffuse. Therefore, you create a study population. Your study population may consist of all students at two identified local colleges who are engaged in a specific club or program after school. You then draw a sample from the study population. A **sample** is the number of individual cases that you ultimately draw and from which/whom you generate data.

How do you determine what the sample size should be? How many individual cases do you need? Sample size varies dramatically, from studies involving a single case to those involving thousands. Guiding questions to determine what size is appropriate are:

- How many cases do you need to answer your research questions or hypotheses?
- What resources do you have available (monetary and time)?
- What research method or methods are you using?
  - What are the corresponding norms when using that particular method?

Quantitative research favors larger sample sizes. For example, in survey research, accuracy increases with larger samples. However, you must also consider the additional costs often associated with larger samples. There are sample size calculators available online that can be used to determine the ideal sample size for a particular study (e.g., *http://surveysystem.com, http://fluidsurveys.com,* or just Google *sample size calculator* for options). You need a few values to plug in:

- **Population size:** The total number of elements in the population about which you will later make claims. You can approximate this number if you aren't certain.
- **Confidence level:** Expressed as a percentage, this value tells you how confident you can be in your results. Researchers use 90%, 95%, or 99%. It is standard practice to use 95%, which is what I recommend.
- **Margin of error or confidence interval:** All surveys have error. This number, expressed as a percent, indicates how much error you are willing to accept. It is standard practice to use 5%, which is what I recommend (this indicates that the survey results will be accurate within a plus or minus 5% range).

Qualitative and arts-based approaches favor smaller sample sizes. There are no hard-and-fast rules for sample sizes. It is a question of how many data are needed to address your questions. Researchers need to provide a rationale or justification of the sample as sufficient to meet the research purpose (Roller & Lavrakas, 2015). In some projects, a single case may be all that is needed (e.g., in some oral history or autoethnography projects), whereas in other cases you may need 20 or more participants (e.g., in some focus group projects).

Methods that are employed in natural settings such as ethnography/field research and some instances of CBPR rarely have predetermined sample sizes. Sample size is based on how many people in those environments elect to participate. The same can be true in quantitative field experiments in which a predetermined period of time is allotted for the study observations, but you can't predict how many people will end up participating (field experiments are reviewed in the next chapter).

In interview or focus group studies, one generally begins planning sample size upfront, although again, there are no rigid guidelines. Consider this advice for interview studies: "Interview as many subjects as necessary to find out what you need to know" (Kvale & Brinkmann, 2008, p. 113). Although researchers have proposed some very loose guidelines (e.g., Svend Brinkmann [2013] suggests that qualitative interview studies typically have no more than 15 participants), these guidelines are somewhat erroneous, as each study will differ. Margaret Roller and

Paul J. Lavrakas note that sample size should be considered during two phases of the research process in interview studies: research design and data collection (their suggestions can be applied to other forms of qualitative research, including ethnography and content analysis). During research design, Roller and Lavrakas (2015, p. 73) suggest considering four factors:

1. The breadth, depth, and nature of the research topic or issue.
2. The heterogeneity or homogeneity of the population of interest.
3. The level of analysis and interpretation required to meet research objectives.
4. Practical parameters such as the availability of and access to interviewees, budget for financial resources, time constraints, as well as travel and other logistics associated with conducting face-to-face interviews.

In addition to the aforementioned considerations, it is also important to avoid generating unnecessary data. During data collection, you revisit the question of sample size. You don't need "more" simply for the sake of more. *Valuable data contribute to new learning.* When additional data do not yield additional insights, you have reached the **saturation point.** Once you have reached this point, you risk inundation and redundancy from additional data (Coffey, 1999). **Theoretical saturation** occurs when you select a small group of participants within a population from whom to collect data, and then select another group from the population and learn nothing new from the additional participants (Agar, 1996). Qualitative researchers employing grounded theory with any method often use "saturation" to determine when to stop data collection (Robson, 2011; Roller & Lavrakas, 2015). Grounded theory involves cycles of collecting and analyzing data in order to adapt to new learning (elaborated in Chapter 5).

There are numerous ways that you might go about drawing a sample. All sampling procedures fit into two umbrella categories: probability sampling and purposeful sampling. These general categories of sampling have different strengths and thus are appropriate in different kinds of projects, based on your goals.

Probability Sampling

Probability sampling relies on probability theory and involves the use of any strategy in which samples are selected in a way that every element in the population has a known and nonzero chance of being selected. This means that the chance that each element in the population will be included in the sample can be statistically determined, and the chance of inclusion, no matter how small, will be a number above zero. Each element has some chance of inclusion.

Probability sampling strategies are typically used in quantitative research, and may also be used in the quantitative phase of mixed methods research.[1] These samples are useful when researchers want to **generalize** their findings to a larger population. The results of studies that rely on probability sampling are typically **statistical** in nature. The following subsections describe the main types of probability sampling strategies.

Simple Random Sampling (SRS)

This is a sampling strategy in which every element in the study population has an equal chance of being selected.

Systematic Sampling

This is a sampling strategy in which the first element in the study population is selected randomly and then every kth element, after the first element, is selected. For example, if your study population is an activism club membership list comprised of students at multiple colleges, you may randomly select student #18 on the list. Then, if you decide that $k = 5$, you would select every fifth student on the list after 18 (so 23, 28, 33, and so on, until you reach the end of the list).

Cluster Sampling

This is a multistage sampling strategy. First, preexisting clusters are randomly selected from a population. Next, elements in each cluster are sampled (in some cases, all elements in each cluster are included in the sample). For example, if your population is all college students who participate in activism clubs, you might get a list of all the universities in the Northeast with such clubs. Then you would randomly select several of those schools—each serving as a cluster—and the students in activism clubs at those schools would comprise your sample.

Stratified Random Sampling

This is a sampling strategy in which elements in the study population are divided into two or more groups based on a shared characteristic (these groups are called *strata*). Then you conduct simple random, systematic, or cluster sampling on each strata. For example, if you want to compare student activism across gender, you might divide the elements into three categories: male, female, and transgender. Or you could compare student activism across class year, dividing elements into four categories: freshman, sophomore, junior, and senior.

Purposeful Sampling

Purposeful sampling (also called *purposive* or *judgment sampling*) is based on the premise that seeking out the best cases for the study produces the best data, and research results are a direct result of the cases sampled (Patton, 2015). This is a strategic approach to sampling in which "information-rich cases" are sought out in order to best address the research purpose and questions (Morse, 2010; Patton, 2015, p. 264). Sampling is a central feature of research design when purposeful strategies are used because the better the participants are positioned in relation to the topic, the richer the data will be (Morse, 2010; Patton, 2015).

Purposeful sampling strategies are typically used in qualitative, ABR, and

CBPR projects. These strategies may also be used in the qualitative phase of mixed methods research. Qualitative, arts-based, and community-based researchers are often after **in-depth understanding** from a small sample and therefore rely on some form of purposeful sampling procedure (Hesse-Biber & Leavy, 2011). Research findings may later be **transferred** from one case to another on the basis of **fittingness** (similarity between the cases) (Lincoln & Guba, 2000). In other words, when cases are similar, we can make inferences about one case based on findings in another.

According to Michael Quinn Patton (2015), there are 40 types of purposeful samples (not all of which can be discussed here), which he groups into eight categories (pp. 264–272):

1. Single significant case
2. Comparison-focused sampling
3. Group characteristics sampling
4. Theory-focused and concept sampling
5. Instrumental-use multiple case sampling
6. Sequential and emergence-driven sampling strategies during fieldwork
7. Analytically focused sampling
8. Mixed, stratified, and nested sampling strategies

Here I review a few of the most commonly used purposeful sampling strategies. (For a full discussion of these categories and all 40 sampling types, see Patton, 2015.)

Snowball Sampling

Also called *chain sampling,* this is a sampling strategy in which one case organically leads to another (Babbie, 2013; Patton, 2015). In Patton's (2015) framework this is a form of sequential and emergence-driven sampling typically used in fieldwork. For instance, participants may suggest additional participants they think could provide important data for the project.

Exemplar of the Phenomenon of Interest

This is a sampling strategy in which a single significant case is selected because it can provide a wealth of rich data that speak directly to the research purpose and questions (Patton, 2015, p. 266). For example, in 1998 I conducted an oral history project about anorexia nervosa and body image with a college student. I conducted the oral history interviews with one woman, given the pseudonym Claire, because she exhibited all of the "classic" issues associated with anorexia in college-age women, was an eager participant, and could provide rich data to illuminate the topic.

Homogeneous Sampling

This is a sampling strategy in which cases are sought out because they share a common characteristic (Patton, 2015). For example, another approach to my study on anorexia nervosa and body image would be to seek out several participants who are the same age, gender, and race (all key factors in the literature on eating disorders). A variation on this method is *heterogeneity sampling* (a strategy in which cases are sought because they differ on key characteristics) (Patton, 2015).

 REVIEW STOP 4

1. _____ is the process by which a researcher selects a number of individual cases from a larger population.

2. When collecting additional data does not yield additional insights, you have reached the _____.

3. What are the two umbrella categories under which all sampling procedures fit?
   a. Explain the premise of each of these two approaches

4. Simple random sampling (SRS) is a sampling strategy in which _____ _____.

5. Snowball sampling is a sampling strategy in which _____ _____.

☛ **Go to the end of the chapter to check your answers.**

Conclusion

This chapter has reviewed some basic research design issues, including topic selection, literature reviews, research purpose statements, hypotheses and research questions, and sampling. The design issues reviewed in this chapter, and how they come together to form the basis for a research project, are elaborated in Chapters 4–8. In the following chapters, each of the five major approaches to research design are reviewed in-depth, including guidance on how to design a research proposal or plan.

 REVIEW STOP ANSWER KEY

Review Stop 1

1. if researchable; significance, value, or worth; personal inventory/preparedness; existing research on topic

2. Search Google Scholar Citations to find authors most frequently cited on topic; if authors are mentioned in multiple pieces of literature, search for their articles.

3. Summarizing involves documenting major features of each source of literature; synthesizing involves connecting and integrating the different sources.

Review Stop 2

1. purpose or objective of the research project
   a. the major objectives/goals/focus, phenomenon under investigation, variables being tested, population, participants or collaborators, setting, research approach, reason for research, arguments, predictions or assumptions
2. community-based participatory research
3. likely affects or influences another variable
4. independent variable: safe sex educational programs; dependent variable: the rate of unplanned pregnancy

Review Stop 3

1. how variables relate to each other
2. null, directional, nondirectional
3. directional
4. central questions that guide a research project
5. quantitative, qualitative, mixed methods
   a. integrated

Review Stop 4

1. sampling
2. saturation point
3. probability and purposeful
   a. Probability sampling relies on probability theory and involves the use of any strategy in which samples are selected in a way that every element in the population has a known and nonzero chance of being selected. Purposeful sampling is based on the premise that seeking out the best cases for the study produces the best data, and research results are a direct result of the cases sampled.
4. Every element in the study population has an equal chance of being selected.
5. One case organically leads to another.

Further Engagement

1. Coming up with the right keywords is an important part of conducting a literature review. Practice doing a keyword search by picking a research topic you can describe in a short phrase. An example from this chapter is "bullying between peers in the workplace." Once you have selected a research topic, conduct a keyword search using words from the phrase. See what kinds of results this yields. You may find that you have too many search results and need to narrow the topic, or that you don't have enough results. Play around with the keywords, trying synonyms, until you get the right combination of words to find what you're looking for.

2. Select a research topic in which you are interested and conduct a preliminary literature review (six to eight peer-reviewed sources).

   a. Read, annotate, and summarize each source.

   b. Synthesize the literature.

   c. Create a sample literature map (only use four to five sources for this exercise).

3. Armed with your literature review, design the basics of your study.

   a. Which of the five approaches will you use and why (one paragraph)?

   b. Create a research purpose statement.

   c. Create two to three sample research questions or two to three hypotheses.

   d. From whom or what are you interested in collecting data? To answer this, identify the elements in your study, the population, and the study population.

   e. What sampling strategy will you use and why (just a couple of sentences)?

Resources

"Literature Reviews Handout" for download from The Writing Center at UNC–Chapel Hill: *http://writingcenter.unc.edu/handouts/literature-reviews*.

Patton, M. Q. (2015). *Qualitative research and evaluation methods* (4th ed.). Thousand Oaks, CA: Sage. —Qualitative and mixed methods sampling is reviewed in Chapter 5, Modules 30–40 (pp. 264–315).

Vogt, W. P., Vogt, E. R., Gardner, D. C., & Haeffele, L. M. (2014). *Selecting the right analyses for your data: Quantitative, qualitative, and mixed methods.* New York: Guilford Press.

Note

1. Sometimes researchers working from qualitative, arts-based, or community-based research approaches also use probability sampling; however, it is far more common in quantitative research.

PART II

Five Approaches
to Research Design

CHAPTER 4

Quantitative Research Design

Quantitative research values breadth, statistical descriptions, and generalizability. Quantitative approaches to research center on achieving objectivity, control, and precise measurement. Methodologically, these approaches rely on deductive designs aimed at refuting or building evidence in favor of specific theories and hypotheses. Marianne Fallon refers to quantitative research as a "top down process" (2016, p. 3). Quantitative approaches are most commonly used in explanatory research investigating causal relationships, associations, and correlations.

Structure of a Research Proposal

Recall in the preface of this book, I noted that research design addresses two questions: What do we want to learn? and How do we execute on our goals? The latter question refers to building our methodology or plan for how research will proceed. Remember, as noted in Chapter 1, a methodology combines methods and theory in order to develop a plan for how the research will proceed. A research proposal can be broken down into three main parts:

1. Basic introductory information
2. The topic (which addresses the question "What do we want to learn?")
3. The research plan (which addresses the question "How will we execute on our goals and build a methodology?")

(Note that these three basic components of a research proposal will not be repeated in Chapters 5–8, although the same applies.)

Of all the five designs reviewed in this text, quantitative studies follow the most rigid and linear designs. This does not mean there aren't differences in how quantitative researchers structure their proposals, but because there are fewer differences, I am presenting the most commonly used template (see Template 4.1).

TEMPLATE 4.1

Title
Abstract   } Basic Introductory Information
Keywords

The Topic under Investigation
  Significance, Value, or Worth
Theoretical Perspective   } Topic
Research Purpose Statement
Research Questions or Hypotheses

Literature Review
Design and Methods of Data Collection
Population, Sampling, and Subjects
Data Analysis and Assessment
Interpretation and Representation   } The Research Plan
Pilot Tests (if applicable)
Ethics Statement
References
Appendices

In the remainder of this chapter, I fill in Template 4.1.

Basic Introductory Information

Basic introductory information, including the title of your project, an abstract, and keywords should be included at the beginning of your research proposal.

Title

Quantitative titles clearly state the main topic (the research problem or phenomenon and central variables) and the method and approach to design being used. In order to develop the title, write a brief list of keywords about your study and build the title out of those words or phrases.

Abstract

Abstracts provide an overview of the study. In quantitative research they typically include the problem under investigation, the research purpose and research questions or hypothesis, basic information about the methods, population of interest, research subjects/respondents, and the main theory or concept guiding the study (if applicable). Abstracts are generally 150–200 words and should be written after you have completed the rest of the research proposal.

Keywords

Keywords may be singular words and/or short phrases. Create a list of five or six keywords by thinking about the words or phrases one would Google if researching your topic online. In quantitative research, keywords let readers know the main problem or phenomenon, the central variables, the primary theory or concept (if applicable), and something about the population and subjects/respondents.

The Topic

The Topic under Investigation

Clearly state the phenomenon under investigation. Break down the phenomenon into measurable variables. Clearly state the variable relationship(s) being tested. It is also advisable to briefly discuss how you came to your topic, including pragmatic issues. Here you can concisely share your personal and/or professional interest in the topic, your ability to access samples in the population of interest, and/or funding opportunities for working on this topic.

Replication Studies

In addition to the ways of selecting a topic discussed in the last chapter (personal interests, previous research experience, funding opportunities), in quantitative research you may also decide to replicate previous research. **Replication studies** involve "the purposeful repetition of previous research to corroborate or disconfirm the previous results" (Makel & Plucker, 2014, p. 2). In quantitative research, replication is important for strengthening our cumulative knowledge and increasing the dependability of research findings (Funder et al., 2014; Makel & Plucker, 2014; Schmidt, 2009). According to Stefan Schmidt (2009), there are two types of replication research: direct and conceptual. In **direct replication,** the same methods are used in order to corroborate or disconfirm previous findings (Makel & Plucker, 2014). In **conceptual replication,** different methods are used to study the hypothesis or theories (Makel & Plucker, 2014).

There are high rates of unsuccessful replications—meaning, research that disconfirms previous findings (Makel & Plucker, 2014). For example, a review of frequently cited health publications found only 44% of replicated studies had corroborated the previous findings (Ioannidis, 2005). This finding suggests that there may be a wealth of unreliable studies out there, and thus replication studies are necessary for building confidence in existing findings and identifying unreliable or even fraudulent research. The Personality and Social Psychology Presidential Task Force on Publication and Research Practices, created in February 2013, found that a considerable amount of time and other resources could be saved if published research were more dependable (Funder et al., 2014).

Despite the importance of replication, very few such studies are conducted. A recent analysis of the entire publishing history for 100 high-impact psychology journals found that only 1.07% were replications (Makel, Plucker & Hegarty, 2012). A study of education journals found a replication rate of only 0.13% (Makel & Plucker, 2014). There are two primary reasons for these low replication rates: **professional disincentives** and **data-sharing deficiencies.**

There is a long-standing bias in favor of original studies, which makes it harder and less motivating to publish replication studies. Bias may be built into submission criteria, publication policies (which may expressly exclude replication studies), and both editor and reviewer bias (Makel, 2014; Makel & Plucker, 2014; Spellman, 2012). Bias also permeates funding opportunities (Makel & Plucker, 2014; Schmidt, 2009) and institutional hiring and promotion practices (Makel & Plucker, 2014). Based on their task force findings, Funder et al. suggest that "funding agencies reserve some proportion of their resources for high-quality replication studies" (2014, p. 9). They also suggest that journals that have published prominent findings have a "special obligation" to publish studies that attempt to replicate those findings (2014, p. 9). Fortunately, replication has been receiving considerable attention in fields, including psychology and education. The tide may be turning. In the inaugural editorial for *AERA Open*, a new open-access education journal, the editors ask authors to include "direct replications of related findings from published research" and to share online appendices such as research instruments and protocols so that their work can be replicated (Warschauer, Duncan, & Eccles, 2015).

This topic brings us to the issue of data sharing. In the social sciences, although large datasets are often shared, meaning they are made available to other researchers, smaller datasets are often lost, hidden, or unavailable, so those studies cannot be replicated (King, 2011). Researchers can contact the authors of the studies and seek access and permission to use their datasets, but there are no rules or guidelines requiring authors to provide them (King, 2011). In their task force report, Funder and colleagues suggest that (1) published manuscripts include an online supplemental appendix with all procedural details from the study, and (2) data sharing be required (all raw data and related coding information) for the purpose of verifying findings or other uses if mutually agreed upon (2014, p. 8).[1]

Despite the obstacles toward replication, it's an important part of quantitative social and behavioral science and may be trending upward. If you are seeking a study to replicate, consider the following points:

> **Expert Tip**
>
> Dr. Marianne Fallon, Associate Professor in the Department of Psychological Science at Central Connecticut State University, suggests incorporating an element of direct replication into your study, saying, "It bridges the past and propels you into the future. Science is strongest when converging evidence mounts; to push science forward, we need to confirm what we think we know and build from there."

- The availability of the information needed to replicate (protocols, instruments, datasets)

- In a field where research can impact public policy, such as the education sciences, select a study whose replicated findings could be used to advance policy changes (Makel & Plucker, 2014).

● The importance of the original findings in your field (e.g., the original study is widely cited)

Significance, Value, or Worth

This section of your research proposal is an opportunity to consider the social or political value of conducting quantitative research on your topic (whether it is an original study or a replication). Outline the project's underlining values system and any social justice or policy initiatives. For example, note if this study replicates previous research, this time using a sample representative of an underresearched population. If the rationale for the study is linked to a current event, social problem, or policy issue, discuss the timeliness of the proposed research. Many funding agencies require "evidence-based" research, so there are often opportunities to conduct quantitative research on timely topics. Additionally, note how the research can be used to impact policy (if applicable). For example, if you are conducting a study that hypothesizes that participation in music education in middle schools correlates with higher grades in math classes, the results of your study can be used during policy discussions regarding funding music programs in public education.

 Ethics in Practice

As discussed at length, quantitative research can be based on replication (e.g., replicating a previously conducted study with new populations). If a group has been neglected in the research on your topic—for example, on the basis of social class or race—consider the value of doing research on that group. Bear in mind that others may replicate the study you conduct as well. How will you make your datasets and protocols available to other researchers for possible replication? Further, your research findings may be generalized to the larger population of interest. How will this research benefit that population? What does it tell us about the selected population that is of value?

Theoretical Perspective

Historically, quantitative research was guided by the philosophy of **positivism**, which originally developed in the natural sciences. This tradition presupposes that reality exists independently of the research process and can be measured via the objective application of the **scientific method**. Laws that govern the social world can therefore be tested and proven. Today, postpositivism, a refined version of these principles, guides quantitative research.

Postpositivism holds that there is an objective reality that exists independently of the research process. Rational researchers can study this reality by employing objective methods grounded in measurement, control, and systematic observation. Laws that govern the social world can be predicted and tested via hypotheses that investigate causal relationships or associations between/among variables. However, differing from positivism, absolute truth claims cannot be made. Postpositivism is based on **probability testing and building evidence to reject or support hypotheses** (but not conclusively prove them) (Crotty, 1998; Phillips & Burbules, 2000). Further, although researcher objectivity and neutrality remain central to this philosophy, it acknowledges that researchers are "knowing subjects" who employ heuristic devices to guide research (Haig, 2013, p. 9).

Although the terms *positivism/postpositivism, empiricism, objectivism, critical realist,* and *scientific realism*[2] also appear in the literature, I employ the term *postpositivism* because it is commonly used in the social and behavioral sciences.

Within the postpositivist tradition, innumerable theories are available to guide your study. Theories are employed deductively as a means of predicting what you expect to find regarding how certain variables relate to each other. The specific theory or theories you employ will be determined by prior research on your topic, most likely within your discipline. John Creswell (2014) suggests that a discussion of your theoretical perspective should include the following: the central propositions of the theory, past uses and applications, and a discussion about how the theory specifically relates to your proposed study (p. 61). For example, if you are conducting a psychological study about eating disorders and self-esteem, you would base your study around a particular theory on this topic from the field of psychology.

Research Purpose Statement

Briefly state the purpose of the proposed study, focusing on the **primary objective or causal relationship(s) being investigated.** To do so, clearly state the main problem or phenomenon, the variables being investigated (at a minimum, the independent and dependent variables), the population of interest, and the theory being tested (if applicable).

Research Questions or Hypotheses

Quantitative research typically employs either research questions or hypotheses. **Research questions** are the **central questions** your study seeks to address. Quantitative research questions are **deductive.** Questions center on how the variables under investigation relate to each other, affect different groups, or how they might be defined. They may employ **directional language,** including words such as *cause, effect, determine, influence, relate, associate,* and *correlate.*

As reviewed in the last chapter, a hypothesis is **a prediction about how variables relate to each other** (the main variables in your study have already been identified in your research purpose statement). When your purpose is to test or measure variables, you may opt to write one or more hypotheses statements. See Chapter 3 for a review of the different kinds of hypotheses: null, directional, and nondirectional.

Note that whether you are conducting experimental or survey research, you will need to provide an **operational definition** for each of the variables under investigation (as discussed in Chapter 3 in the section on variables and measurement). This topic is expanded in the following discussion of literature reviews.

Literature Review

As discussed in Chapter 3, the literature review provides a synthesis of the recent and landmark studies on your topic. The review should focus on primary sources. A quantitative literature review describes the study you are replicating or modifying in your research. Even if you are including a separate section on the theoretical perspective, your literature review also typically cites the origins of the primary theory you are employing in your study (as a means of predicting how variables relate to each other). Although I discussed literature reviews in depth in the last chapter, there are particular issues unique to quantitative research. Because quantitative research is based on studying the relationships between/among variables, each variable investigated in the study must be defined in operational terms. To do so, seek previous quantitative research studies about each variable *and* those studies that examine the relationship between/among the variables in your study. The literature review should provide clear examinations of what is known about the variables from prior research, including precisely how they have been defined.

 REVIEW STOP 1

1. What is a replication study?
   a. Why are replication studies needed?
   b. What are the two main reasons for low replication rates?

2. Today _____ is the theoretical perspective that guides quantitative research.

3. Experimental and survey research require that each of the variables under investigation are operationally defined. How does a researcher do this?

☛ **Go to the end of the chapter to check your answers.**

The Research Plan

Design and Methods of Data Collection

Research methods should be selected on the basis of their ability to best address your research purpose and to help you test your hypothesis or answer your research questions (bearing in mind pragmatic issues such as time, resources, and researcher skill set). The primary quantitative designs are experimental research and survey research.

Experimental Research

Experimental research is the oldest form of quantitative research. After the scientific revolution in the 17th century, experiments in research came to mean "taking a deliberate action followed by systematic observation" (Shadish, Cook, & Campbell, 2002, p. 2). However, we encounter the basic principles of experiments in our daily lives. For example, when you're cooking a pot of marinara sauce, you might taste it, then add a little salt, and then taste it again. You are checking to see if adding the salt improved the taste of the sauce. As a college student, you may decide to skip a class one day to see if it impacts your performance in the class, or if you're able to miss a class with no difference to your grade-point average (GPA). A teenage girl may experiment with makeup. She may try wearing liquid eyeliner one day to see how her friends react at school, whether they think she looks better or not. She may adjust her makeup the next day based on her friends' reactions the previous day. As a research method in the social and behavioral sciences, experiments are systematic and controlled but still involve the basic protocol of creating a test to see if what you predict will happen, does happen.

Experiments rely on **hypothesis testing** (testing variable relationships). The basic use of experiments is to test how introducing an intervention (a variable) affects what happens. In other words, you select research subjects, do something to them, and observe the effect of what you've done (Babbie, 2013). In order to be certain that you are measuring the effect of the intervention (variable) you have introduced, you need to **control** for all other factors.

Settings for experiments include natural environments, labs, and the Internet. **Field experiments** occur in **natural environments.** When your study relies on observing people in their normal activities, including those who may not know the study is occurring, a natural setting is appropriate (an example is given at the end of this section). **Research or scientific labs** are the most common setting for experiments. Although they are "artificial" settings, meaning they exist for the sake of the research, they allow researchers the greatest measure of control. Finally, experiments may be conducted on the **Internet.** This setting is appropriate when you are studying people's beliefs and attitudes (Babbie, 2013). Your research purpose and hypothesis will ultimately dictate the setting of your experiment as well as the kind of experiment you design.

Experiments are used in **explanatory research** and are based on **causal logic (or cause-and-effect logic).** This logic looks at identifying causal relationships between variables (e.g., *A* causes *B* or *A* causes *B* under *C* circumstance). There are **necessary conditions** in order to support the presence of a causal relationship. The cause must precede the effect (temporal order), the cause must be related to the effect, and there must be no alternative explanation for the effect (Shadish et al., 2002). Explained in terms of variables:

The independent variable precedes the dependent variable.

The independent variable must be related to the dependent variable.

There must be no alternative explanation for the dependent variable (no extraneous variable).

Experimental groups are those that receive the experimental intervention (also called the *experimental stimulus*). **Control groups** do not receive the intervention (in some cases, they may receive a placebo). All experiments have at least one experimental group, but not all experiments have control groups. Control groups are used to compare the results of the experimental group (whose members received the intervention) with a similar group whose members have not received the intervention. Experiments may involve one, two, or four groups in total, depending on the type of experiment. Some experiments involve pretests and/or posttests in addition to the experimental intervention. A **pretest** determines a subject's baseline prior to introducing the experimental intervention. A **posttest** is given after the experimental intervention to assess the impact of the intervention.

For example, let's say you want to study middle-aged people's biases against hip hop music because previous research indicates that people carry assumptions that hip hop music promotes violence. Research indicates that some people who hold these negative attitudes aren't actually familiar with hip hop music. You create the following hypothesis: *People's negative attitudes about hip hop music will decrease with exposure to hip hop music.* You give research subjects a pretest, such as a questionnaire, to determine their current attitudes toward hip hop music. Then, for the experimental intervention, you expose the subjects to 30 minutes of hip hop music by various artists. A posttest questionnaire determines if their attitudes have changed after exposure to hip hop (see Figure 4.1)

There are many possible variations on this experiment, involving control groups and so forth, but this provides you a basic illustration of what is meant by a pretest, experimental intervention, and posttest.

FIGURE 4.1. Hip hop music research example.

✋ REVIEW STOP 2

1. In experimental research, what are the three conditions needed to support the presence of a causal relationship?

2. Define experimental and control groups.

3. Explain the purpose of pretests.

4. Explain the purpose of posttests.

☞ **Go to the end of the chapter to check your answers.**

There are three primary categories of experiments: preexperiments, true experiments, and quasi-experiments. There are additional designs within each broad category. Campbell and Stanley (1963) identified 16 types of experimental designs (I review only the most commonly used, drawing on their work). Regardless of the type of experimental design, you must operationally define the independent and dependent variables.

Preexperimental designs are focused on studying a single group that is given the experimental intervention (experimental groups only). Campbell and Stanley (1963) identified three types of preexperiments. In a **one-shot case study,** a single group is given the experimental intervention and then observed to see if the intervention causes any changes. These are the weakest forms of experiments. With a **one-group pretest–posttest design,** a single group is given a pretest (to determine the subject's baseline), then given the experimental intervention, and then given a posttest. Pretest and posttest scores are compared and any differences are attributed to the experimental intervention. Finally, the **static-group comparison** involves two groups. First, a single group is given the experimental intervention. Then a comparison group (a group that is like the experimental group) is selected. Then both groups are given a posttest. The posttests of both groups are compared, and any differences are attributed to the experimental intervention. (See Table 4.1.)

True experimental designs (also called *classical experiments*) are based on randomization. Research subjects are randomly assigned to experimental and control groups. Because both randomization and control groups are used, true experiments

TABLE 4.1. Preexperimental Designs

Design	Groups	Actions
One-shot case study	Single group	One group experimental intervention
One-group pretest–posttest design	Single group	Pretest, experimental intervention, posttest
Static-group comparison	Two groups	One group experimental intervention, both groups posttest

are considered the strongest form of experiments. Campbell and Stanley (1963) identified three types of true experiments. The **pretest–posttest control-group design** involves two groups, with each given a pretest; only one group is given the experimental intervention, and then both groups are given a posttest. The group that receives the experimental intervention is the *experimental group,* and the group that receives only the pretest and posttest is the *control group.* In the **Solomon four-group design,** all groups receive the posttest, but the pretest and experimental intervention combination differs for each group. The first group receives a pretest, the experimental intervention, and a posttest. The second group receives the pretest and posttest. The third group receives the experimental intervention and the posttest. The final group receives only the posttest. This rigorous design controls for both the effect of the pretest and the effect of the intervention on posttest scores. The **posttest-only control-group design** involves two groups. One is given the experimental intervention and a posttest, and the second group is given only the posttest. The group that receives the experimental intervention is the experimental group, and the group that receives only the posttest is the control group. (See Table 4.2.)

Quasi-experimental designs involve taking advantage of natural settings or groups, and thus subjects are not randomly assigned. For example, these designs are often used in education research when researchers have access to specific educational institutions in which to conduct the study, in management research when researchers have access to specific businesses, in health research when researchers have access to specific medical institutions, and so on. Quasi-experimental designs may involve experimental groups only or experimental and control groups. Campbell and Stanley (1963) noted that quasi-experiments are appropriate when "better designs are not feasible" (p. 34). They identified 10 types of quasi-experiments (I review three commonly used designs here). The **time-series experiment** involves taking measures of a single group for a predetermined period of time, then giving the group the experimental intervention, and then again taking measures of

TABLE 4.2. True Experimental Designs

Design	Groups	Actions
Pretest–posttest control group design	Two groups randomly assigned	Both groups pretest, one group experimental intervention, both groups posttest
Solomon four-group design	Four groups randomly assigned	One group pretest, experimental intervention, posttest
		One group pretest and posttest
		One group experimental intervention and posttest
		One group posttest only
Posttest-only control-group design	Two groups randomly assigned	One group experimental intervention, posttest,
		One group posttest only

the group for a predetermined period of time. The **multiple time-series experiment** involves taking measures of two groups for a predetermined period of time, then giving one group the experimental intervention, and then again taking measures of both groups for a predetermined period of time. The group that receives the experimental intervention is the experimental group and the group that does not is the control group. The **nonequivalent control-group design** involves two groups. One group receives a pretest, experimental treatment, and posttest. The second group receives only the pretest and posttest. (See Table 4.3.)

Whereas research subjects do not know if they have been placed in an experimental or a control group, in **double-blind experiments** neither the subjects nor the researchers know which subjects are in the experimental group and which are in the control group. This design eliminates the possibility that researchers' observations will be skewed based on their desire to see changes in the experimental group.

In addition to the preceding types of experimental designs, there are also **single-subject designs** (also known as *N*-of-1 designs). A single-subject design involves multiple observations of one individual. First, multiple observations are recorded to determine the individual's baseline; then the experimental intervention is introduced, and additional observations are recorded (Creswell, 2014). (See Table 4.4.)

No matter which design you use, in your research proposal describe every step of the experiment and the instruments or materials being used in any pretest, experimental, and posttest phases of the research, as applicable. You will also need to consider how to safeguard your study against a range of possible biases and errors (reviewed in the upcoming section on analysis and assessment). As a general matter in all experimental research, one must consider the "Hawthorne effect" (first discussed in Chapter 2). The **Hawthorne effect** (also referred to as *testing effect*) refers to how participation in a research study may, on its own, impact subjects' responses. For instance, in the hip hop music example given earlier, if subjects are asked to complete a pretest prior to the experimental intervention, they may believe, when they are completing the posttest, that the researchers want to see a change

TABLE 4.3. Quasi-Experimental Designs

Design	Groups	Actions
Time-series experiment	Single group	Measures taken over time, experimental intervention, measures taken
Multiple time-series experiment	Two groups	Measures of both groups taken over time, one group experimental intervention, measures of both groups taken
Nonequivalent control-group design	Two groups	One group pretest, experimental intervention, posttest, one group pretest and posttest only

TABLE 4.4. Single-Subject Designs		
Design	Subject	Actions
Single-subject	One individual	Record multiple observations to determine baseline and then introduce the experimental intervention and record multiple observations

in their attitudes, so their answers may reflect their desire to "do well" for the researchers. There are several available measures to account for the effect of the study. **Control groups** are used in experiments in order to mitigate against the effect of the experiment itself, which is why designs that do not rely on single groups are preferable when possible. Pretests may also be a possible source of testing effect, which is why some designs, such as the posttest-only control-group design, omit them altogether.

 Ethics in Practice

The issue of deception can be a concern in experimental research. Given their subject matter, many experiments require you to hold back on what you share with your research subjects about the study until their participation is complete. For example, if you are studying people's prejudice toward homosexual adoption, and showing a documentary film educating subjects about gay families and adoption, you can't tell subjects you want to see how homophobic or biased they are. Studying any form of prejudice likely requires sharing a minimum of information about the study. In some instances, people may not know they are participating in a study at all. As we'll see in the following example, this is true in field experiments in which you want to observe people behaving naturally and can't risk informing them of this intention lest they adjust their behavior.

Now that we've reviewed experiments, let's look at a published example. The following is an excerpt from Tara Goddard, Kimberly Kahn, and Arlie Adkins's (2015) field experiment studying if racial bias impacts whether drivers stop at crosswalks for pedestrians. They hypothesized that drivers would be less likely to stop for Black pedestrians as compared with White pedestrians. As participants crossed the street in a controlled manner, two trained observers stood 30 feet away from the crosswalk recording whether the first car yielded, how many cars it took to yield, and the total seconds it took for each pedestrian to be able to cross the street from the time he or she stepped off the edge of the curb. Their hypothesis was supported: It took longer for the Black participants to be able to cross the street safely.

Three white and three black research participants were recruited to participate in the study as the crossing pedestrians. All six were men in their 20s, and were matched based on their height and build. Each research participant was clearly identified as either white or black and was phenotypically representative of their racial group (Eberhardt, Davies, Purdie-Vaughns, & Johnson, 2006; Kahn & Davies, 2011). As is commonly done in racial bias research, in order to isolate the effect of race, participant pedestrians wore an identical outfit of long-sleeve gray shirt and khaki pants to achieve a neutrally colored palette that did not indicate any obvious socioeconomic status or social characteristics. Participants were trained in walking speed, body posture, and safety protocols in an earlier field session so that they approached and crossed the crosswalk in an identical manner. Having all participants use the same walking speed and body posture helped control for any differences in our pedestrians' behavior that might affect drivers' decisions to yield. (Goddard, Kahn, & Adkins, 2015, p. 3)

In the preceding example, you can see the principles of experiments at work. A hypothesis about how one variable impacts another variable is tested (in this case, how racial bias effects drivers' yielding behavior). Controlling for factors such as participant size, posture, and dress allowed the researchers to isolate race as the only variable at play. Further, drivers were not told they were participating in an experiment, or they would have adjusted their behavior and rendered the study useless.

✋ REVIEW STOP 3

1. _____ designs are based on studying a single group who are given the experimental intervention.

2. True experimental designs are considered the strongest form of experiments because they include what two features?

3. A researcher has access to a specific bank on Wall Street in which to conduct an experiment. What kind of experimental design will they use?

4. Define a double-blind experiment?
   a. What is the advantage of a double blind experiment?

5. Explain the Hawthorne effect.
   a. What measures are available to mitigate against the Hawthorne effect?

☞ **Go to the end of the chapter to check your answers.**

Survey Research

Survey research is the most widely used quantitative design in the social sciences. Common uses of survey research with which you are probably familiar include the census, polling on political issues or public opinions, and market research. In social science, education, and health care research you are more likely to use a **special-purpose survey** (Fowler, 2014). Surveys rely on asking people **standardized questions** that can be **analyzed statistically**. They allow researchers to collect a breadth of data from large samples and **generalize** to the larger population from which the sample was drawn. Surveys are typically used for ascertaining individuals' attitudes, beliefs, opinions, or their reporting of their experiences and/or behaviors. The data from these surveys are called **subjective data**, although that term is controversial, because they can be ascertained only from the respondents (Vogt, Vogt, Gardner, & Haeffele, 2014). Surveys may also ask for facts, which are termed **objective data**, because they can be ascertained elsewhere (e.g., age, place of birth) (Vogt et al., 2014). Most likely you will be seeking subjective data; however, you may also ask for some demographic information that could be termed *objective data*.

There are two primary methodological designs in survey research: cross-sectional and longitudinal (Ruel, Wagner, & Gilllespie, 2016). **Cross-sectional designs** seek information from a sample at one point in time. **Longitudinal designs** occur at multiple times in order to measure change over time. There are three types of longitudinal designs: **repeated cross-sectional, fixed-sample panel design**, and **cohort study** (in which a sample that experienced the same event or starting point completes the survey at multiple times) (Ruel et al., 2016). In longitudinal designs **attrition** (respondents pulling out of the study) is potentially an issue. Build strategies into your design in order to minimize attrition. Such strategies may include updating respondents regularly through a newsletter, letting them know in the cover letter how and when they will receive information about the progress of the study (Ruel at al., 2016), or providing a refrigerator magnet as a gift so they have a visual reminder of the study (Bengtson, 2000; Ruel at el., 2016).

Questionnaires are the primary data collection tool in survey research. A questionnaire is also referred to as the **survey instrument**. Questionnaire construction and delivery to respondents are very involved processes, and I discuss them in detail. In survey research, this phase is considered the "upfront" work, and it determines everything else (Vogt et al., 2014, p. 24). In fact, although we often think of coding as occurring during the data analysis stage, in survey research the first phase of coding focuses on the format and content of the survey questions or survey items (Vogt et al., 2014). In survey research you are already explicitly thinking about assessment and evaluation as you construct your data collection instrument. There must be clear and justifiable links between your indicators (questions) and the concepts you say you are measuring in order to produce a valid instrument (Vogt et al., 2014; see Figure 4.2).

There are many **preexisting surveys** available on a wide range of topics. It is advisable to consult published research on your topic and available online databases to determine whether or not there are preexisting surveys that you can use or draw from to answer your research questions. Often you do not need to design a brand-new survey instrument. In psychology it is more common to use preexisting surveys than to construct a new one (Vogt et al., 2014). If you are using one or more preexisting surveys, or parts of them, make sure to secure any necessary permission rights and cite your sources appropriately. Although it is common to use preexisting

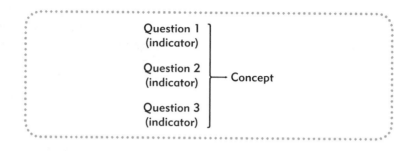

FIGURE 4.2. Linking questions (survey items) to the concept measured.

surveys, it is also useful to know how to construct your own survey instrument/questionnaire using new questions and/or questions pulled from preexisting surveys. Hence I provide a detailed discussion of this task next.

Survey items (questions in the questionnaire) are designed to help you test your hypotheses or answer your research questions. The hypotheses or research questions have been constructed in terms of the variables you want to measure. To begin thinking about survey question construction, you need to return to those variables and build a definition of each variable concept in the study (this process was reviewed in Chapter 3). Survey questions are designed to measure the concept in which you are interested as precisely as possible. The questions you design around each concept in the study are how you **operationalize your variables.** They are the indicators that a variable is or is not present.

Let's say you want to conduct a study investigating whether or not there is a relationship between college students' satisfaction with their roommate and their overall satisfaction with their college experience.

> **Expert Tip**
>
> In addition to preexisting survey instruments, secondary data may also be available on your topic. Dr. Michael J. Stern at the University of Chicago's Center for Excellence in Survey Research suggests that you see if there are data already available on the question you are interested in, because there is a wealth of accessible secondary data, and using these sources saves considerably on costs. He says, "Don't reinvent the wheel" if you don't have to.

First, you would have to define "satisfaction with roommate" and "satisfaction with college experience." These are both multidimensional concepts. For illustrative purposes, let's consider "satisfaction with roommate." Based on your literature review, you determine satisfaction with roommate is comprised of three concepts (each of which is also multidimensional): respect, cleanliness, and friendship. Next you need to determine the dimensions for each of those concepts, again drawing on preexisting research. Let's say you come up with the following three dimensions of "cleanliness": personal items kept orderly, communal items kept orderly, and personal hygiene. You would then come up with several questions to measure each of those dimensions of "cleanliness." All of those questions together measure the concept of "cleanliness."

Following Vogt and colleagues (2014), I suggest using a **two-column-table approach** to create your **first draft** of survey questions. To do so, make a list of all of the variables and put them in one column. In the second column, put a draft of the question or questions you will employ to collect data on each variable. These might be questions you have constructed or that you have found from preexisting surveys. You will need to determine how many questions it takes to ascertain the data you seek for each variable. The more multidimensional a variable concept is, the more questions you will likely ask in regard to that specific variable. It could take many questionnaire items to address one concept. Let's return to the example of roommate satisfaction and the variable "cleanliness." Table 4.5 illustrates the beginning of a two-column-table approach to this study.

The table merely illustrates your initial draft of ideas for questions. There is a long process of refining your questions and putting them into an appropriate format. For example, the word *regularly* is vague and problematic and will need to be specified. Further, the entries are currently presented as a series of statements that need to be turned into questions.

Question construction is at the heart of survey research. Never lose sight of your goal, which is measuring the phenomenon of interest as precisely as possible ("getting at" what you really want to get at). There are some general dos and don'ts for creating effective survey questions. Beginning with dos, it's vital to **use clear, understandable,** and, whenever possible, **highly specific language** (Ruel et al., 2016). Pay careful attention to how you word sensitive questions, as they are more likely to elicit nonresponses from respondents (Ruel et al., 2016; Tourangeau & Yan, 2007). There is a long list of things to avoid when constructing survey questions, including double-barreled questions; double-negative questions; negatively phrased questions; biased or leading questions; questions with built-in assumptions, abbreviations, slang and contractions, or ambiguous phrases; and questions that ask respondents to recall information from an unrealistic time frame (Ruel et al., 2016, pp. 51–56).

TABLE 4.5. Example of a Two-Column Approach	
Variable: Cleanliness	**Draft questions (in idea form)**
Personal items kept orderly.	Roommate regularly makes his/her bed.
	Roommate puts away his/her clothes in drawers/closet.
	Roommate keep personal items on his/her side of the room.
Communal items kept orderly.	Roommate hogs the common-use items in the room.
	Roommate returns common-use items to designated places.
	Roommate cleans common-use items if he/she dirties them.
Personal hygiene.	Roommate has good personal hygiene habits.
	Roommate cleans bedding regularly.
	Roommate wears clean clothing.

The nature of your questions is also determined in part by whether you are creating open-ended or forced-choice questions. Although there are examples of surveys that use open-ended questions, the vast majority opts for a forced-choice format, which is what I discuss (if you have the human and financial resources to collect data for both types of questions, you can attain cross-validation, but this typically occurs only in a very well-funded project) (Vogt et al., 2014). With **forced-choice or fixed-choice questions,** respondents are provided with a range of response options from which to select. This kind of question design allows you to collect a breadth of data, provide data that are easy to quantify, and has high generalizability when large samples are used (Vogt et al., 2014). Different types of forced-choice questions include, but are not limited to, multiple choice, dichotomous, checklists, and scales (rating scale, Likert scale) (Ruel et al., 2016).

To illustrate these types of forced-choice questions, I return to the example of roommate satisfaction. One dimension of the variable "roommate satisfaction" is "friendship," which was further broken down into three dimensions: enjoy spending time with him/her, spend time together outside of dorm, and talk to him/her about personal matters. Let's take the last one as our example (see Figure 4.3).

Here are examples of how to address the above issues using different types of forced-choice questions. In these examples I focus on the dimension of friendship "talk about personal matters."

Multiple choice: A question with several response options (typically four to five) is provided, and respondents select a single response.

When are you most likely to confide something personal to your roommate?

- O When I have a problem and need advice
- O When something good has happened
- O When I have a secret I want to share
- O Never

Dichotomous: Provide a statement with two response options (such as yes/no or true/false).

I talk to my roommate about personal matters.

- O True
- O False

Checklist: Provide a question with several response options and direct respondents to check all that apply.

I talk to my roommate about personal matters when (please select *all* that apply) . . .

- O I need to confide in someone about a secret
- O I need to seek advice about a problem
- O I want to share good news
- O Never

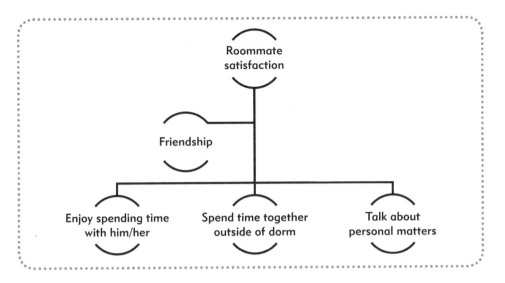

FIGURE 4.3. Breaking down the dimensions of a variable.

Rating scale: Provide a statement or question with response options on a continuum and instruct respondents to select a single response.

How often do you talk to your roommate about personal matters?

- O Very frequently
- O Somewhat frequently
- O Occasionally
- O Rarely
- O Never

Likert scale: Provide a statement with responses that indicate level of agreement and ask respondents to select a single response. There are usually four or five response choices, depending on whether you include a neutral, midpoint option or force a non-neutral choice.

When I have a problem, I greatly value the advice of my roommate.

- O Strongly agree
- O Somewhat agree
- O Neutral
- O Somewhat disagree
- O Strongly disagree

In the final example, please note that there are an **equal number of positive and negative responses.** Also note the choice of a **neutral option.** One could just as easily decide not to include the neutral option and force respondents to lean one way or another. In this case, one can see potential problems with the neutral option. What exactly does it mean when respondents select it? Does it mean they "sort of" value their roommates' advice, or does it mean they never seek that advice (which may also be indicated by the "strongly disagree" response)? As you can see, constructing survey questions is a difficult process (and some of these issues may be worked out in a pretest).

Regardless of which type of response format you choose (and there are more than what I have reviewed), there are general guidelines for creating the response options.

As noted earlier, whenever it is possible to **specify,** do so, avoiding vague words that are open to multiple interpretations. For example, take the statement *My roommate regularly makes his/her bed*. The word *regularly* is vague. A more specific way of phrasing this would be to offer choices based on days per week.

Response choices must be mutually exclusive and exhaustive. **Mutually exclusive** means that there is no overlap in response items, and **exhaustive** means that all of the possible responses a respondent might wish to select are available. Let's look at these in practice.

My roommate makes his/her bed:

O 1–2 times per week   ⎫
O 2–3 times per week   ⎬   Not mutually exclusive
O 4–5 times per week   ⎭
O 6–7 times per week
O Never

Note: The above answers are *not* mutually exclusive. If the roommate makes the bed twice a week, there are two possible response options when there should only be one.

My roommate makes his/her bed:

O 1–2 times per week   ⎫
O 3–4 times per week   ⎬   Not exhaustive
O 5–6 times per week   ⎭
O 7 days per week

Note: The above answers are *not* exhaustive. If the roommate never makes his/her bed, there is no accurate option for the respondent to select.

Now let's look at a final example in which the response options are both mutually exclusive and exhaustive.

My roommate makes his/her bed:

O 1–2 times per week
O 3–4 times per week
O 5–6 times per week
O 7 days per week
O Never

The **organization** of your survey instrument (questionnaire) is also critical to research design. The goal is for the questionnaire to be easy for respondents to understand and for you to later process the data (Ruel et al., 2016). The **layout** should be simple, clear, and uncluttered (Fowler, 2014). Consider type style and size as well as the spacing of items on the document. Begin with a short **introduction** to the survey, providing general instructions. Next carefully consider **question order,** beginning with engaging questions, locating highly sensitive questions in the middle, logically ordering questions and subsets of questions, and placing demographic questions last in order to reduce respondent fatigue for the substantive questions (Ruel et al., 2016, p. 42). Finally, provide a brief **conclusion** in which you thank respondents for their participation and possibly include an open-ended space for their comments regarding their experience (Ruel et al., 2016, p. 37).

As you create the survey instrument by determining the number of items, the content of questions, the format of questions and responses, and the organization of the instrument, always bear in mind the experience of respondents. **Respondent burden** occurs to the degree that respondents experience their participation as too stressful and/or time-consuming (Biemer & Lyberg, 2003; Ruel et al., 2016). High burden causes **respondent fatigue,** which leads to a higher nonresponse rate and lower-quality responses (Ruel et al., 2016). Consider these issues carefully as you determine how many questions are needed to ascertain the data you are after and how many more "burdensome" questions there will be, such as those on highly sensitive or personal topics, those that require respondents to recall past events (Ruel et al., 2016), and those with longer statements or vignettes for respondents to read.

Survey delivery is another important decision. Balance your desire to maximize **response rate** against pragmatic concerns, such as time and budget. Available delivery methods include in person, online, mail, and telephone. **In-person** surveys generally occur in group settings and have the highest response rate. However, a researcher is needed to administer the survey, and the geographic location of respondents is an issue. **Online** surveys can be done via -mail or Web-based software such as Survey Monkey. These are self-administered (no researcher is present) and allow you to include geographically dispersed respondents. **Mail** surveys are self-administered and typically have a low response rate. These days, most favor online options over "snail mail." However, the snail mail format has a long, successful history in census research and is appropriate when respondents are geographically dispersed and perhaps do not have online access (e.g., older respondents who are not active online). Be sure to include a self-addressed stamped envelope for easy return. Finally, **telephone** surveys are administered by a researcher, differing from online and mail surveys. However, they typically also have a low response rate. These too may be appropriate when respondents are geographically dispersed and perhaps not accessible online.

A final issue to consider is creating a **respondent inventory** (also called a *respondent audit*), in which you keep track of respondents and reduce the risk of multiple responses from one individual (Ruel et al., 2016). Each respondent can be assigned a number for anonymity.

Ethics in Practice

In survey research, question construction is a vital component of ethical praxis. There are numerous issues to consider as you word your questions (sensitive topics, built-in assumptions, bias)—for example, weighing bias (the use of loaded terms) against respondents' familiarity with a term. Consider the terms *used car* and *previously owned vehicle*. The term *used car* is more commonly used, but it may also have negative connotations.

Now that we've reviewed survey research, let's consider a published example. Kathryn S. Whitted and David R. Dupper (2007) conducted survey research via a written questionnaire with students in an alternative school setting to investigate the extent to which students report being psychologically or physically bullied by teachers or other adults in school, and whether peers or teachers/adults were involved in their self-reported "worst school experiences" (WSE). They used a preexisting instrument, which they modified for the study.

> One of our most surprising findings was that almost twice as many students reported that an adult, rather than a peer, was involved in their WSE. It appears that bullying in schools extends beyond our current focus or fixation on peer-on-peer bullying and suggests teacher-on-student bullying is largely a hidden problem that demands much more attention than it currently receives. Although some previous studies in the nascent area of research have suggested teacher-on-student bullying is primarily psychological in nature, our findings suggest that teachers engage in many more forms of physical bullying than was anticipated prior to conducting this study. (Whitted & Dupper, 2007, p. 338)

REVIEW STOP 4

1. Surveys in social research studies typically focus on subjective data. Why?

2. Is it advisable to use preexisting surveys when they're available?

3. Question construction is at the heart of survey research. Which of the following are good, or "dos," for creating good questions?

   a. Double negative questions

   b. Abbreviations

   c. Highly specific language

   d. Ambiguous phrases

   e. Clear and understandable language

      i. _____ questions mean that respondents are provided with a range of response options from which to select.

     ii. How does a researcher create a Likert scale?

    iii. When using a Likert scale, researchers have to decide whether or not to include a _____ option.

    iv. What are the two criteria response choices must meet?

4. High respondent burden causes respondent _____, which leads to a higher nonresponse rate and lower-quality responses.

5. Surveys delivered in what way have the highest response rate?

☛ **Go to the end of the chapter to check your answers.**

Population, Sampling, and Subjects

In which population are you interested in learning? How will you access members of that population? Who will your subjects or respondents be? What size sample will you draw? How will your sampling strategies maximize the reliability and generalizability of your findings?

    Research subjects or respondents should be identified and recruited in accord with your research purpose and hypothesis or research questions. Quantitative research typically relies on **probability sampling,** which, as noted in Chapter 3, is based on probability theory and involves the use of any strategy in which samples are selected in a way that every person (element) in the population has a known and nonzero chance of being selected. Each element in the population will have a chance to be included in the sample, which can be statistically determined, and the chance of inclusion, no matter how small, will be a number above zero for all elements.

    After identifying the population and the study population, you will need to determine the size of the sample (how large the sample needs to be depends on your design and the extent to which you want to generalize your findings) (consult Chapter 3 for guidance). Figure 4.4 illustrates the process of moving from the general

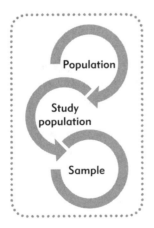

FIGURE 4.4. The process of moving from the population to your sample.

population to your sample. (Later you will see that if you select your sample well and implement a well-conceived design, this process occurs in reverse as you generalize from your sample to the larger population of interest.)

Once the study population is in place and you've selected a sampling strategy, there are computer programs you can use to determine your sample. The following probability sampling strategies were reviewed in Chapter 3, but I repeat them here for your convenience.

Simple random sampling (SRS; also called *random selection*) allows every element in the study population an equal chance of being selected.

Systematic sampling is a strategy in which the first element in the study population is selected randomly and then every *k*th element, after the first element, is selected. Take the study population list of potential subjects and randomly select the first subject. Then decide *k* is the number based on the size sample you are ultimately seeking. So, if you're study population has 1,000 names and you want 250 in your sample, *k* = 4. You may randomly select the third person on your list. The research subjects would then be numbers 3, 7, 11, 15, and so on.

Cluster sampling is a multistage strategy. First, preexisting clusters are randomly selected from a population. Next, elements in each cluster are sampled (in some cases, all elements in each cluster are included in the sample).

If you are interested in comparing groups within the population based on some characteristic (e.g., gender, race, age, political affiliation), **stratified random sampling** is appropriate. Elements in the study population are divided into two or more groups based on a shared characteristic (these groups are called *strata*). Then you conduct simple random, systematic, or cluster sampling on each strata.

It is important to note that although, generally speaking, probability sampling methods are preferred in quantitative research, there are instances when **purposeful sampling** is used. For example, **convenience sampling** involves identifying research subjects based on their accessibility to the researcher (Hesse-Biber & Leavy, 2005, 2011). This approach is often used when the researcher has access to subjects within a particular institution, organization, business, group, and so forth. Quasi-experimental designs typically use this kind of sampling procedure.

In experimental research involving experimental and control groups, there are additional issues to consider. It is important that the different groups are truly comparable so that inferences can be drawn about the effect of the experimental intervention. Two techniques for achieving comparability are randomization and matching. **Randomization** refers to randomly assigning subjects to the experimental and control groups. **Matching** is the process of creating pairs of research subjects who are similar, based on either a list of predetermined characteristics (e.g., gender, race, age) or on their scores on a pretest. Pairs of similar subjects are then split into different groups (one member of a pair is placed in the experimental group and one in the control group).

In survey research it is important to consider sampling error when you draw your sample. **Sampling error** occurs when you have a biased sample. For example, if you are conducting a Web-based survey with respondents ages 18–65, but people over 55 are less likely to respond to Internet surveys, respondents in that age group may end up underrepresented in your sample, causing bias as you later attempt to generalize from the sample to the larger population of interest (Fowler, 2014). Bear these issues in mind as you design your study and develop your sampling protocol.

 Ethics in Practice

Avoiding sampling error, to the extent that you are reasonably able to do so, is a part of ethical practice in quantitative research.

Data Analysis and Assessment

Data analysis procedures allow you to determine your findings. Has the hypothesis been supported or refuted? What are the answers to the research questions? In quantitative research, the analysis process leads to a statistical rendering of the data generally represented in a set of tables or charts along with a discussion. I recommend using a statistical methods book to assist you through this entire process.

First, **prepare the data** by entering it into a spreadsheet or statistical software program. It is common in both experimental and survey research to first report descriptive statistics and then conduct inferential statistical tests to examine the research questions or hypotheses (in some instances of survey research, you may report only descriptive statistics—it depends on your purpose and questions). In survey research, before getting into statistical data analyses, it's important to report on the members of the sample who did and did not complete the survey, and note **response bias** (the effect of nonresponses on the results) (Creswell, 2014; Fowler, 2009). There are numerous statistical tests you can run on your dataset. It depends what you want to learn from the data.

Descriptive statistics describe and summarize the data (Babbie, 2013; Fallon, 2016). There are three kinds of descriptive statistics (Fallon, 2016, pp. 16–18):

1. **Frequencies:** Count the number of occurrences of a category. Frequencies are generally reported as percentages. For example, in a sample of 100 female respondents, you count the number who reported being on a diet. Sixty-seven out of 100 reported being on a diet. You report this as 67% of female respondents reported being on a diet.

2. **Measures of central tendency:** Use a single value to represent the sample.
   a. **Mean:** the average
   b. **Median:** the "middle" value
   c. **Mode:** the most frequent value in the sample

3. **Measures of dispersion:** Illustrate how spread out the individual scores are and how they differ from each other.
   a. **The standard deviation:** The most commonly used measure of dispersion

lets you see "how individual scores relate to all scores within the distri-bution" (p. 18).

Once the analysis is conducted, all of these descriptive statistics can be repre-sented visually (discussed in the next section on interpretation and representation).

Inferential statistics test the research questions or hypotheses and make infer-ences about the population from which the sample was selected (Adler & Clark, 2011). One common approach to inferential statistics is **null hypothesis significance testing (NHST)** (Vogt et al., 2014). **NHST** or **statistical significance tests** are used to test the null hypothesis (which states that there is no relationship between/among the variables). Even though you are actually interested in the alternative hypotheses (the relationships that *do* exist between variables, and in some cases, the direc-tion of those relationships), you test the null hypotheses in order to avoid a Type I error (Fallon, 2016). A **Type I error** occurs when you infer that a relationship exists that does *not* exist (Adler & Clark, 2011). Significance testing results in a *p*-value (*p* refers to probability). You are looking for a *p* score of less than .05, which is expressed as follows: $p < .05$. A *p* score of .05 means 5 in 100. If your *p* score is higher than .05, you should not infer a relationship between the variables. (A **Type II error** occurs when you do *not* infer a relationship that *does* exist.)

Typically, you would conduct a significance test on the null hypotheses and any number of inferential statistical tests depending on your questions/hypotheses and the kind of variable relationship(s) you wish to test. There are many statistical significance tests you could run, so explain your decision. Consult Table 4.6 for an overview of commonly used statistical tests.

 REVIEW STOP 5

1. During sampling, what two techniques increase the comparability of experimental and control groups so that inferences can be drawn about the effect of the experimental intervention?

2. A researcher conducts a telephone survey using landlines with respon-dents ages 18–65, but people under 30 are less likely to have a landline. _____ may occur because the sample may be biased.

3. What is the purpose of descriptive statistics?

   a. _____ use a single value to represent the sample.

4. _____ statistics test the research questions or hypotheses and make inferences about the population from which the sample was selected.

   a. What is a common approach to this form of statistics?

5. Type I error occurs when you infer a relationship that does or does not exist?

☛ **Go to the end of the chapter to check your answers.**

The two main criteria for evaluating quantitative research are validity and reliability. **Validity** refers to the extent to which a measure is actually tapping what we think it is tapping. **Reliability** refers to the consistency of results. A good measure should be both valid (measure what it's supposed to measure) *and* reliable (the results are dependable) (Babbie, 2013, p. 153). There are several forms of validity and reliability.

Validity

Although it isn't possible to prove conclusively that a measure is valid, there are different types of validity we can try to achieve, thus imbuing our measure with credibility (Adler & Clark, 2011). **Face validity** is a judgment call we make that,

TABLE 4.6. Overview of Inferential Statistical Tests		
Statistical test	**Type of measure**	**Overview**
t-Test	Comparison	Used to compare the results of two groups (statistical significance of differences in groups' means) (Babbie, 2013)
Analysis of variance (ANOVA)	Comparison	Used to compare the results of more than two groups (statistical significance of differences in groups' means) (Babbie, 2013)
Analysis of covariance (ANCOVA)	Comparison	Used to compare the results of more than two groups, controlling for covariates (Creswell, 2014)
Chi-square (X²)	Association	A test of significance based on the null hypothesis (Babbie, 2013), used to test the association between two categorical variables (Creswell, 2014)
Cramer's V	Association	Used to test the strength of the relationship between two variables. Results in a score between 0 and 1 (0 indicates no relationship whatsoever and *1* indicates a perfect relationship) (Adler & Clark, 2011)
Pearson product–moment correlation	Correlation	Used to determine the strength and direction of a relationship between two variables (Adler & Clark, 2011)
Multiple r regression	Correlation	Used to relate three or more continuous variables

at face value, based on common sense, the measure is tapping what we claim it is tapping. If you presented the measure to someone walking down the street, he/she would know what the measure was supposed to examine or consider. **Content validity** is a judgment call made by experts in the particular area that the measure is valid. If you present the measure to a group of experts, they would agree it is legitimate. **Construct validity** means the measure is tapping into the concept and the related concepts into which we propose that it is tapping. Achieving construct validity requires us to create highly specific operational definitions (Fallon, 2016). **Statistical validity** refers to whether the statistical analysis chosen was appropriate and whether the conclusions drawn are consistent with the statistical analysis and the rules of statistical laws. **Ecological validity** means that the findings are generalizable to a real-world setting. In other words, the results would not occur only in a lab or other artificial setting, but could also be applied to the real world.

Beyond these specific types of validity, there are two major forms of validity: internal and external. **Internal validity** centers on "factors that affect the internal links between the independent and dependent variables that support alternative explanations for variations in the dependent variable" (Adler & Clark, 2011, p. 188). There are numerous possible threats to internal validity. For example, are there prior differences in the experimental and control groups that might account for differences in the dependent variable? Have subjects in the experimental and control groups shared information with each other? Have subjects who are likely to respond to the experimental stimulus in a particular way been included? What all of these threats center on is the possibility that an extraneous variable (an additional factor not being tested) may influence the results. To combat threats to internal validity, researchers can use pre- and posttests, keep subjects in the experimental and control groups separate, and randomly assign subjects to the experimental and control groups.

External validity centers on whether we have generalized to populations beyond those that are supported by our test. For example, if the setting or the research subjects have highly unique characteristics, you cannot generalize to other settings or groups. Additional studies with other subjects and/or settings would be needed to see if the results could be extended. Table 4.7 summarizes the various types of validity.

Reliability

If a measure, a survey instrument, or an experimental intervention is reliable, it will yield consistent results. **Interitem reliability** refers to the use of multiple questions or indicators intended to measure a single variable (Fallon, 2016). For example, in a survey about body image, there may be many questions aimed at assessing "negative body image." The questions related to that variable should yield consistent responses from a subject. If they don't, it would indicate a problem with one or more of those questions. Reliability tests commonly used to check the internal consistency of scales in survey research are Cronbach's alpha and factor analysis. **Test–retest reliability** involves testing the measure twice with the same subjects to

TABLE 4.7. Types of Validity

Type of validity	Description
Face validity	A judgment call made by regular people that, at face value, the measure is tapping what we think it is
Content validity	A judgment call made by experts that the measure is tapping what we think it is
Construct validity	The measure is tapping into the concept and related concepts, as we propose, which requires us to create highly specific operational definitions
Statistical validity	The statistical analysis chosen is appropriate and the conclusions drawn are consistent with the statistical analysis and the rules of statistical law
Ecological validity	The findings are generalizable to a real-world setting
Internal validity	Precautions have been taken to safeguard against the possibility that an extraneous variable influenced the results
External validity	The findings have only been generalized to populations supported by the tests

see if the results are consistent (Fallon, 2016). For example, in a survey on a topic for which you'd expect consistent results over time (the subjects' responses are not prone to change over time), the retest method is appropriate. In a study in which responses may naturally change over time due to mood or maturation, such as in a study about happiness, this type or reliability is not a concern. **Interrater reliability** combats against the effect of the particular researcher/observer on the results. For example, by having more than one researcher record his/her observations during an experiment, even for part of the time, the researchers' observations can be compared. The greater the consistency between the two sets of observations, the more reliable the data are (Fallon, 2016). Interrater reliability can help safeguard against poor or improper training, researcher fatigue, and inadvertent bias. Table 4.8 summarizes the three types of reliability.

TABLE 4.8. Types of Reliability

Type of reliability	Description
Interitem reliability	Consistency of results across multiple questions or indicators intended to measure a single variable
Test–retest reliability	Consistency of results testing the measure with the same subjects twice
Interrater reliability	Consistency of results using two or more researchers/observers

Interpretation and Representation

After analyzing the data, you need to ask two questions: (1) What does it all mean? and (2) What are the implications of this study? As you interpret the results, it is important to stick closely to the data. Use logic as you make sense of the data and support every claim with evidence (data) and the logic you applied. Results are typically presented in a journal article and/or at a conference.

Quantitative research is generally **visually depicted in tables or graphs.** There are four primary ways of visually depicting statistical data (Fallon, 2016, pp. 91–96):

1. **Tables:** good for clearly presenting data on any number of variables and can be used for descriptive or inferential statistics.

2. **Histograms:** good for presenting distributions for a single variable.

3. **Scatterplots:** illustrate the relationship between two continuous variables to help you see:
   a. Whether the relationship is linear
   b. The direction of the relationship (upward left to right indicates a positive relationship and downward left to right indicates a negative relationship)
   c. The strength of the relationship
   d. Outlying points
   e. If you have an intervening (moderating) variable

4. **Bar and line graphs:** good for illustrating one or more categorical variables that are the independent variables and one continuous variable that is the dependent variable. Typically the independent variable(s) is on the x-axis (horizontal) and the dependent variable is on the y-axis (vertical).

Finally, it is customary to include **implications for future research** on your topic (including if you personally plan to conduct further research in the area). What are the implications of the results of your study for others who want to research this topic?

Pilot Tests (If Applicable)

A **pilot test** is a complete run-through of your study. If you are using a pilot test of your proposed study, describe the methodology in detail, including the data collection instrument, sampling method, and findings. If you are making changes to your design, including to any data collection or measurement instruments, explain your rationale for doing so.

Ethics Statement

Begin by clarifying the **values system** guiding your research. Possible topics to address include (as applicable) the values or timeliness driving your topic selection and the use of underrepresented groups (e.g., replicating previous research with a more inclusive sample).

Next provide a detailed discussion of your attention to **ethical praxis.** Topics to address include (as applicable) the status of necessary IRB approvals; informed consent (explaining the risks and benefits of participation, the voluntary nature of participation, confidentiality, and participants' right to ask questions); how you have made your datasets and protocols available to other researchers (allowing for the possibility of replication); and dealing with subjects/respondents at the completion of data collection (debriefings, making findings available). Any use of deception, which is often necessary in experiments (particularly field experiments), should be explained and justified. Finally, describe all efforts to reduce or eliminate the Hawthorne effect or testing effect and sampling error.

✋ REVIEW STOP 6

1. Why is ecological validity important?

2. Threats to _____ validity all center on the possibility that an extraneous variable may influence the results.

3. Define reliability.

4. How are quantitative findings generally depicted?

5. What is a pilot test?

☞ **Go to the end of the chapter to check your answers.**

References

Include a full reference list for your proposal, properly attributing credit for all citations. Check for reference style requirements at your institution (e.g., APA , MLA, Chicago), and if those are not provided, follow the norms in your discipline. (Reference sections are required in all research proposals regardless of the design, so this section is not repeated in Chapters 5–8.)

Appendices

Timeline

Present a proposed timeline for the project, noting the time period allotted for each phase of the research process. Things usually take longer than you anticipate, so bear that in mind so that you come up with a reasonable timetable and avoid undue stress.

Proposed Budget (If Applicable)

If your research is funded or you are seeking funding, you will need to include a detailed proposed budget. Your budget may include the cost of equipment (data analysis software), payments to subjects/respondents (including reimbursement for travel expenses), and any other anticipated expenses. In well-funded research you may be hiring experts or assistants, such as consultants, to help design your survey instrument, or statisticians to analyze the data; however, students and novices typically do this work themselves.

Recruitment Letter and Informed Consent Document

If you are working with research subjects/respondents, include these documents.

Instruments

Include copies of all instruments and protocols used in the study (e.g., pretest, survey instrument [questionnaire], experimental intervention, measurement instrument, posttest).

Conclusion

As reviewed in this chapter, quantitative research is particularly useful to learn deductively about variable relationships. Quantitative research allows us to build statistical descriptions of phenomena, refute or support existing theories, and test hypotheses about variable relationships. This approach values breadth, control, and precise measurement. Large, randomly selected samples are generally favored.

Here is a brief summary of the template for a quantitative research design proposal.

Title: Includes your main topic (including the central variables, if possible) and the method being used.

Abstract: This 150- to 200-word overview should be composed at the end. Include the problem under investigation, the research purpose and hypothesis or research questions, the basic methods, the population of interest, the research subjects/respondents, and the main theory or concept guiding the study (if applicable).

Keywords: Provides five to six keywords a reader would be likely to Google to find your study, including the main phenomenon, the variables, and the concepts and theories guiding the study (as applicable).

The Topic under Investigation: Discusses the phenomenon to be investigated in your study; the variable relationships being tested; pragmatic issues; and the significance, value, or worth for the study (including timeliness if applicable).

Theoretical Perspective: Discusses the specific theory or theories you are using. As suggested by Creswell (2014), this section should include the central propositions of the theory, past uses and applications, and a discussion about how the theory specifically relates to your proposed study.

Research Purpose Statement: Outlines the primary objective or causal relationships studied. Includes the main problem, the independent and dependent variables (at a minimum), the population of interest, and the theory being tested.

Research Questions or Hypotheses: A list of the central deductive questions your study seeks to answer may be provided, or these clearly identify the variables in your study and provide a statement or statements predicting how the independent variable affects the dependent variable (if any intervening variables are also under investigation, these should be noted as well).

Literature Review: Synthesizes the most relevant research on your topic, focusing on primary sources, demonstrating how your project contributes to the literature by replicating or modifying previous research, and including precise definitions of variables.

Design and Methods of Data Collection: Describes in detail the strategies you will use to collect data, making note of how you will address the primary issues associated with the method you are employing.

Population, Sampling, and Subjects: Describes the population in which you are interested, the study population, and your sampling procedure (i.e., probability or purposeful). Discusses any additional strategies used in experimental designs such as randomization or matching.

Data Analysis and Assessment: Describes the strategies you will use to prepare the data and which descriptive and inferential statistical tests you will run. Notes the measures you will take to increase the validity and reliability of your results.

Interpretation and Representation: Notes how you will interpret and represent the results, including anticipated visual depictions of the data.

Pilot Tests (if applicable): Describes the data collection instrument, sampling procedure, and findings. If you are making changes based on the pilot test, discuss these here.

Ethics Statement: Discusses your attention to ethics, including your values system, ethical praxis, and attempts to minimize testing effect and sampling error.

References: Includes a full list of citations, properly crediting all those from whom you've borrowed ideas or quoted. Follow your university reference style guidelines (if applicable) or the norms within your discipline.

Appendices: Includes your proposed timeline, budget, copies of your recruitment letter and informed consent, and copies of all instruments (e.g., pretests, survey instruments [questionnaires], experimental interventions, measuring instruments, posttests).

✓ REVIEW STOP ANSWER KEY

Review Stop 1

1. a study that purposefully repeats previous research to support or disconfirm the previous results

    a. to build confidence in existing research and identify unreliable or fraudulent research

    b. professional disincentives (e.g., harder to publish, receive funding, or earn jobs and promotions) and data-sharing deficiencies

2. postpositivism

3. through a literature review

Review Stop 2

1. The independent variable precedes the dependent variable (temporal order); the independent variable must be related to the dependent variable; there must be no alternative explanation for the dependent variable (no extraneous variable).

2. experimental groups: receive the experimental intervention; control groups: do not receive the experimental intervention

3. to determine the subject's baseline prior to the experimental intervention

4. to assess the impact of the experimental intervention

Review Stop 3

1. preexperimental

2. randomization and control groups

3. quasi-experimental design

4. Neither the subjects nor the researchers know which subjects are in the experimental or control groups.

    a. Eliminates the possibility that researchers' observations will be skewed based on their desire to see changes in the experimental group.

5. how participation in the study alone may impact subjects' responses

    a. control groups; omit pretests

Review Stop 4

1. The data can be ascertained only from the respondents.

2. yes

3. c and e

   i. forced-choice/fixed choice

   ii. Provide a statement with responses that indicate level of agreement, and respondents select a single response.

   iii. neutral

   iv. mutually exclusive and exhaustive

4. fatigue

5. in person

Review Stop 5

1. randomization and matching

2. sampling error

3. to describe and summarize the data

   a. measures of central tendency

4. inferential

   a. null hypothesis significance testing

5. does not

Review Stop 6

1. so the findings have relevance in a real-world setting

2. internal

3. a measure that yields dependable/consistent results

4. visually (in tables or graphs)

5. a complete run-through of a study

Further Engagement

1. Select a published survey research study from a peer-reviewed journal in your discipline and evaluate the methodology based on:

   a. The types of validity and reliability reviewed in Tables 4.7 and 4.8.

   b. What was done to minimize sampling error

   c. What worked well in the study and what could be improved upon (one to two paragraphs).

2. If you want to design an experiment to study the effect of a documentary film about being transgender on college students' perceptions of this topic, what might you do? Briefly explain your rationale (one paragraph).

3. Take a research topic you are interested in and locate two preexisting surveys on the topic. How could you combine questions from the two surveys to develop a new study (one page maximum)?

Resources

Fallon, M. (2016). *Writing quantitative research.* Rotterdam, The Netherlands: Sense Publishers.

Hayes, A. F. (2013). *Introduction to mediation, moderation, and conditional process analysis: A regression-based approach.* New York: Guilford Press.

Johnson, R. L., & Morgan, G. B. (2016). *Survey scales: A guide to development, analysis, and reporting.* New York: Guilford Press.

Little, T. D. (Ed.). (2014). *The Oxford handbook of quantitative methods* (2-vol. set). New York: Oxford University Press.

Suggested Journals

AERA Open (SAGE)
http://ero.sagepub.com

Journal of Education and Behavioral Statistics (SAGE)
http://jeb.sagepub.com

Multivariate Behavioral Research (Routledge)
www.tandfonline.com/loi/hmbr20#.VsC2e5XQCM8

Organizational Research Methods (Sage)
http://orm.sagepub.com

Psychological Methods (American Psychological Association)
www.apa.org/pubs/journals/met

Sociological Methods Research (Sage)
http://smr.sagepub.com

Notes

1. There are other issues regarding data sharing that are currently being debated within research communities. Specifically, there are enormous sources of data available, collected by commercial entities (via social media posts, customer shopping and online clicking patterns, etc.) (King, 2011). Often commercial companies are able to purchase this data, but social researchers are not. If researchers had access to this data, in ways that maintained privacy and confidentiality, it would save the need for many data collection efforts and would open up new research possibilities (and because the data are aggregate

data, meaning group and not individual data, it seems there would be ways of protecting privacy) (King, 2011). See Gary King (2011) for an excellent discussion of this topic.

2. It is important to note that although I am suggesting that these terms are all similar and used interchangeably, some view postpositivism and empiricism as different from scientific realism (e.g., see Greenwood, 1992; Haig, 2013; Manicas & Secord, 1983). Haig (2013) provides a detailed overview of scientific realism, identifying seven features of the tradition. Likewise, some view critical-realist philosophy differently than positivism (e.g., see Cook & Campbell, 1979).

CHAPTER 5

Qualitative Research Design

Qualitative approaches to research value depth of meaning and people's subjective experiences and their meaning-making processes. These approaches allow us to build a robust understanding of a topic, unpacking the meanings people ascribe to their lives—to activities, situations, circumstances, people, and objects. Methodologically, these approaches rely on inductive designs aimed at generating meaning and producing rich, descriptive data. Qualitative approaches are most commonly used in exploratory or descriptive research (although they can be used in research with other goals).

Structure of a Research Proposal

The qualitative paradigm is extremely diverse methodologically and theoretically. Additionally, qualitative research projects often follow malleable designs in which the methodology is revised in accord with new learning acquired as the research unfolds. For all of these reasons, templates are highly problematic. Every research proposal will look somewhat different, just as each project will follow a different plan. However, to some extent, even if the order and weight differ, research proposals typically include some mention of most of what is suggested in Template 5.1. Bear in mind that the template can be greatly modified or reimagined to suit your specific project.

TEMPLATE 5.1

Title
Abstract
Keywords
} Basic Introductory
Information

The Topic under Investigation
   Significance, Value, or Worth
   Literature Review
Research Purpose Statement
Research Questions
} The Topic

Philosophical Statement
Genre/Design and Methods of Data Collection
Sampling, Participants, and Setting
Data Analysis and Interpretation Strategies
Evaluation
Representation
Ethics Statement
References
Appendices
} The Research Plan

In the following boxes, I present two common alternative templates in which the ordering of information varies. However, I again stress that in qualitative research, projects differ.

TEMPLATE 5.2

Title
Abstract
Keywords
The Topic under Investigation
Significance, Value, or Worth
Literature and Theory
Philosophical Statement
Ethics Statement
Research Purpose Statement
Research Questions
Genre/Design
Methods of Data Collection
Sampling, Participants, and Setting
Data Analysis and Interpretation Strategies
Evaluation
Representation
References
Appendices

TEMPLATE 5.3

Title
Abstract
Keywords
The Topic under Investigation
Significance, Value, or Worth
Literature Review
Philosophical Statement
Ethics Statement
Research Purpose Statement
Research Questions
Genre/Design
Sampling, Participants, and Setting
Methods of Data Collection and Analysis
Theory and Interpretation Strategies
Representation
Evaluation
References
Appendices

For remainder of this chapter, I fill in Template 5.1.

Basic Introductory Information

Title

Qualitative titles clearly state the main topic (the primary phenomenon, the method, and the approach to design being used). If you have already collected data and have a clever turn of phrase from an interview, field note, and the like, use it as a hook.

Abstract

In qualitative research this 150- to 200-word overview of the project typically includes the phenomenon you are studying; the research purpose; basic information about the methods, participants, and setting; and why the study is needed (e.g., how it fills a gap in previous research).

Keywords

Keywords let readers know the main problem or phenomenon, the theoretical framework, and any central concepts guiding the project.

The Topic

The Topic under Investigation

Clearly state the phenomenon under inquiry or the dimension of it on which your study will focus. It is also important to give readers a sense of how you came to the topic, including pragmatic issues. Briefly share your personal interest in the topic, any special skills you have that drew you to this topic, funding opportunities for working on this topic, and/or how you are well positioned to have access to the participants or data needed to study this topic.

> **Expert Tip**
>
> Dr. David M. Fetterman, of Stanford University and Fetterman and Associates Evaluation Consultations, gives this all-too important advice: Find a mentor and colleagues off whom to bounce ideas.

There are two additional issues to address when writing about the topic: (1) the significance, value, or worth of studying this topic; and (2) how your understanding of the topic is shaped by existing literature and how the proposed study will contribute to that literature. You can discuss the significance of research on your topic as subsections of the section on "The Topic under Investigation" or in separate sections of the proposal.

Significance, Value, or Worth

This section is an opportunity to consider the social or political value of conducting the proposed research. Outline the project's underlying values system and any social justice imperatives. For example, note if the research focuses on a group currently underrepresented in research on this topic, which has created a gap in the literature. If the rationale for the study is linked to a current event, social problem, or policy issue, discuss the timeliness of the proposed research. For example, if you are proposing a study on arts integration programming in public schools at a time when there are proposed federal cuts to public education or art programming more specifically, you should address the timeliness of the project and the uses to which it could be put.

 Ethics in Practice

The social significance of the topic bears directly on your values system and is thus a part of the philosophical substructure of the project. When weighing and writing about the benefits of research on the topic as you have conceived it, consider the question "How are my values as a researcher and citizen reflected in this topic selection?"

Literature Review

A qualitative literature review provides a solid base from which readers gain an understanding of what is already known about your topic through your synthesis of the recent and landmark studies in this area. Point to what is lacking and how your study will fill a gap or otherwise contribute to our body of knowledge. Note what prior qualitative studies have contributed to our understanding of the topic, or if no such studies exist, point to their absence and what your research will add to prior quantitative studies. The literature review may include relevant theories or conceptual frameworks (which may shape the research purpose statement and research questions), or you could review theoretical frameworks as a part of your philosophical statement later in the proposal.

Research Purpose Statement

Briefly state the purpose of the proposed study by focusing on the **primary focus or goals.** To do so, clearly state the main topic, problem or phenomenon, the participants and setting, the methodology (data collection method, how the methods will be employed, and, if applicable, theoretical framework guiding the study), and the primary reason for conducting the research. With respect to your reason for carrying out the project, your primary purpose may be to explore, describe, or explain.

Research Questions

In qualitative research it is typical to write one to three **central research questions,** although there may be ancillary questions. There are no hard-and-fast rules, and it is possible to design a study with more questions. Bear in mind that research questions need to be researchable—that is, they can be answered by your proposed research. It is better to focus on less and do that well, especially as a student or early career professional.

Qualitative research questions are **inductive** (open-ended) and often begin with the words *what* or *how.* These questions may employ **nondirectional language,** including words and phrases such as *explore, describe, illuminate, unearth, unpack, generate, build meaning,* and *seek to understand.*

The Research Plan

Philosophical Statement

Qualitative research centers on holistic approaches to the research process, whereby choices in methods and methodology are informed by philosophical belief systems. Therefore, it is necessary to provide a philosophical discussion. A qualitative philosophical statement provides a **discussion of the paradigm or worldview** guiding the research project. Typically the statement focuses on the **theoretical school of**

thought (also known as the *theoretical framework*) that is shaping your perspective and design choices.

As noted in Chapter 1, there are two major paradigms within which qualitative researchers typically work: interpretive/constructivist and critical.[1] Each is an umbrella term for numerous theoretical schools of thought.

Interpretive or Constructivist Paradigm

This paradigm examines **how people engage in processes of constructing and reconstructing meanings through daily interactions.** When working within this paradigm, attention is drawn to people's patterns of interaction and the interpretive processes by which they assign meanings to events, situations, and so forth. If you are working within this paradigm, you prioritize people's subjective understandings and multiple meanings in the research process. The major theoretical schools of thought within this paradigm are symbolic interactionism, phenomenology, ethnomethodology, and dramaturgy.

Symbolic interactionism, pioneered by George Herbert Mead (1934/1967) and Herbert Blumer (1969), examines how individuals and small groups use shared symbols, such as language and gestures, during interactions in order to communicate meaning (Hesse-Biber & Leavy, 2011, p. 17). Symbolic interactionists believe that the meanings we attach to interactions, people, or objects are not inherent but rather develop out of "ongoing social interactions" (Hesse-Biber & Leavy, 2011, p. 17). Shared meanings help people understand how to act "appropriately" (Hesse-Biber & Leavy, 2011, p. 18). We all act differently with different people, in different situations, and/or with different objects because of the meanings we attach/ascribe to them. For example, doctors act differently with their patients than they do with their families. College students act differently with professors than they do with peers. People act differently with objects they consider family heirlooms than they do with other objects, deemed less sentimental. A diamond given in the form of an engagement ring will be ascribed meanings that another diamond, such as one in the form of a pendant, will not carry.

The field of **phenomenology** was developed by Edmund Husserl (1913/1963), Martin Heidegger (1927/1982), Maurice Merleau-Ponty (1945/1996), and Alfred Schutz (1967). Phenomenologists are "interested in human consciousness as a way to understand social reality, particularly how one 'thinks' about experience; in other words, *how consciousness is experienced*" (Hesse-Biber & Leavy, 2011, p. 19, emphasis in original). You may be working from this perspective if you are asking how people experience the topic under investigation. For example, you investigate how people experience bullying, grief, or miscarriage. To demonstrate how researchers' philosophical belief systems impact their choice of methods, phenomenologists frequently use ethnography and interview methods.

Harold Garfinkel (1967) was a leading force in the field of **ethnomethodology,** which draws on phenomenology to examine the specific strategies people use to negotiate meanings through their interactions with others and thus how they make sense of their lives. The assumption is that "social life is created and re-created" as a result of the "micro-understanding individuals bring to their everyday social context" (Hesse-Biber & Leavy, 2011, p. 20). Again, to demonstrate how researchers' philosophical belief systems impact their choice of methods, ethnomethodologists frequently use ethnography and interview methods.

Dramaturgy was developed by Erving Goffman (1959). This theoretical school of thought uses the metaphor of theatre to understand social life. Dramaturgy suggests that just as in theatre, so too in social life there is a front and back stage. The "front stage" is where we enact our public roles or faces as we engage in interactions others see and judge. When we are "back stage" we are able to act differently, because we are not putting on a social or public face. For example, Facebook is a public platform—or front stage—and people tend to use it accordingly, presenting the most flattering pictures of themselves and the like. Backstage they may have taken many pictures, and edited them, in order to get the one they shared publicly.

Critical Paradigm

The theoretical frameworks that comprise the critical paradigm grew out of the interplay between theoretical developments, changes in the academy that included the development of numerous interdisciplinary areas of study, and the social justice movements. The social justice movements were discussed in Chapter 2, so here I only briefly note that one result was the development of areas studies "forged in critique" (Klein, 2000). In other words, area studies such as Black studies or African American studies, women's studies or gender studies, Chicano/Chicana studies, and queer studies all developed in **critique of the unequal relations of power** within the broader society. The main theoretical schools of thought within this paradigm are postmodernist, poststructuralist, feminist, critical race, indigenous, and queer theoretical frameworks.

In different ways the theoretical bodies in the critical paradigm all consider issues of **power** in social life and the research process. In qualitative research these theoretical frameworks are often used to consider the **micro-politics of power,** how power is negotiated, maintained and resisted by/within small groups. Further, these perspectives assume people are operating within power-rich environments, meaning power is always at play.

Postmodern theorists investigate dominant ideology. More specifically, theorists in this perspective critique the **discourses that normalize dominant ideology—** that is, those lines of thinking that become so "taken-for-granted" that people may fail to realize that they are power-laden discourses. The argument is that there is nothing accidental about dominant ideology and the discourses that create and maintain it. Antonio Gramsci (1929), an early leader in the field, argued that people partly consent to their own oppression through the internalization of the dominant ideology, which poses as "commonsense" ways of thinking that seem to make sense of the world. This theoretical framework draws our attention to the **symbolic and discursive contexts** (images, objects, language, phrasing) that have been constructed in power-rich environments and through which power operates and ideas of normalcy are created. (Hesse-Biber & Leavy, 2011, p. 21). Stephen Pfohl (2007) warns that social constructions always push alternative ideas and perspectives to the periphery. As such, the images and stories that circulate in the media, for instance, are haunted by what they exclude. For example, Venus Evans-Winters (Facebook post, April 29, 2015) considers the language that might be used to describe the Black Lives Matter protests of 2014–2016 versus the incendiary and racialized language repeatedly employed by the media:

"Protests vs. Riots"
"Citizens vs. Thugs"
"Youth vs. Black Community"

Under postmodern theoretical approaches, research claims must be situated in their particular social–historical contexts and not assumed to represent "The Truth" but rather **partial and situated truths.**

Poststructuralism is also concerned with challenging **dominant ideology.** Jacques Derrida (1966), a pioneer in poststructuralism, promoted a strategy of **critical deconstruction** as a way to break down unities to expose what has been rendered invisible. Poststructuralism focuses on breaking down unified narratives to see how dominant ideology works. For example, from this perspective, a qualitative researcher might conduct a critical content analysis of media representations of the 2014–2016 Black Lives Matter protests in order to deconstruct how the media created and re-created a cohesive narrative using the language of *riots* instead of *protests* and how such a narrative reinforced dominant ideologies that systematically disadvantage people of color and serve to depoliticize their actions.

Feminist, critical race, indigenous, and **queer** theoretical frameworks focus on issues of **equality, inequality, hierarchy, justice, privilege, power, and oppression** for women; people of color; indigenous people; and lesbian, gay, bisexual, transgender, and queer (LGBTQ) people, respectively. These perspectives consider inequality at all levels, including institutional and cultural, and they examine how interactions between individuals and small groups may reinforce or resist dominant ideologies that maintain White supremacy and patriarchy. For example, from a feminist perspective, a qualitative researcher might conduct an ethnographic field study on a college campus to unpack and describe the dimensions of rape culture and how they impact campus life differently for male, female, and transgender students. Additionally, these theoretical bodies contain specific theories that also consider issues of *intersectionality* (a term first coined by Kimberlé Crenshaw in 1989): that is, how these status characteristics intersect to create "vectors of privilege and oppression" (Hill-Collins, 1990). Researchers influenced by any of these perspectives may seek out participants from underrepresented groups and/or construct research purposes and questions designed to access the experiences of those disenfranchised, or that may produce research that can be put in service of social justice. Table 5.1 summarizes the main paradigms and their related theoretical schools of thought.

TABLE 5.1. Paradigms and Theoretical Schools of Thought

Paradigm	Theoretical school	Focus
Interpretive or constructivist	Symbolic interactionism	Individuals and small groups use shared symbols during interactions to communicate meaning
Interpretive or constructivist	Phenomenology	How individuals experience
Interpretive or constructivist	Ethnomethodology	Strategies people use to negotiate meanings in their interactions
Interpretive or constructivist	Dramaturgy	People's presentation of self in "front" and "back" stages of social life
Critical	Postmodernism	Dominant ideologies and symbols and discourses of power
Critical	Poststructuralism	Deconstruction of unified narratives to expose how dominant ideology works
Critical	Indigenous	Resist colonizing research practices and value indigenous knowledge
Critical	Critical race	Injustice and difference based on race
Critical	Queer	Injustice and difference based on sexual orientation and identity
Critical	Feminist	Injustice and difference based on sex and gender

 Ethics in Practice

The worldview guiding your project is linked to your philosophical belief system, including your values system. It is important to be cautious about how you enact your belief system, even when well intentioned. For example, if you are applying a critical race theoretical framework, it may impact your sampling choices. You may seek out participants in minority racial groups as a part of your theoretical commitments. However, be cautious that you are not, in fact, exploiting those communities merely to serve your own research agenda. At the 2015 annual American Educational Research Association (AERA) conference, scholars Donna Y. Ford and Ivory Toldson warned about the dangers of "drive-by scholarship"—by which they mean going into communities of color in which you are not otherwise invested simply to collect data and then leave (thereby objectifying the research participants).

✋ REVIEW STOP 1

1. How is topic selection an ethical decision?

2. Which of the following research questions are inductive?

    a. How would you describe your childhood?

    b. Did you have a good childhood?

    c. What is your favorite childhood memory?

    d. Do you remember much of your childhood?

3. The _____ paradigm examines how people engage in processes of constructing and reconstructing meanings through daily interactions.

    a. Match the theoretical school of thought with its description:

    Dramaturgy

    Symbolic Interactionism

    Ethnomethodology

    Phenomenology

    i. examines how individuals and small groups use shared symbols, such as language and gestures, during interactions in order to communicate meaning

    ii. examines the specific strategies people use to negotiate meanings through their interactions with others and thus how they make sense of their lives

    iii. uses the metaphor of theatre to understand social life

    iv. examines how consciousness is experienced

4. In different ways the theoretical schools of thought in the critical paradigm all consider _____.

👉 **Go to the end of the chapter to check your answers.**

Genre/Design and Methods of Data Collection

As noted earlier, methods should always be selected because of their ability to best address the research purpose and help answer the research questions (bearing in mind pragmatic issues such as time, resources, and the researcher's skill set). In qualitative research, your philosophical point of view comes to bear as particular theoretical traditions lend themselves to the use of particular research methods. For example, the principles of phenomenology and ethnomethodology are in accord with the methodological techniques of ethnography and interview, and thus your philosophical point of view may impact your method selection as much as your research purpose and questions.

Qualitative research is characterized by numerous available research methods (consult Table 1.2 in Chapter 1). They cannot all be adequately covered in this text, so I review four popular genres and the corresponding methods.

Field Research (Ethnography)

> The office space of investment banking analysts is literally called the bullpen. The bullpen that I observed at DLJ was a long hallway about 150 feet long and 20 feet wide, demarcated by the high desks of administrative staff, who sat in the center of the floor, and the associates' small offices. The entrance to the bullpen was an actual plastic gate, meant as both a joke and a commentary on life at the bank. Inside the gate, cramped desks, shelves, and floors overflowed with pitch books, PowerPoint presentations, and old binders of previous deal books, not to mention soda cans, footballs, gym bags, weights, change of clothes, deodorant, and an extra suit hanging just in case. The bullpen on one of Merrill Lynch's corporate finance floors was a U-shaped area with a similar lived-in feel, peppered with the detritus of work and work distractions: suction basketball hoops, paper airplanes, a pile of take-out containers. (Ho, 2009, p. 90)

The preceding is an excerpt from Karen Ho's ethnography of Wall Street. This brief example illustrates the rich descriptions that distinguish field research. Further, we see how much we can learn about daily life for people in various settings or groups through these detailed descriptions. For example, in the preceding excerpt we learn not only about the physical environment but also the mood and some of the unexpected activities that speak to larger issues in the environment.

Field research (ethnography) is the oldest qualitative genre, with its roots in cultural anthropology. The terms *field research* and *ethnography* are often used interchangeably in the literature; however, they have slightly different meanings. **Ethnography** refers to writing about culture. **Field research** takes place in natural settings, referred to as *the field*. The result of field research is an ethnography. These approaches to research rely on the researcher engaging in **direct observations** of people in their **natural settings** in order to **understand social life from the perspective of the participants** (Bailey, 2007).[2] Ethnographers aim to **describe the culture** in which the research participants are enmeshed. These approaches to research result in "thick descriptions" of social life (Geertz, 1973).

The primary research methods in this genre are participatory and nonparticipatory observations. **Participatory observation** requires the researcher to engage in the activities of those he or she is researching, and to record systematic observations. Often ethnographers spend extended periods of time in the field, at times even living with their research participants. **Nonparticipatory observation** also typically occurs over a long period of time; however, the researcher observes the participants in the setting without engaging in the same activities. In practice, the researcher's level of participation may occur along a continuum, ranging from nonparticipatory to fully participatory (see Figure 5.1).

The success of ethnographic research is inextricably bound to the researcher's ability to gain access to the setting and build productive relationships in the field. The first issue to consider is gaining entrance. Do you have access to the setting in which the participants are located? There can be both formal and informal **gatekeepers** preventing you from accessing the site. Formal gatekeepers may be present in both private and public spaces. For instance, if you wish to conduct research in a private or members-only environment, such as a country club or health club, it is unlikely you will be able to gain entrance unless you are already a member or know a member who can assist you. If you wish to conduct research in public schools, you will need formal permission from a host of gatekeepers before you are able to gain entrance. In addition, every setting also has informal gatekeepers. Each person in the setting in which you are conducting your research can decide whether or not he/she will participate, and in that sense each person is, at a minimum, a gatekeeper to his/her own knowledge. If multiple participants in a setting do not want you there, then even if they can't keep you out of the space, they can still deny you the kind of access you need to conduct your research. Ethnographic research necessitates relationships in the field. So even in a public space such as a park, there are gatekeepers.

As you attempt to gain entrance into the field and cultivate relationships once you are there, **insider–outsider status** comes to bear. You may share some status characteristics in common with the participants, such as gender, race, and/or age, but you may be an outsider as well based on different characteristics such as education, job, and so forth. It is important to be aware of these similarities and differences as you build relationships. In order to collect data, it is necessary to develop **rapport** with the participants in your setting—which is how you build relationships in the field. Some participants may become **key informants** who share not only their own experiences but also introduce you to other possible participants and/or provide an overview picture of people and activities in the setting. In addition to following the protocols of informed consent, in this kind of research it is also important to **set expectations** about your role in the setting, including how long you intend to be there, whether or not you intend to maintain relationships once you have left the setting, and if so, in what capacity. Setting expectations with

Nonparticipatory ⬅️➡️ **Fully participatory**

FIGURE 5.1. Continuum of researcher's level of participation.

participants with whom you are developing relationships is important so that when it is time to leave the field, the participants are properly prepared for your departure.

In terms of data collection, researchers in both participatory and nonparticipatory approaches engage in a process of systematic note taking—called *field notes*. **Field notes** are the written or recorded notes of your observations in the field—they are the data. It is important to record the date and time of your field notes to maintain a chronological record. It is also good practice to note the location, and, if the field note refers to an interaction with a particular participant or group of participants, note that as well. Field notes should be written systematically. Typically, ethnographers set aside a certain time or times in the day for extensive note taking.

It is always advisable to have a small notepad or a cellphone with a voice-recording feature in order to "jot" down words or phrases that you want to remember. Those jottings are referred to as **on-the-fly notes.** There are numerous types of field notes you might collect, including those labeled **thick descriptions, summary notes, reflexivity notes, conversation and interview notes, and interpretation notes** (Bailey, 1996, 2007; Hesse-Biber & Leavy, 2011). Table 5.2 summarizes the different kinds of field notes (not an exhaustive list).

Try to capture as many details as possible, including the exact words of participants, whenever possible. Given the breadth of data you will be collecting, it is vital to have a good **organizational system and to catalog your field notes** regularly. Handwritten notes should either be typed and filed away regularly or scanned and organized in an electronic database. Although you may handwrite or voice-record your field notes during data collection, during analysis and interpretation it will be much easier to work with an electronic version of the data—which is why I highly recommend typing your field notes.

While on the subject of analysis and interpretation, it is important to mention memo notes. "Memo-ing" is also a vital part of data production in ethnographic research. **Memo notes** help you develop your ideas about your data (field notes), synthesize your data, integrate your ideas, and discern relationships within the data (Hesse-Biber & Leavy, 2005, 2011). Memo notes are reviewed at length in the section on data analysis and interpretation; however, because qualitative research—and field research, in particular—is a recursive process wherein some data are collected and analyzed, and then new data are collected, and so forth, you may well be writing memo notes while in the field.

In addition to observations (field notes), analysis, and impressions (memo notes), researchers may also **informally and/or formally interview** participants. It

TABLE 5.2. Types of Field Notes

On-the-fly notes

Words or phrases you want to remember

Thick descriptions

Highly detailed descriptions of the setting, participants, and activities observed. When describing the setting, use your senses to paint the scene, and when describing participants and activities, use their exact language and other specifics when possible

Summary notes

Daily or weekly summaries of what you learned in the field and things you intend to look for or follow up on

Reflexivity notes

An ongoing accounting, or regular gut-check, of your role as researcher in the process; comment on your feelings, ethical dilemmas or issues, relationships in the field

Conversation and interview notes

Notes about each informal or formal topic, details of what was said (using exact words when possible); include follow-up questions or others with whom you want to speak

Interpretation notes

Notes about your sense-making process (including what you think something means)

is advisable to keep a small recorder or a cellphone with voice-recording capacity on you to audio-record interviews (with your participants' consent). This allows you to type up a verbatim transcript of interviews, which will serve as a part of the data.

Field research typically produces an abundance of data in the form of field notes, memos, and interview notes or transcripts. As this kind of research occurs over a lengthy period of time, you'll know it is time to exit the field and cease data collection when you have reached the **saturation point.** As discussed in Chapter 3, this means that you are not learning new information and may even be losing clarity. If you are engaging in a recursive process of collecting and analyzing data, sometimes referred to as **data analysis cycles** (Tenni, Smith, & Boucher, 2003), the process can help you realize when you've reached data saturation (Coffey, 1999).

Expert Tip

Dr. Christopher Pole, Pro Vice-Chancellor Academic Directorate at Nottingham Trent University, suggests that we "ask the dumb question"—questions that may seem naïve and challenge taken-for-granted assumptions. For example, he suggests that if you're in an unfamiliar setting, ask people "Why is that like that?" and "Why is it always done that way?"

✋ REVIEW STOP 2

1. Field research occurs in _____ settings.

2. How do field researchers collect data?

3. What is the purpose of field research?

4. Define field notes.

   a. Name two out of the six kinds of field notes reviewed.

   b. What is the relationship of memo notes to field notes?

👉 **Go to the end of the chapter to check your answers.**

Interview

The following is excerpted from an in-depth interview study that two student researchers and I conducted about body image and attraction ideals in a sample of heterosexual female and male college students. The following excerpt is what some of the female participants had to say.

When prompted with the question: "what do you dislike about your body?" the female participants were quick to respond with specific examples. They uniformly expressed dissatisfaction with numerous parts of their bodies. Almost all of the participants shared the common frustrations encompassed in the following excerpt:

> "Well my midsection is one and I think that's a lot, I think a lot of females have that problem with their midsection. Definitely my thighs and my butt and my abs are definitely areas I would improve if possible, if at all possible."

Nearly all of the participants stressed frustrations with *specific* parts of their bodies that they identified as areas of concern, dissatisfaction, and insecurity. Each body part the participants noted were the same parts that they continuously attempt to make *smaller.*

> "Ugh . . . My thighs! Because I have fat thighs! I hate it! And I think, I feel like no matter how long I go to the gym, I'm never going to have skinny thighs. That just pisses me off."

Another participant noted:

> "If I'm going to be wearing a shirt that shows my stomach or something I should exercise a little or work on my abs."

Even participants who did not point out specific parts of their bodies admitted to the desirability of being thinner and smaller:

"We have a thin mirror in our room and my roommate and I stare at ourselves and analyze ourselves in the mirror, and I definitely love it when I can look in the mirror and like what I see . . . when I can it makes me feel like everything I've done is totally worth it and like it doesn't even matter that I haven't eaten macaroni and cheese in months."

Another participant contributed:

"And I mean I still . . . like being thin, I do it (work out) to stay in shape and to look decent." (Stiman, Leavy, & Garland, 2009)

Interview is a commonly used research genre across disciplines. There are numerous interview methods available to qualitative researchers, including in-depth, semistructured, oral history or life history, biographic minimalist, and focus groups (in which multiple participants are interviewed at once in a group). In general, interview methods use **conversation as a learning tool.** People are naturally conversational, and so interview methods draw on something people are accustomed to participating in, even if not typically in formal settings (Brinkmann, 2012, 2013). As a research method, an interview is **an event** that is likely preplanned (Brinkmann, 2012, 2013). Narrative approaches have increased in recent years and view "storytelling as a communicative activity" that allow people to ascribe meanings to their experiences (Bochner & Riggs, 2014, p. 202).

Different methods of interview impose various **levels of structure.** Interview structures range from **unstructured to semistructured to highly structured,** the latter of which resembles survey research discussed in the last chapter. These levels of structure exist on a continuum with innumerable possibilities (see Figure 5.2).

I focus on in-depth interviews, which are commonplace and occur between the researcher and one participant at a time. **In-depth interviews are inductive or open-ended** and range from unstructured to semistructured. In other words, questions do not have a predetermined set of acceptable responses, such as true or false. Rather, participants are able to use their own language, provide long and detailed responses if they choose, and go in any direction they want in response to the question. Here are examples:

Is your dorm room nice? (closed-ended)
Describe your dorm room. (open-ended)

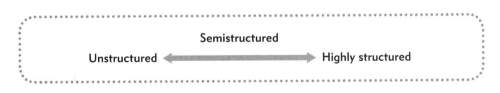

FIGURE 5.2. Continuum of level of structure in interviews.

Do you like your roommate? (closed-ended)
How do you feel about your roommate? (open-ended)

In order to prepare for data collection, researchers create interview guides that range from a list of general **lines of inquiry** or themes they intend to cover to detailed lists of open-ended questions (Weiss, 1994). In the most inductive studies, interview guides provide general lines of inquiry, perhaps peppered with a few questions in case you get stuck. It's advisable for novice researchers to create more detailed interview guides. Even if you turn away from them during data collection, you have them if needed. As you prepare your interview guide, consider the order of questions. In their discussion of focus group interviews, Margaret R. Roller and Paul J. Lavrakas (2015) suggest a "funnel" organization that begins with broader, more general questions and leads to more specific questions (p. 140; see Figure 5.3). This format allows participants time to get more comfortable while you build rapport, and also allows you to learn some things that may impact your later, more specific, questions.

When designing your study, consider the **level of structure** you will impose. Will you ask all participants the same questions? Will the questions be asked in the same order? To what extent will you allow participants to take the interviews in different directions and go with their flow? If you plan to impose a high degree of structure, you need to create a detailed interview guide in advance so that you can ask each participant the same questions in the same order.

Successful interview research is dependent on building **rapport** with your participants through **active listening.** Eye contact and gestures can go a long way to showing participants that you are interested in what they are saying and you want them to continue. **Probes** can also be used to demonstrate active listening and to collect richer data. A probe might be a simple as "Can you give me an example of that?" or "Do you have a story about that?" or "Please tell me more," or may even be a nonverbal gesture such as a nod that indicates you would like the participant

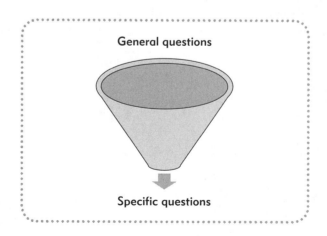

FIGURE 5.3. Inductive interview question organization.

to continue on with whatever he/she is discussing. Active listening can also help you to pick up on markers, which may be the keys to vital information.

Participants often drop **markers** when they are talking about something else (Weiss, 1994). In other words, while they are speaking on one topic, they say something about a different topic that you think may be worth returning to for exploration. You do not want to interrupt the participant until he/she has completed his/her response, but you can jot down markers when you hear them, ideally noting just a word or short phrase to remind you, so you don't distract your participant or fail to hear what he/she is saying. Then when the participant has finished his/her current line of talking, you can return to the marker. For example, in an interview about marriage, you may ask a participant about her wedding. In the context of telling you about her wedding, she describes the food and says, "Each plate looked like art, and I was glad we splurged on the salmon because the sauce was incredible and everyone loved it, except my mother who complains about everything, but it was amazing. It had champagne and caviar. . . . " While your participant is speaking, you may pick up on the marker she dropped about her mother, which you could note on a small notepad with the word *mother*. Once she has finished describing the food, you could say, "That sounds great. You mentioned when you were talking about the food that your mother has a habit of complaining. Can you tell me about that?" Although not all markers lead to information that is important for your project, often they do. In this example it is possible the participant could go on to describe a rocky relationship with her mother, or that her mother is a difficult person to get along with and that has impacted her parents' marriage, or many other things. In those instances, what is revealed might bear directly on the larger topic of marriage and how your participant thinks about and experiences relationships. In short, there may be vital data that would not come out otherwise, simply because you wouldn't know to ask.

In addition to "direct questioning," there are alternative techniques for ascertaining data in interview contexts. "Enabling techniques" are a way of modifying a question to make it easier for participants to express themselves. These strategies can be quite useful in social research (Roller & Lavrakas, 2015, p. 140). Examples noted by Roller and Lavrakas include:

- Sentence completion/fill in the blank (e.g., "During my wedding ceremony I felt _____").

- Word association (e.g., "What is the first word you think of when you hear *wedding*?").

- Storytelling (e.g., "Tell me a story about something that happened at your wedding").

Your ability to employ these various techniques will depend in part on how your interviews are taking place. A benefit of **face-to-face interviews** is the opportunity to build rapport, pick up on visual cues, and use gestures. However, in-person interviews are not always possible (due to resources, geographic location, etc.). Interviews may also be conducted via video conferencing or Skype, telephone, or e-mail. Although not identical to face-to-face experiences, **video-conferencing and Skype interviews** have many of the benefits of in-person interviews *and* allow you to talk to people whom you might not be able to reach in person because they are located far away. **Telephone interviews** eliminate your ability to communicate through gestures; however, you can still ask probing questions and pick up on verbal markers. **E-mail interviews,** which are written interviews, don't allow you to capture verbal or physical cues. However, written interviews have the benefit of allowing you to interview people in disparate locations, to allow participants more time to respond to questions thoughtfully, and may be appropriate for research on sensitive topics that participants are more comfortable responding to privately. Written interviews via e-mail result in more highly structured interviews, wherein you are using the same interview guide with every participant. When using this approach, you may ask participants follow-up questions after you have read their initial responses. There may even be more than one round of follow-up questions.

Once you have collected the interview data, it is customary to **transcribe** the interviews. Many researchers transcribe each interview verbatim to preserve a complete record of the interview. In other instances researchers decide to transcribe only what they deem to be the relevant parts of the interview. Although this approach saves time, you do risk losing valuable data early in the process. A benefit of written interviews is that you can avoid the monotonous transcription process (although that reason alone is insufficient for selecting that approach). It is important to **clearly label and mark up your transcript** so that it is in a form that is easy to analyze—for example, the use of bold and italic fonts consistently (e.g., to mark when the researcher is talking, or when the participant emphasized something). By going the extra mile during data preparation, the process of data analysis and interpretation is made easier. Transcription is a tedious process and ample time for it should be built into the research design. Transcription software programs are available to assist this process, but it is still labor intensive. If you're applying for funding for your research, you may consider budgeting for a transcriber. If so, they must be informed to maintain the confidentiality of participants. When using a hired transcriber, I strongly urge you to at least listen to the audio recordings to get to know the data, the participants' voices, and how they place emphasis.

You will need to make decisions about whether or not to **edit or beautify** your transcripts. For example, people often say things like "um" or "like" repeatedly. People also use colloquialisms. Will you leave these speech elements in or leave them out? There are ethical implications to consider. You have an obligation to present people sensitively. You also have an obligation not to erase cultural differences and homogenize the participants' voices. If you hire a transcriber, you will need to give him/her specific instructions regarding editing.

As with field research, memo writing is also a vital part of data production and later analysis in interview research (discussed in greater detail in the section on analysis).

✋ REVIEW STOP 3

1. In-depth interviews are inductive. Which of the following questions are inductive?

    a. What do you do during a typical day at work?

    b. Do you like your job?

    c. Do you have your dream job?

    d. How do you feel about your boss?

2. When designing an interview study, researchers consider whether all participants will be asked the same questions, if questions will be asked in the same order, and the latitude participants will have in responding to questions and directing the flow of interviews. These all speak to the _____ the researcher imposes.

3. What are some ways to demonstrate active listening during interviews?

4. What are the advantages and disadvantages of conducting interviews via e-mail?

👉 **Go to the end of the chapter to check your answers.**

Self-Data (Autoethnography)

The following is an excerpt from Anne Harris's (2014) autoethnography "Ghost-Child," which explores her experience as an adoptee attempting to meet her birth mother.[3] She ultimately uses her experience to explore larger issues regarding adoption, identity, and mother–daughter relationships.

> She keeps shifting from one window to the next, peeping out until I look up, then pulling away. What a tease.
>
> "You're a ghost and I want you to leave."
>
> "I'm not a ghost," I say, but she doesn't hear me. No one hears me.
>
> "I'm not a ghost, I'm a person," I say again.
>
> Nothing.
>
> I sit down.
>
> For a while I cried. Then I sob. I sit there for more than five hours, and she never opens the door.

I speak everything I ever needed to say, everything I've dreamed of saying for so many years. It doesn't matter in the end that no one heard me. All of a sudden, something shifts, the pain eases.

It comes like a sentence:

"There's nothing here for me."

It's my release. I realize she can't give me anything I crave, that the mother I dreamed of is gone. What's done is done. Dorothy is a ghost too.

I see myself from a distance, over the 30 years leading up to that day, and it seems to me in that moment that I have spent my entire life banging on somebody's metaphorical door wanting to be let in.

I suddenly feel free.

I stand up, wipe my eyes, and walk away. (p. 73)

Genres of qualitative research that rely on **self-data,** also referred to as **autobiographical or personal data,** have rapidly grown over the past 20 years. This genre has expanded as research into identity, identity politics, and the relationship between the personal and the public has expanded. Approaches within this genre rely on **researchers viewing themselves as a knowing subject** and valuing their own experiences as worthy of the starting point for investigation into the larger culture.

Autoethnography has emerged as the primary research method in this genre. The term *auto-ethnography* first appeared in Karl Heider's work in 1975 and was changed to *autoethnography* (no hyphen) in the 1980s, becoming popular in the 1990s (Adams et al., 2015). Like ethnography, autoethnography is a method of **writing about culture.** To do so, autoethnography uses the **researcher's personal experience** as a method for connecting the personal to a larger cultural context or phenomenon (Adams et al., 2015). In other words, autoethnography values the researcher's personal experiences as a way of studying culture. This method is useful when the researcher has personal experience with the topic under investigation and is willing to delve into that experience as a starting point for inquiry. For example, if you are interested in studying the experience of living with chronic pain or illness, divorce, domestic violence, sexual assault, grief, homophobia, or racism, and you have personal experience with the topic, you can rigorously investigate your own experience as a way of connecting it with larger cultural, social, or political processes (Ellis, 2004).

It is important to understand that not all personal writing is autoethnographic. Stacy Holman Jones, Tony Adams, and Carolyn Ellis provide a list of four characteristics that distinguish autoethnography, which you can build into your research design and also use to evaluate your work: "1. purposefully commenting on and/or critiquing of culture and cultural practices, 2. making contributions to existing research, 3. embracing vulnerability with purpose, and 4. creating a reciprocal relationship with audiences in order to compel a response" (2013, p. 22).

Methodologically, an autoethnographic project necessarily involves a **rigorous writing practice** (e.g., daily journaling and a process of memo writing). It is important to capture details and descriptions, including the emotional aspects of your experience. Develop a systematic writing plan. In any given project, this approach may also include **fieldwork, formal or informal interviewing, and content analysis** (the study of texts such as diaries, historical documents, photographs, etc.). Autoethnographic projects often begin with a personal experience, epiphany, or transformative moment (Adams et al., 2015.) For example, Adams (2011) used his personal experience as a gay man coming out of the closet in order to explore sexuality in American culture and how cultural and institutional norms impact the lives, relationships, and coming-out processes of gay people. Derek Bolen (2014) notes that "aesthetic moments," often centered on the mundane, can inspire a project. Adams and colleagues (2015) suggest beginning your project by finding yourself in the story. What is your experience with the topic? Once you have located yourself in the story, you can begin to build your methodology, which may include fieldwork, talking with others, interviewing others, and collaborative conversations in addition to your writing practice (Adams et al., 2015).

Insider–outsider status, discussed in the section on field research, is complicated in autoethnography. You are explicitly working from an **insider status** and with insider knowledge (Holman Jones et al., 2013). When using this method, you use your own "insider accounts" to address "outside forces" (Adams et al., 2015, p. 27). Doing this kind of work requires **vulnerability** on the part of the researcher. You need to be able to dig deeply into your own experiences, which may release unexpected emotions. You also need to be prepared to share your personal experiences in order to prompt a response in audiences. However, you cannot control the nature of their response, and so it is important to make sure that you are comfortable sharing on this level before engaging in this kind of work. An ethic of **self-care** is necessary in the practice of autoethnography. Some strategies for keeping track of yourself in the project include journaling about your experience in the project and sharing with trusted peers.

Finally, autoethnography uses the **conventions of literary writing** in order to make research **engaging and accessible** (Ellis, 2004). The further you get into data collection and analysis, the more you can begin to piece together the narrative. Ultimately, autoethnography has a **storytelling** quality that can be achieved in numerous ways—for example, consider the excerpt from Anne Harris's "Ghost-Child."

Unobtrusive Methods (Content Analysis)

The following is an excerpt from a study conducted by Ashley Merianos, Rebecca Vidourek, and Keith King (2013) that analyzed the content in 21 brochures from three cosmetic surgery centers. In this excerpt we see how qualitative content analysis revealed the language and concepts used to create particular portrayals in these brochures, as well as the size of the font and space allotted to the physical risks associated with these procedures.

The [study] also revealed females are targeted to view cosmetic procedures as beauty services that provide medical therapy as well as therapeutic therapy. All of the brochures including noninvasive and invasive cosmetic procedures were portrayed through a medical lens as well as therapeutic healthy alternatives and safe options to enhance the female body. For example, the majority of the brochures employed medicalization of the female body by describing the natural process of aging as a medical problem that can be solved by receiving treatments. It is important to note that the bodily risks associated with medicalization are minimally discussed and typically found in small print in the brochures. Perhaps portraying elective female cosmetic surgeries in terms of medicine minimizes the risks associated as the surgeries seem to be needed instead of elected. (p. 11)

Content analysis developed in the field of communication but is now widely used across the disciplines. There are both qualitative and quantitative approaches to content analysis; here I review qualitative content analysis. Content analysis or document analysis is a method for **systematically investigating texts.** Some refer to content analysis as a way of studying documented human communications (Adler & Clark, 2011; Babbie, 2013). Qualitative researchers use content analysis to understand the meanings that circulate in texts. For example, this method has been widely used to study the portrayal of gender in advertising and other media, the representation of minority groups in history textbooks, and the content of news and political programming, both the overt and implied messages. Qualitative researchers analyze not only "textual content" but also the context in which it was created. Roller and Lavrakas (2015) define qualitative content analysis as "the systematic reduction . . . of content, analyzed with special attention to the context in which it was created, to identify themes and extract meaningful interpretations of data" (p. 232). Differing from all of the other methods reviewed in this chapter, content analysis relies on **nonliving data.** Because the data are nonliving, they possess two distinct features: These data (1) **are noninteractive** and (2) **exist independent of the research** (Reinharz, 1992, pp. 147–148). Because the data exist in the world regardless of whether or not the research is occurring, the data are considered **naturalistic** (Reinharz, 1992). Qualitative content analysis allows researchers to investigate the meanings embedded within texts.

Many different kinds of **texts** and materials can be studied via content analysis, including (but not limited to) historical documents, transcribed speeches, newspapers, magazines, books, blogs, and diaries. **Visual data** are used within visual research. Visual images studied often include photographs or images from advertising. Texts may also include **audio data,** such as music. Finally, **audiovisual data** are considered a **multiple field** because they contain visual and audio/textual components (Rose, 2000). Examples of audiovisual data might include movies, television, videos, or Web series. It is important to carefully consider how you will sample your content (choose your texts). For example, if you are studying history textbooks, how will you select them, how many will you use, and from what period of time?

Content analysis generally involves initial immersion into the content to get a sense of the "big picture," determining the units of analysis, coding, analysis, and interpretation (there are typically multiple rounds of coding and analysis). During initial immersion, or what Roller and Lavrakas (2015) call "absorbing the content," take notes on your overall impressions and ideas for how you might approach coding based on what you are seeing. Next determine the units of analysis you will study and begin coding.

Units of analysis can be thought of as **chunks of data.** For example, in a written text such as a newspaper, you may define the units of analysis as individual stories, each column of text, each paragraph of text, or each sentence of text. Or, instead of predetermining the unit of analysis based on the "amount" of text, you may do it thematically. So, every time X theme (something in your study) is mentioned, that is considered a unit of analysis. For instance, if you are conducting a content analysis to understand how female politicians are portrayed by the television media with respect to marriage, motherhood, and gender presentation (e.g., body, clothing, femininity), you may decide that each time one of those topics is mentioned in a chunk of reporting constitutes a "unit of analysis."

The process of coding data can begin once the units of analysis are determined. Some researchers use a computer-assisted qualitative data analysis software (which goes by the acronym CAQDAS), lauded for its efficiency, reliability, and ability to handle large quantities of data. CAQDAS can be used to code, group codes, memo, collapse codes, as well as other functions (Roller & Lavrakas, 2015; Silver, 2010). Roller and Lavrakas note the following programs for conducting content analysis: ATLAS.ti, MAXQDA, NVivo, HyperRESEARCH, Ethnograph, and Qualrus (p. 248), to which I would add NUD*IST and Deedoose. Other researchers choose to code manually, without a software program. CAQDAS may miss important nuances or latent meanings, and further, each program's utility differs (Roller & Lavrakas, 2015). Roller and Lavrakas remind us that even when using CAQDAS, it is merely a "tool" and researchers remain "instrumental" to the research outcomes and their quality by the questions they ask, how they code, and how they explore latent or underlying meanings (p. 252).

Whether doing so by CAQDAS or manually, during initial immersion into the data it is customary to generate a **code** for each unit of analysis. So if you are using sentences as your unit of analysis, for each sentence you would assign a word or phrase that captures the essence of that sentence. Typically this process starts with literal codes (exact words, concrete ideas). As you continue to analyze or re-analyze the data, you may refine your codes, collapse several literal codes into a larger category or more abstract code. Eventually you identify themes. Memo writing can assist you during this process. The coding process is described in greater detail later in the section on analysis; however, due to the unique nature of content analysis, I briefly raise these issues now so that you can better understand what is at stake as you define your units of analysis.

Qualitative content analysis is **inductive,** with codes and themes developing out of a **recursive process of data collection and analysis** (Hesse-Biber & Leavy, 2005, 2011). One inductive approach to employ is grounded theory. Developed by

Barney Glaser and Anselm Strauss in 1967, **grounded theory** refers to an approach by which one collects and analyzes data, develops new insights, and then uses those insights to inform the next round of data collection and analysis. These steps are repeated until the saturation point is reached. Codes, concepts, and insights develop directly out of the data, and hence are *grounded* in the data. Qualitative researchers used grounded theory to develop concepts and ideas that directly emerge from data. Grounded theory approaches to content analysis involve an inductive coding process in which data are analyzed, typically line by line, and code categories emerge directly out of the data (see Charmaz, 2008). Using this approach, you sample a small portion of data (content), analyze the data-generating codes, and based on what you learn, you collect and analyze more data, refining your codes and creating memo notes, continuing on until you reach data saturation.

✋ REVIEW STOP 4

1. Define autoethnography.

2. Methodologically, what does autoethnography involve?

3. Define content analysis
   a. Because the data are nonliving, they possess what two distinctions?

4. A researcher interested in how sexuality is portrayed in women's magazines through "relationship articles" collects a small sample of articles and codes them line by line, allowing code categories to develop directly out of the data. Based on the insights learned, the researcher selects more articles and repeats this process several times, refining the coding process. The result is the development of a new conceptual framework through which to understand the topic. What approach to content analysis have they employed?

👉 **Go to the end of the chapter to check your answers.**

Sampling, Participants, and Setting

Who will participate in your study? How will you find them? What kinds of relationships do you intend to foster with the participants? Where will the research occur?

Participants should be identified and recruited in accord with the research purpose and research questions. Qualitative research typically relies on **purposeful sampling,** which, as noted in Chapter 3, is based on the premise that seeking out the best cases for the study produces the best data (Patton, 2015). Therefore, it is important to be strategic when sampling, in order to find "information-rich cases" that best address the research purpose and questions (Morse, 2010; Patton, 2015, p. 264).

An overview of the sampling procedures that qualitative researchers commonly use follows here.

Snowball sampling is a process whereby each participant leads to the selection of another participant (Adler & Clark, 2011; Patton, 2015). You may directly ask participants, for example, in interview situations to suggest others who would make good interviewees (Babbie, 2013). So, if a participant is a particularly good source of information and/or seems to be well connected with members in the larger group in which you are interested, you may ask him/her to suggest additional participants.

Convenience sampling involves identifying participants based on their accessibility to you (Hesse-Biber & Leavy, 2011).[4] For example, if you are interested in studying how college students experience a particular topic and you work in a university setting, you may begin your sampling process on your own campus. You look for the best cases within the larger group that you have access to.

Quota sampling is a strategy whereby you identify the relevant characteristics of the population you are interested in and their overall presence in the population. Then you select cases (participants) to represent each of the relevant characteristics in the same proportion as they are represented in the population.

In some projects you may be looking for a single case. For example, oral history or life history interview, case study research, and autoethnography may involve the selection of one robust case. There are numerous strategies for selecting a single case, two of which I briefly review. First, you may seek a **single significant case that is an exemplar** (Patton, 2015, p. 266). In other words, you identify a particularly robust case that promises to yield rich data. Second, in the case of autoethnography, you may seek a **single significant case based on self-study** (Patton, 2015, p. 266). This means you make yourself the case under investigation.

There are also **mixed sampling strategies** (Patton, 2015). In addition to straightforward purposeful sampling strategies, some qualitative researchers opt for a two-phase sampling procedure, either combining two purposeful sampling strategies or combining probability and purposeful samples.

As well as locating the participants, you need to consider the kind of **relationships** you intend to cultivate during the process. When working with participants in qualitative research, it is necessary to build rapport, but there is a wide range between building professional rapport and developing friendships to aid the research (the latter of which often occurs in field research and autoethnography). What will be the extent of your collaboration with the participants? What boundaries will you collaboratively set up? How will you clarify and set expectations?

In addition to determining the participants, or "the data" in the case of content analysis, you also need to determine the **setting** for the research. The first decision is whether the research will occur in a natural or artificial setting. This decision is typically made indirectly when you choose the data collection method, as has been discussed through this chapter. For example, ethnography or field research data collection occurs in a **natural setting,** interview research likely occurs in an **artificial setting,** and content analysis may be dictated by where the necessary documents are available (e.g., you may need access to a special library or archive).

When research occurs in a natural setting, you will be selecting the participants (at least initially) and the setting in conjunction with each other. In essence, you are selecting a setting in which you will have the best participants available to you (bear in mind the issues of gatekeepers/access discussed earlier).

Data Analysis and Interpretation Strategies

The process of data analysis and interpretation helps us to answer the question "What does it all mean?" This process allows us to create "intelligible accounts" of our data (Wolcott, 1994, p. 1). It is important to remember that "the data do not speak for themselves. We have to speak for them" (Vogt et al., 2014, p. 2).

Allen Trent and Jeasik Cho define analysis as "summarizing and organizing data" and interpretation as "finding or making meaning" (2014, p. 652). These phases may blur because analysis and interpretation are often a **recursive process,** with analysis leading to interpretation leading to analysis, and so forth. For the sake of clarity, the general phases of analysis and interpretation include (1) data preparation and organization, (2) initial immersion, (3) coding, (4) categorizing and theming, and (5) interpretation.

Data Preparation and Organization

The first thing you need to do is prepare the data for analysis. Depending on the kind of data you have generated, you will need to **transcribe** the data (e.g., transcribing interview recordings) or **scan** the data (e.g., historical documents) (Hesse-Biber & Leavy, 2011).

The data should be **organized in a repository** for easy access, with backups for all files (Saldaña, 2014). Because qualitative research produces a wealth of data, you will also need to **sort** the data for analysis as a part of the organizational process. The nature of the sorting process will depend on how much data you have collected. Saldaña (2014) recommends a separate file for each "chunk" of data—for instance, one day's worth of field notes, one interview, and so forth. If you are a visual thinker, you might consider using a color-coding system (different colored files, highlighting, etc.).

Initial Immersion

It is vital to get a sense of the data as a whole before beginning a systematic analysis process. Read, look at, and think about the data (Hesse-Biber & Leavy, 2005, 2011). Take the time to stew on it and let your ideas develop. Initial immersion into the data has three main benefits.

First, immersion helps you "to feel" **the pulse of the data** (Saldaña, 2014). It is easy to lose sight of the big picture through the daily grind of data collection and then data preparation. To get back to the heart of your data, immerse yourself in it. Saldaña beautifully explains that this immersion allows you to "gain deep emotional insight into the social worlds you study and what it means to be human" (2014, p. 583).

Second, immersion helps you **develop your initial ideas** (Creswell, 2014). During this review of the data, take brief notes about your thoughts, ideas, and points for which you want to remind yourself (Hesse-Biber & Leavy, 2005, 2011; Saldaña, 2014). Whether you are doing so by hand on hard copies or electronically, you can use sticky notes; write notes in the margins; and/or circle, underline, or highlight words or phrases.

Third, as you are likely working with an extensive amount of data, initial exploration may help you begin **data reduction** (Hesse-Biber & Leavy, 2005, 2011). You may begin to "prioritize" the data for analysis by noting which data will best help you address the research purpose and answer the research questions (Saldaña, 2014, pp. 583–584).

Coding

The coding process allows you to **reduce and classify** the data generated. Coding is the process of **assigning a word or phrase to segments of data.** The code selected should summarize or capture the essence of that segment of data (Saldaña, 2009). Coding may be done by hand or using computer-assisted software (CAQDAS). As noted in the section on content analysis, there are many programs available. (For an outstanding discussion and lengthy list of available programs with their URLs and whether they are available for purchase, rent, or free, consult Christina Silver and Ann Lewins, 2014.)

Whether you are coding by hand or with a computer software program, there are numerous approaches to coding qualitative data, a few of which follow:

- *In vivo* **coding:** This strategy relies on using participants' exact language to generate codes (Strauss, 1987). *In vivo* coding is favored by many qualitative researchers because it prioritizes and maintains participants' language. Some researchers who employ this strategy do so in conjunction with a grounded theory approach (discussed in the content analysis section). When in doubt, I suggest using this strategy because it doesn't limit your focus and it allows you to maintain the participants' language, such that codes develop organically.

- **Descriptive coding:** This strategy mainly uses nouns to summarize segments of data (Saldaña, 2014).

- **Values coding:** This strategy focuses on conflicts, struggles, and power issues (Saldaña, 2014).

Your approach to coding should be linked to your research purpose and research questions. In other words, select a coding procedure based on what you want to learn from the data. Table 5.3 presents an example of coding the same interview transcript using the three approaches reviewed (the interview was with a 60-year-old woman on the topic of body image; see Leavy & Scotti, 2017).

TABLE 5.3. Examples of Analytic Coding Strategies

Interview transcript	In-vivo coding	Descriptive coding	Values coding
I do not like looking in mirrors and feeling unattractive. I am a presenter and would love to feel good about how I look. Part of what makes me suffer is the mismatch of how I feel I look and then the mirror's confrontation	dislike mirrors unattractive presenter suffer mismatch how I feel mirror's confrontation	mirrors presenter mirror	dislikes feeling unattractive appearance important to job suffers with mismatch between how looks and feels mirror's confrontation

Categorizing and Theming

Once you have coded your data, it is important to look for patterns and the relationships between codes. **Categorizing** is the process of **grouping similar or seemingly related codes** together (Saldaña, 2014).

As you work with your coded data, you may also engage in a process of **theming** the data. As you study your codes and categories, what themes emerge? Differing from short codes, a theme may be an **extended phrase or sentence that signals the larger meaning behind a code or group of codes** (Saldaña, 2014).

During the processes of coding, categorizing, and theming, which are likely occurring cyclically, qualitative researchers engage in memo writing. **Memo writing** involves thinking and systematically writing about data you have coded and categorized. **Memos are a link between your coding and interpretation,** and they document your impressions, ideas, and emerging understandings (they also assist you later in your write-up; Hesse-Biber & Leavy, 2011; see Figure 5.4).

Each memo further articulates your understanding of that particular topic/concept/data and thus allows you greater insight into the data (Saldaña, 2014). You may write different types of memos, including (but not limited to) detailed descriptions or summaries, key quotes from the data, analytic memos about different codes, interpretive ideas about how codes and categories are related and what you think something means, and interpretive ideas about how a theory or piece of literature relates to a segment of coded data (Hesse-Biber & Leavy, 2011, p. 314).

Interpretation

Interpretation addresses the question "So what?" (Mills, 2007). How do you make sense of what you have learned? What does it all mean?

In order to develop meaning out of your coded data, **use your memo notes,** look for **patterns** across your data, make note of **anomalous data,** and look for **links between different categories, concepts, and/or themes.** You can also turn to

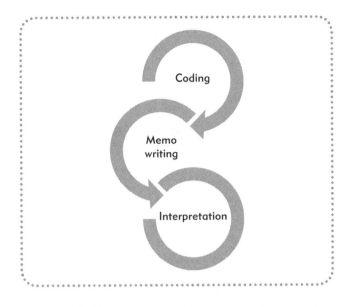

FIGURE 5.4. The process of linking coding to interpretation.

strategies of triangulation in order to build confidence in the summary findings you are developing. **Triangulation** is a commonly used strategy for using multiple methods or sources of data to address the same question (Greene, 2007; Greene, Caracelli, & Graham, 1989; Hesse-Biber & Leavy, 2005, 2011). There are multiple types of triangulation. **Data triangulation** refers to using multiple sources of data to examine an assertion (Hesse-Biber & Leavy, 2011, p. 51). Explicitly use literature and/or theory to coax meaning out of your data and to put it in a framework for understanding. **Theoretical triangulation** refers to looking at the data through more than one theoretical lens in order to allow different interpretations to emerge (Hesse-Biber & Leavy, 2011, p. 51). **Investigator triangulation** refers to having two or more researchers study the same topic and compare their findings (Hesse-Biber & Leavy, 2011, p. 51). As you interpret your data and create meaning, return to the research purpose and questions and ask yourself the following:

- What are the relationships between categories, themes, and concepts?
- What patterns have emerged?
- What seems most salient in the data? What is the essence of the data telling me?
- What do I learn by placing the data in the context of existing literature?
- What do I learn by considering the data through more than one theoretical lens?
- Using what I have learned, how might I respond to my research questions?

✊ REVIEW STOP 5

1. Qualitative research typically relies on _____ sampling.
   a. What is the premise of this kind of sampling?

2. In what two kinds of settings can qualitative research occur?

3. Define qualitative data analysis.
   a. What are the four phases of analysis?

4. Define data interpretation.

5. What is data triangulation?

☛ **Go to the end of the chapter to check your answers.**

Evaluation

It is important for those who read or otherwise consume your research findings to be able to understand what you did as well as your rationale for doing so. **Explicitness** means that you have clearly accounted for the methodological strategies employed as well as your own role as researcher (Leavy, 2011b; Whittemore, Chase, & Mandle, 2001). In other words, the methodology is disclosed.

A qualitative study can also be evaluated based on thoroughness and congruence. **Thoroughness** refers to the comprehensiveness of the project's components, including sampling, data collection, and representation (Whittemore et al., 2001). **Congruence** refers to how the various components of the project fit together, including the fit between the questions, methods, and findings; the fit between data collection and analysis; and the fit between your project and previous research on the topic (Whittemore et al., 2001). In order to evaluate thoroughness and congruence, you can ask the following questions:

- Can you see what was done and why? (Leavy, 2011b, p. 135)
- Do the components of the project fit together? (Leavy, 2011b, p. 138)

It is also important to consider the extent to which readers can trust the process and ultimately the research findings.

In qualitative practice, **validity** speaks to the credibility and trustworthiness of the project and any assertions or conclusions (Leavy, 2011b). Some researchers prefer the term **credibility** (Agar, 1986), whereas others use the term **trustworthiness** (Mishler, 1990, 2000; Seale, 1999). Regardless of the term employed, validity or trustworthiness speaks to the quality of the project, the rigor of the methodology, and whether readers of the research findings feel you have established trustworthiness (Aguinaldo, 2004; Lincoln & Guba, 1985). Do readers have confidence in your findings (Hesse-Biber & Leavy, 2011b)? Do readers trust your data and interpretation? What have you done in order to establish confidence? Yvonna Lincoln and Egon Guba (1989) explain this as follows:

> The basic issue in relation to trustworthiness is simple: how can an inquirer persuade his or her audiences (including self) that the findings of an inquiry are worth paying attention to, worth taking account of? What arguments can be mounted, what criteria invoked, what questions asked, what would be persuasive on this issue? (p. 398)

Validation is a process of confidence building that occurs in community (Koro-Ljungberg, 2008) through the development of intersubjective judgment (Polkinghorne, 2007). Validation of a particular project would require that research methods were used appropriately for a particular research purpose and that the data gathered and the conclusions from the research findings are also determined to be appropriate (Maxwell, 1992). The strategies of triangulation reviewed earlier can help establish validity.

There are no cookie-cutter approaches to qualitative research because each project differs, and therefore it is also important to consider whether it is a well-crafted project. **Craft** refers to how the project has been conceived, designed, and executed (Leavy, 2011b, p. 155). There are several specific practices that may speak to craft. **Innovation or creativity** may come to bear as we develop a unique methodology by employing methods of data collection or analysis in new ways that allow us to examine what might otherwise remain invisible or out of reach (Hesse-Biber & Leavy, 2006, 2008; Leavy, 2009, 2011a; Whittemore et al., 2001). In the next section on representation, we will see that **artfulness,** including producing an elegant representation of the project, is also a part of the craft of qualitative research and a criterion by which it can be evaluated (Leavy, 2011a).

Your project can also be evaluated for its **vividness.** Providing detailed and rich descriptions and highlighting the particulars of the data produce vividness (Whittemore et al., 2001). Can you see the setting, hear the dialogue, and imagine the interactions? Not only does vividness help build trustworthiness into the findings, but it can also be used to establish fittingness, which in turns allows for transferability (Leavy, 2011b; Lincoln & Guba, 1985). **Transferability** is the ability to transfer research findings from one context to another (Lincoln & Guba, 1985). In other words, transferability is a way of making the research findings useful in other contexts, thereby extending the findings beyond your own data. The extent to which you can transfer findings from one context to another depends on the similarity, or what Lincoln and Guba (1985) termed the "**fittingness,**" of the two contexts. That is, the more similar the contexts are, the greater the extent to which you can transfer your findings from one to the other. Therefore, the more vivid your account, accomplished through detailed descriptions, the greater a case you can make for fittingness.

To summarize, in your research proposal you will need to discuss appropriate criteria for evaluating your project as well as strategies you will employ to fulfill those criteria (see Table 5.4).

Representation

Research proposals generally require you to say something about how you intend to represent the findings. In qualitative research, the findings may be represented in any number of **formats,** including a journal article, a conference presentation, a monograph (book), and/or a popular form of writing such as a story or blog. **Identify the intended audience**(s) and how the format chosen allows you to reach that audience. The voices of the participants are primary in qualitative research (Gilgun, 2014), so state how you intend to emphasize their perspectives (e.g., through ample excerpting from interview transcripts). Successful qualitative research is known for producing engaging, descriptive, interesting, and memorable writing (Gilgun, 2005, 2014). It's a process of storytelling. You may briefly talk about your approach to writing, including the extent to which you will draw on literary conventions such

---

TABLE 5.4. Qualitative Evaluation Criteria

Explicitness

Methodology disclosed

Thoroughness

Comprehensiveness of project

Congruence

Components of project fit together

Validity/credibility/trustworthiness

Quality of project and establishment of confidence in assertions

Triangulation

Multiple sources address same question

Craft

How the project was conceived, designed, and executed, including innovation, creativity, and artfulness

Vividness

Detailed and rich descriptions that can be seen, heard, and imagined

Transferability

Ability to transfer findings from one context to another based on "fittingness" (the similarity between the contexts made clear by a vividness in the data)

as narrative, description, detail, and dialogue to create your account. When you are actually writing up your research findings, bear in mind that qualitative research allows for rich descriptions, storytelling, and narrative—in other words, the features that make writing good. Qualitative writing should be compelling. Use literary tools to strengthen your writing. There are many approaches to writing in qualitative research, which themselves comprise books, so please consult the suggested resources at the end of this chapter.

 Ethics in Practice

The representation stage is critical to ethical practice in three primary ways. First, have you gotten to the heart of what really matters? That is, have you represented the essence of what you have learned and done justice to the participants and the topic? Second, have you carefully thought through the relevant audiences and made an effort to make your research accessible to them? Finally, have you shared your findings with your participants?

Ethics Statement

A qualitative ethics statement provides a **discussion of the ethical substructure** of your project, addressing your values system, ethical praxis, and reflexivity.

Begin by clarifying the **values system** guiding your research. Possible topics to address include (as applicable) the moral or social justice imperative driving your topic selection; the use of underrepresented groups; special attention paid to language that is accessible and culturally sensitive during all interactions with participants and the representation of research findings; and intentions toward using the project to promote positive social change or to impact public policy. Values are central to qualitative research, so provide a robust discussion.

Next provide a detailed discussion of your attention to **ethical praxis.** Topics to address include (as applicable) the status of necessary IRB approvals; informed consent (explaining the risks and benefits of participation, the voluntary nature of participation, confidentiality, and participants' right to ask questions); permissions rights (in content analysis); relational ethics (what kinds of relationships you intend to develop with participants and how you will do so, including setting appropriate expectations); dealing with participants at the completion of data collection (debriefings, making resources available); and the representation and dissemination of findings (format, sharing with participants, sharing with research communities, efforts toward public scholarship, and archival storage).

Finally, describe how you will practice **reflexivity.** Because qualitative researchers have advanced the role of reflexivity in research practice, it is customary and advisable to address this final dimension of ethics. Topics to address include (as applicable) your place in the research project (documenting your feelings, impressions, assumptions); and your attention to power issues in the research process (attempts to structure nonhierarchical relationships with participants, and/or share authority and deal with issues of "voice").

✋ REVIEW STOP 6

1. If researchers fail to account for their methodological strategies, and readers can't understand what they did and how they reached their conclusions, the researchers have not reached the evaluative criterion of _____ _____.

2. _____ is a process of building confidence in the project and the conclusions.

3. Explain transferability.

4. Identify the three ways in which representation is critical to ethical practice.

☛ **Go to the end of the chapter to check your answers.**

References

See Chapter 4.

Appendices

Timeline

See Chapter 4.

Proposed Budget (If Applicable)

If the research is funded or you are seeking funding, include a detailed proposed budget. The budget may include the cost of equipment (audio recorders, tapes, pens/paper, CAQDAS); payments to participants (including reimbursement for travel expenses); the cost of reproducing documents and/or fees for access to special library or archival collections; and any other anticipated expenses. In well-funded research, you may be hiring experts or assistants, such as transcribers to transcribe interview data; however, students and novices typically do this work themselves.

Recruitment Letter and Informed Consent Document

If you are working with participants, include these documents.

Permissions

If you are working with textual/material data (e.g., in content analysis), include any necessary permissions with appropriate citations.

Instruments (If Applicable)

If you have created an interview guide, or even an outline containing general lines of inquiry, include it.

Conclusion

As reviewed in this chapter, qualitative research is particularly useful to learn inductively about a social phenomenon from the perspective of individuals and small groups. Qualitative research allows us to unpack the meanings people ascribe to activities, situations, events, people, or artifacts, build a depth of understanding about some dimension of social life (Leavy, 2014), or to study the meanings embedded in texts. This approach values people's subjective experiences and meaning-making processes. Small, information-rich samples are generally favored.

Here is a brief summary of the template for a qualitative research design proposal.

Title: Includes keywords and a hook.

Abstract: This 150- to 200-word overview should be composed at the end. Includes the phenomenon you are studying; the research purpose; basic information about the methods, participants, and setting; and why the study is needed.

Keywords: Provides five to six words a reader would Google to find your project, including the main problem or phenomenon, theoretical framework, and any main concepts guiding the project.

The Topic under Investigation: Describes the phenomenon investigated in your study; personal and pragmatic reasons; and the significance, value, or worth (ethical call) for the study.

Literature Review: Provides a synthesis of the most relevant research on your topic, demonstrating how your project contributes to the literature.

Research Purpose Statement: Outlines the primary purpose of your study, the methods employed, the participants, and the rationale.

Research Questions: Provides one to three open-ended questions your project aims to answer.

Philosophical Statement: Discusses the paradigm or worldview guiding the proposed research project, typically focusing on the selected theoretical school of thought (theoretical framework).

Genre/Design and Methods of Data Collection: Describes in detail the strategies you will use to collect or generate data, making note of how you will address the primary issues associated with the method you are employing.

Sampling, Participants, and Setting: Describes your desired participants (demographics and particular experiences), the purposeful sampling strategy that will be used, and how the process will result in participants able to yield rich data. Also discuss where the research will occur.

Data Analysis and Interpretation Strategies: Describes in detail the strategies you will use to analyze and interpret your data, such as your coding and memo-writing process and your use of theory and literature to make sense of your data.

Evaluation: Explains the rationale for your methodology, including steps taken to achieve validity/credibility, your attention to craft, and the transferability of your findings (if applicable).

Representation: Identifies your intended audience(s) and the format to represent your findings to that audience through vivid and engaging writing. Notes any efforts at public scholarship (if applicable).

Ethics Statement: Discusses the ethical substructure of your project, addressing your values system, ethical praxis, and reflexivity.

References: Includes a full list of citations, properly crediting all those from whom you've borrowed ideas or quoted. Follow your university reference style guidelines (if applicable) or the norms within your discipline.

Appendices: Includes your proposed timeline, budget, and copies of your recruitment letter, informed consent and permissions, and copies of any instruments such as an interview guide (if applicable).

 REVIEW STOP ANSWER KEY

Review Stop 1

1. because the researcher considers the social significance of the topic, which bears directly on his/her values system

2. a and c

3. interpretive or constructivist

    a. dramaturgy, iii; symbolic interactionism, i; ethnomethodology, ii; phenomenology, iv

4. power

Review Stop 2

1. natural

2. direct observations

3. to understand social life from the perspective of the participants

4. The written or recorded notes of observations in the field (the data).

    a. on-the-fly notes, thick descriptions, summary notes, reflexivity notes, conversation and interview notes, interpretation notes

    b. memo notes help the researcher develop their ideas about the field notes (synthesize and integrate the researcher's ideas)

Review Stop 3

1. a and d

2. level of structure

3. eye contact and gestures, probes, markers

4. *advantages:* can interview people in different locations, allows participants more time to respond to questions, no transcription needed; *disadvantages:* no verbal or physical cues

Review Stop 4

1. a method for writing about culture using the researcher's experience

2. a rigorous writing practice that may also include fieldwork, interviews, and/ or content analysis

3. a method for systematically investigating texts

    a. noninteractive and the data exist independent of the research

4. grounded theory

Review Stop 5

1. purposeful

    a. seeking out the best cases produces the best data

2. natural or artificial

3. summarizing and organizing data

    a. data preparation and organization, initial immersion, coding, categorizing and theming

4. making meaning

5. using multiple sources of data to examine an assertion

Review Stop 6

1. explicitness

2. validation

3. the ability to transfer research findings from one context to another based on the "fittingness" (or similarity) of the two contexts

4. did justice to the participants and topic (got to the heart of the matter), determined relevant audiences and made the research accessible to them, shared findings with participants

Further Engagement

1. Take a research topic in which you are interested and develop an interview study.

   a. Conduct a short literature review to learn more about what research exists on the topic (six to eight sources).

   b. Write a research purpose statement and one to three research questions.

   c. Determine your ideal participants and sampling strategy.

   d. Create an interview guide following the "funnel" model presented in this chapter (two pages).

2. Conduct a small "mock" content analysis. Take a research topic in which you are interested and select a small sample of sources from which to extract your data (e.g., three to four magazines, newspapers).

   a. Determine the unit of analysis.

   b. Code your data, refining your codes as you go.

   c. Write memo notes about your impressions and ideas.

3. Select a published qualitative study from a peer-reviewed academic journal and briefly evaluate the methodology based on:

   a. The evaluation criteria outlined in Table 5.4.

   b. Identify what worked well and what could be improved upon (two paragraphs).

Resources

Faulkner, S., & Squillante, S. (2016). *Writing the personal: Getting your stories onto the page*. Rotterdam, The Netherlands: Sense Publishers.

Gullion Smartt, J. (2015). *Writing ethnography*. Rotterdam, The Netherlands: Sense Publishers.

Roller, M. R., & Lavrakas, P. J. (2015). *Applied qualitative research design: A total quality framework approach*. New York: Guilford Press.

Leavy, P. (Ed.). (2014). *The Oxford handbook of qualitative research*. New York: Oxford University Press.

Saldaña, J. (2011). *The fundamentals of qualitative research*. New York: Oxford University Press.

Understanding Qualitative Research book series, Oxford University Press. *https://global.oup.com/academic/content/series/u/understanding-qualitative-research-uqr/?cc=us&lang=en*

Suggested Journals

International Journal of Qualitative Methods (University of Alberta)
https://ejournals.library.ualberta.ca/index.php/IJQM

Qualitative Health Research (SAGE)
http://qhr.sagepub.com

Qualitative Inquiry (SAGE)
http://qix.sagepub.com

Qualitative Psychology (American Psychological Association)
www.apa.org/pubs/journals/qua

Qualitative Social Work (SAGE)
http://qsw.sagepub.com

The Qualitative Report Online (NOVA)
http://tqr.nova.edu

Notes

1. As noted in Chapter 1, many current research texts also include the transformative paradigm in their discussion of qualitative research, but in those instances authors classify CBPR as a qualitative approach. The transformative paradigm is reviewed in detail in Chapter 8.
2. Digital or virtual ethnography is focused on observing people in digital social environments. Research occurs in mediated or online settings.
3. From Harris (2014, p. 73). Copyright © 2014 Sense Publishers. Reprinted by permission.
4. Some don't consider convenience sampling a true purposeful sampling strategy because it involves selecting the most convenient cases, not necessarily the best cases.

CHAPTER 6

Mixed Methods Research Design

Mixed methods research (MMR) involves collecting and integrating quantitative and qualitative data in a single project and therefore may result in a more comprehensive understanding of the phenomenon under investigation. This is a problem-centered approach to research in which methods and theories are used instrumentally, based on their applicability to the present study. Mixed methods designs value both quantitative and qualitative approaches to research. Methodologically, MMR approaches rely on (1) combining deductive and inductive designs to generate both quantitative and qualitative data, and (2) integrating the datasets in some way. These approaches are appropriate when your purpose is to describe, explain, or evaluate, and are particularly useful for studying complex problems or issues.

It is important to note that *multimethod* research involves the use of two or more methods within one research tradition in a single project (i.e., combining two quantitative methods or two qualitative methods). Multimethod research is not the focus of this chapter; however, after reading Chapters 4, 5, and 6, you will have all the tools needed to build a multimethod design. Community-based participatory research (CBPR) often relies on multimethod designs, so you can also consult Chapter 8 for examples.

Structure of a Research Proposal

The mixed methods paradigm is extremely diverse methodologically and theoretically. Every research proposal will look somewhat different, just as each project will follow a different plan. However, to some extent, even if the order and weight differ, research proposals typically include most of what is suggested in Template 6.1. Bear in mind that the template can be greatly modified or reimagined to suit your specific project.

TEMPLATE 6.1

Title Abstract Keywords	Basic Introductory Information
The Topic under Investigation Research Purpose Statement Research Questions and Hypotheses Philosophical Statement and Theoretical Perspective	The Topic
Literature Review Design and Methods of Data Collection Sampling and Participants Data Analysis and Interpretation Strategies Representation Ethics Statement References Appendices	The Research Plan

For the remainder of this chapter, I fill in Template 6.1.

Basic Introductory Information

Title

MMR titles clearly state the main research problem and the mixed methods design.

Abstract

In MMR this 150- to 200-word overview of the study typically includes the problem or phenomenon you are studying, the research purpose, basic information about the methods (noting the mixed methods design), the participants, and why a mixed methods study on the topic is needed.

Keywords

Five to six keywords let readers know the main problem, the guiding theory (if applicable), and the mixed methods design.

The Topic

The Topic under Investigation

MMR is **problem-centered** with the research problem guiding all aspects of research design. Clearly state the phenomenon under inquiry. You may identify different dimensions of the topic as appropriate.

It is also important to give readers a sense of how you arrived at the topic, including values-based and practical issues. Your values system includes the **social, political, or justice imperatives** of studying this topic. What social reasons compel you to study this topic? What good might it do and for whom? Any number of practical factors might also lead you to the **topic**, including your **disciplinary background, personal interests, and prior research or professional experiences**. With respect to prior research or professional experiences, skills you have acquired come to bear. MMR requires experience with both quantitative and qualitative data collection and analysis (or at least a general understanding in the context of team research). Your **professional network** may also lead you to a topic. A professional network may include professors, peers, researchers, and colleagues as well as associates at relevant organizations. In this regard, you may have an opportunity to join a team conducting MMR. If your expertise is on one dimension of your topic, or with one approach to research (quantitative or qualitative), the opportunity to join forces with a team of researchers may afford you an opportunity to conduct research on a topic of interest that would otherwise be out of reach. Because MMR is increasingly attractive to funding agencies, **funding opportunities** may also steer you to a particular problem. Searching for available grants or contacting people in your network to see if they are working on any grant proposals in which you could be included are two strategies. **Timeliness** may also impact topic selection. Current events or hot topics, such as those receiving national attention, may be appealing. Funding opportunities and timeliness are often interconnected.

Research Purpose Statement

Briefly state the **primary purpose(s) or objective(s)** of the study. Include the research topic (phenomenon), the participants and setting, the methodology (quantitative and qualitative data collection methods, the selected mixed methods design, and the theoretical framework guiding the study as applicable), and the primary rationale for conducting the research. Your primary purpose in carrying out the project may be to describe, explain, or evaluate. The different components of the research (quantitative and qualitative) may have different but interlinked purposes. If so, explain. For example, qualitative interviews may be used to *explore* the topic and then develop an experimental intervention aimed at *explanation*.

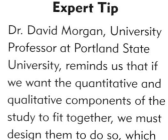

Expert Tip

Dr. David Morgan, University Professor at Portland State University, reminds us that if we want the quantitative and qualitative components of the study to fit together, we must design them to do so, which requires advance planning.

Research Questions and Hypotheses (as Applicable)

MMR necessarily involves at least one quantitative research question or hypothesis, at least one qualitative research question, and generally at least one mixed methods question (although there are published studies that do not include a mixed methods question, I strongly recommend including one). Bear in mind that in order to effectively conduct MMR analysis, it is necessary to have **integrated research questions** (Brannen & O'Connell, 2015; Yin, 2006). Integration can take various forms. Depending on a number of factors, including the specific research purpose, the type of design used, and whether the same participants are used for the different components of the research, the quantitative and qualitative questions will be linked, but to various degrees and in different ways. For example, the qualitative question may be formulated to explain or contextualize the answer to the preceding quantitative question. Or, the quantitative question may be formulated in response to what was learned by addressing the qualitative question. MMR has the "capacity to address different aspects of a research question," so often the quantitative and qualitative questions simply investigate different aspects of the same topic (Brannen & O'Connell, 2015, p. 259).

As discussed in Chapter 4, quantitative research employs either hypotheses or research questions. A hypothesis is **a statement about how variables relate to each other,** which is then tested (see Chapter 4 for assistance with writing a hypothesis). Quantitative research questions are **deductive.** Questions center on how the variables under investigation relate to each other, affect different groups, or how they might be defined. They may employ **directional language,** including words such as *cause, effect, determine, influence, relate, associate,* and *correlate.*

As discussed in Chapter 5, qualitative research questions are **inductive** (openended) and often begin with the words *what* or *how.* They may employ **nondirectional language,** including words and phrases such as *explore, describe, illuminate, unearth, unpack, generate, build meaning,* and *seek to understand.*

The MMR question(s) directly addresses the mixed methods nature of the study by asking something about what is learned by combining the quantitative and qualitative data, or it may ask something about how the mixed methods design aided the research project. These questions may employ **relational language,** aimed at addressing the relationship between the quantitative and qualitative phases of research, including words and phrases such as *synergistic, integration, connection, comprehensive, fuller understanding,* and *better understanding.*

Given the complexity of question formulation in MMR, here's an example:

- *Study:* A mixed methods study of college students' attitudes regarding gender roles (combining survey research and in-depth interviews)

- *Quantitative hypothesis:* Male undergraduates have more traditional attitudes about gender roles than female undergraduates.

- *Qualitative question:* How do male and female undergraduates describe their views on gender roles?

- *Mixed methods question:* How did the combination of survey research and in-depth interviews provide a more comprehensive understanding of male and female college students' attitudes about gender roles?

As you can see in the preceding example, the quantitative and qualitative components are linked. Survey research will be used to determine if, as predicted, male undergraduates have more traditional attitudes regarding gender roles. The interview research will allow participants to describe their views in their own words. The mixed methods question may reveal that there is a disjuncture between what people self-report in the surveys versus how they describe their attitudes (they may think their views are more or less traditional than their survey responses suggest), or the two datasets may confirm each other, with the qualitative data yielding insight into the meaning of the quantitative data. These are just possibilities of what might be learned. The takeaway is that the themes of three questions—quantitative, qualitative, and mixed methods—should be integrated. You aren't simply collecting "more" data, but rather adding *valuable data* that together provide a greater understanding of the topic.

Philosophical Statement and Theoretical Perspective

MMR developed as a problem-centered approach to research design. Additionally, by utilizing both quantitative and qualitative approaches, mixed methods researchers necessarily embrace and draw on the very different assumptions guiding both practices. MMR therefore relies on what Jennifer Greene calls "a mixed methods way of thinking," which necessarily assumes that there are "multiple legitimate approaches to social inquiry" (2007, p. 20). A mixed methods way of thinking values "multiple ways of seeing and hearing, multiples ways of making sense of the social world, and multiple standpoints on what is important and to be valued" (Greene, 2007, p. 20). For these reasons, differing from all of the other traditions reviewed in this book, MMR is not committed to a particular philosophical belief system and corresponding set of theoretical frameworks. Although there is considerable debate in the MMR community, a pragmatist position is the prevailing norm.[1]

Pragmatism is an American philosophical belief system that developed at the start of the 20th century out of the work of Charles Sanders Peirce (1839–1914), William James (1842–1910), John Dewey (1859–1952), and George Hebert Mead (1863–1931) (Biesta & Burbules, 2003; Greene, 2007; Hesse-Biber, 2015; Patton, 2015). This worldview holds no allegiance to a particular set of rules or theories but rather suggests that different tools may be useful in different research contexts. Researchers value utility and what works in the context of a particular research question. Pragmatists "focus on the outcomes of action" (Morgan, 2013, p. 28), suggesting that whatever theories are useful in a particular context are thereby valid. The major criteria for design decisions are that they be "practical, contextually responsive, and consequential" (Datta, 1997, p. 34). Leaders in the field, Abbas Tashakkori and Charles Teddlie (1989), state that pragmatism supports using both qualitative and quantitative methods, places the research question(s) at the center of inquiry, and links all methodological decisions to the research question(s). R. Burke Johnson and Anthony J. Onwuegbuzie (2004, p. 18) list the following among the primary features of pragmatism:

- The natural/physical world as well as the social and psychological world (including subjective thoughts) are both recognized.

- Knowledge is both constructed and based on the reality of the world we experience and live in.

- Theories are valuable instrumentally; they are true to the extent that they are applicable in a particular circumstance.

- Action is emphasized over philosophizing.

Given this pragmatic viewpoint, any of the methods and theories reviewed in this text may become a part of an MMR study. An MMR philosophical statement provides a discussion of the **theoretical school(s) of thought and specific theories** shaping design choices. Consult Chapters 4 and 5 regarding the major theoretical traditions guiding quantitative and qualitative research, respectively, and conduct a literature review to locate specific theories that may be employed in your study. Depending on the overall research design, theories may be used both deductively and inductively.

Literature Review

An MMR literature review provides a foundation for readers to understand what is already known about the topic through a synthesis of the recent and landmark studies. This type of literature review is complex, drawing on prior quantitative, qualitative, and mixed methods research. If there is a gap in previous research, such as a lack of quantitative, qualitative, and/or MMR, note this and how the proposed study will fill the gap in research on this topic. The literature review should also include relevant theories (and their origins) and conceptual frameworks (as applicable). Because you are not bound to any particular set of theories or disciplinary bodies in MMR, Sharlene Hesse-Biber (2010, p. 39) suggests considering the following questions when reviewing literature for a mixed methods study:

- How are topics defined in the research?
- What key terms and phrases do authors employ?
- How have other researchers approached the topic?
- What controversies emerge in the literature?
- What are the most important findings from the literature?
- What findings seem most relevant to your interests?
- What pressing questions still need to be addressed concerning your topic?
- Are there gaps in the literature?

If you are following a pragmatic approach, it is possible you are including studies or theories from outside of your discipline, selected because of their utility in your study. Accordingly, I suggest also asking the following questions:

- What are the relevant disciplinary bodies of knowledge?
- What methodological designs have been used to study the topic in each relevant discipline (quantitative, qualitative, mixed methods)?
- What is beyond the scope of each discipline or area?

Creating a **literature map,** as reviewed in Chapter 3, may be helpful as you work through the literature, seeking synergies.

 REVIEW STOP 1

1. In MMR, a researcher's professional network may assist in topic selection. Who might a professional network include?

2. MMR relies on an integrated set of research questions. Briefly explain this.
   a. What are the three types of questions an MMR study should include?
   b. What does the mixed methods question address?

3. What do pragmatists value?

4. Why is an MMR literature review complex?

☛ **Go to the end of the chapter to check your answers.**

The Research Plan

Design and Methods of Data Collection

There are examples of MMR studies throughout social science history (Small, 2011). Donald T. Campbell and Donald W. Fiske used the term *triangulation* in 1959, which some view as a turning point for MMR. As noted in the last chapter, triangulation refers to using multiple sources of data or multiple theories to examine an assertion. MMR grew exponentially from the 1950s to 1980s (Creswell & Plano Clark, 2011) and has been a methodological field for approximately 25 years (Creswell, 2015).

MMR studies may use any quantitative and qualitative research methods, so consult Chapters 4 and 5 for instruction on specific methods. What differs from the single use of quantitative or qualitative research methods in MMR is the **combination** *and* **integration of the two methods (from different paradigms).** Although the major tenets of designing a quasi-experiment or content analysis, for instance, are the same, there are new issues to consider with regard to overall design construction—specifically, the relationship between the quantitative and qualitative methods and how they are integrated in a particular study.

With respect to research design, there are two primary schools of thought regarding MMR. One school of thought suggests that there are **identifiable components or elements** of an MMR design. The way a researcher addresses each of those components influences the particular design of the study (Maxwell, 2012; Maxwell, Chmiel, & Rogers, 2015; Shadish, Cook & Campbell, 2002). However, the prevailing school of thought in MMR design proposes that there is a finite set of **existing designs or design typologies** that researchers use and adapt in their studies (Creswell, 2015; Creswell & Plano Clark, 2011; Morgan 1998, 2013; Teddlie & Tashakkori, 2009). I focus on these design typologies, each of which can be adapted to suit your needs.

There are three primary types of design: sequential, convergent, and nested.[2] Sequential and nested models each offer two design options, for a total of five primary design types. As these types of designs are reviewed, bear in mind that the type of design you select should be directly linked to your research purpose and questions. In particular, consider the following:

- Why are you collecting both quantitative and qualitative data?
- What is the relationship between the quantitative and qualitative aspects of the study?
- In what ways will the two datasets inform each other? Put differently, how *and* to what extent will you integrate the two datasets during data collection and/or analysis?

Before reviewing the five types of MMR design, it is important to discuss integration, which is a key feature of MMR. **Integration** refers to how the researcher relates the quantitative and qualitative datasets. There is a continuum of integration. That is, the extent to which the two methods and datasets are related to each other varies. At one end of the continuum there are "component designs" (in which integration occurs only during data analysis and interpretation) (Greene, 2007; Maxwell et al., 2015). Component designs offer minimal integration. At the other end of the continuum there are "integrated designs" (in which integration is built into the entire design structure) (Greene, 2007; Maxwell et al., 2015). Integrated designs offer maximum integration (see Figure 6.1).

As we get into specific types of integration, the process becomes more complex, as we take into account additional issues such as the time order of the qualitative and quantitative phases (the direction of integration) and, when applicable, the relative priority of the qualitative or quantitative datasets. In general, the integration factor gets at the question of *why* you are using an MMR approach. It is important to answer this question *before* selecting a type of design. Doing so will lead you to

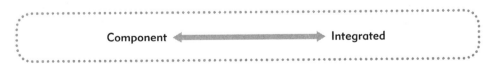

FIGURE 6.1. Continuum of integration.

the best design option. Often texts review design options before talking about the different ways of integrating the qualitative and quantitative aspects of the study; however, this is putting the cart before the horse. For example, if your goal is to use qualitative findings to inform the construction of a quantitative survey—one form that integration may take—that goal will lead you to a particular design in which the qualitative phase of research occurs before the quantitative phase. Knowing your *intent* in selecting a mixed methods approach—that is, identifying the relationship you seek between the quantitative and qualitative aspects—will lead you to the most appropriate design option.

John Creswell (2015, p. 83) identifies four types of integration:

1. **Merging the data:** The quantitative and qualitative results are brought together and compared.

2. **Explaining the data:** The qualitative data are used to explain the results of the quantitative data.

3. **Building the data:** The qualitative findings are used to build the quantitative phase of the study.

4. **Embedding the data:** One set of data is used to augment or support the other set of data.

 REVIEW STOP 2

1. There is a continuum of integration in MMR with _____ designs on one end of the continuum and integrated designs on the other.

2. Why is it important for a researcher to consider why they are using an MMR approach before selecting a type of design?

3. What are the four types of integration outlined by John Creswell?

☛ **Go to the end of the chapter to check your answers.**

To introduce each of the five primary mixed methods designs, I first ask a question about your intent in using both a qualitative and quantitative method. I then review the form of integration you are seeking, and follow that up with the appropriate design type.

Sequential designs are based on time order, with either the quantitative or qualitative data collection phase preceding the other. Creswell (2015) identifies two basic sequential designs (with numerous possible adaptations to suit a particular study): explanatory sequential designs and exploratory sequential designs.

- Are you gathering qualitative in order to explain the quantitative findings? If so, the form of integration you are seeking is an *explanation of the data*. The relationship between datasets: *One dataset is used to explain the other.*

Explanatory sequential designs begin with quantitative methods, which are followed up by qualitative methods designed to explain the quantitative findings in depth (Creswell, 2015; see Figure 6.2). For example, in a study about prevention of STDs (sexually transmitted diseases) and STIs (sexually transmitted infections) among high school students, you might conduct survey research with a large sample of high school students to quantify the prevalence of specific sexual behaviors as well as attitudes toward STDs and STIs. You might follow up the survey by conducting in-depth interviews with a small sample of high school students in order to contextualize and explain the survey results. For instance, if the survey revealed that most students who are engaged in sexual activity are not actively concerned about transmitting or catching an STD or STI, the in-depth interview research could seek to find out why. What do the survey results mean? Or if the survey revealed that a high proportion of female students are concerned about their sexual health but engage in at-risk behaviors anyway, the interviews could provide an opportunity to find out why. What is the context in which they are making choices about their sexual activity? How do they balance different concerns, pressures, or motivations? What is the nature of their decision making and how does it impact their choices?

- Are you using qualitative data to develop a quantitative phase of a study? If so, the form of integration you are seeking is *building the data*. The relationship between the datasets: *One dataset of results is used to design the other phase of research.*

Exploratory sequential designs begin with exploring a topic through qualitative methods and then using the findings to develop a quantitative instrument and phase of the research study (Creswell, 2015). This approach is commonly used when the topic or the population of interest is underresearched (Creswell, 2015; see Figure 6.3). For example, if you are interested in learning whether adding audiovisual teaching material to augment textual material improves the test scores of high school students with learning disabilities, but there isn't a lot of previous research on the topic, you may begin by conducting exploratory focus groups to discover

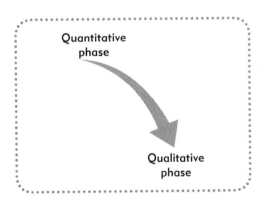

FIGURE 6.2. Explanatory sequential designs.

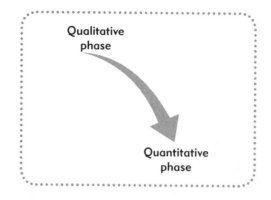

FIGURE 6.3. Exploratory sequential designs.

what students perceive as helpful in their learning. The analyzed qualitative data may then inform the creation of an experimental intervention. For instance, if the focus groups revealed that most students reported that audiovisual material was helpful, the experimental group could be shown a short documentary in addition to reading a segment of text. The control group might receive only the text, and then both groups could be given a posttest to ascertain their knowledge on the subject. Or, one group could be shown the documentary, one group could be given the text and shown the documentary, and one group could be given the text only. There are additional versions of this experiment in which groups may also be given pretests (see Chapter 4 for experimental design options).

As reviewed, explanatory and exploratory sequential designs are both based on the sequencing or time ordering of the quantitative and qualitative methods. The assumption guiding these designs is that both the quantitative and qualitative phases of the study are of relatively equal importance to the overall research purpose. However, Janice M. Morse suggests that MMR includes a core and supplemental method. Accordingly, she developed a notation system to denote when a method is core and when it is supplemental. Under this typology, uppercase words denote the primacy of the method within the study, and lowercase words denote secondary status (see Morse 1991, 2003)[3]:

QUANT: Quantitative method is core
QUAL: Qualitative method is core
quant: Quantitative method is supplemental
qual: Qualitative method is supplemental

David Morgan (1998) embraces Morse's typology and suggests four sequential designs based on both **time order** *and* **priority** (the relative importance of each method within the study). The assumption guiding these designs is that in a given study, either the quantitative or qualitative phase may be dominant.

Design 1: qual followed by QUANT
Design 2: quant followed by QUAL
Design 3: QUANT followed by qual
Design 4: QUAL followed by quant

Similarly, Janice M. Morse and Linda Niehaus (2009) claim that MMR studies necessarily have a core and a supplemental method (the first of which is the primary method, and the latter of which is secondary). In sequential designs, they suggest that you first use the core method and follow it up with the supplemental method. Morse's (1991, 2003) notation system also employs arrows to denote the time sequence and direction of sequential designs. For example:

$$QUANT \rightarrow qual$$
$$QUAL \rightarrow quant$$

- Are you using qualitative and quantitative methods in order to combine and compare the datasets? If so, the form of integration you are seeking is *merging the data*. The relationship between the datasets: *Two sets of findings are brought together and compared to develop a more holistic view of the research problem.*

Convergent or concurrent designs[4] involve collecting both quantitative and qualitative data, analyzing both datasets, and then integrating the two sets of analyses in order to cross-validate or compare the findings (Creswell, 2015; see Figure 6.4). In sequential designs the collection and analysis of one form of data *inform* the second method of data collection and analysis. In convergent designs, a plan for how to enact both the quantitative and qualitative methods is determined in advance of data collection. In the case of concurrent designs,[5] data collection with both methods is carried out simultaneously, more or less (Hesse-Biber & Leavy, 2011). For example, if you are conducting a study about cheating in college, you might conduct survey research to learn about rates of different cheating behaviors and students' attitudes about them from a large sample of students. You could simultaneously conduct focus group interviews with a small sample of students to elicit descriptions of the contexts of these behaviors in detail (e.g., motivations,

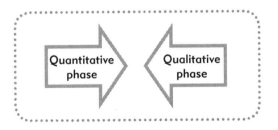

FIGURE 6.4. Convergent or concurrent designs.

pressures, opportunities, attitudes). Morse's (1991, 2003) notation system denotes convergent data collection with a plus sign. For example:

QUANT + QUAL

- Are you using one method in order to augment or support the other set of data? If so, the form of integration you are seeking is *embedding the data*. The relationship between the datasets: *One dataset is nested within the other for support.*

Nested designs are those in which one method is used as the primary method, and additional data are collected using the secondary method (Creswell, 2003; Hesse-Biber & Leavy, 2011). The data from the secondary method are "nested" within the primary study to enhance the primary method. I should note that the term *intervention design* is frequently used in the literature instead of the term *nested design*; however, this term is used only to consider designs in which qualitative data are nested within a quantitative study (Creswell, 2015). I review nested designs instead to account for both directions in which embedding may occur.

- Are you using qualitative data in order to augment or support quantitative data? If so, the form of integration you are seeking is *embedding the data*. The relationship between the datasets: *The qualitative dataset is nested within the quantitative.*

Nesting qualitative data in quantitative designs involves using a quantitative method (e.g., an experiment) as the primary method and nesting a qualitative component in the design (see Figure 6.5). You may collect the datasets simultaneously or one before the other (in either order), depending on how you are using the

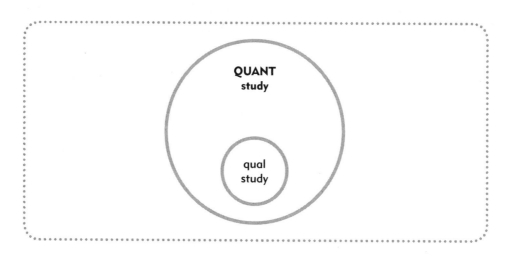

FIGURE 6.5. Qualitative nested in quantitative designs.

qualitative data to enhance the quantitative component. For example, let's say you are conducting an experiment to see if being in a group (as opposed to watching alone) impacts how football fans respond to televised games. During the experiment, you decide to collect qualitative observations about how subjects in the experimental group respond to other "props" in the room, such as the kinds of seating provided, how close people sit to each other, the snacks provided, and so on. Based on these qualitative observations, you may make modifications to the experiment, or you may simply include a discussion of the qualitative findings in your research report.

- Are you using qualitative data to augment or support quantitative data? If so, the form of integration you are seeking is *embedding the data*. The relationship between the datasets: *The qualitative dataset is nested within the quantitative*.

Nesting quantitative data in qualitative designs involves using a qualitative method (e.g., field research) as the primary method, and nesting a quantitative component in the design (see Figure 6.6). You may collect the datasets simultaneously or one before the other (in either order), depending on how you are using the quantitative data to enhance the qualitative component. For example, let's say you're conducting a field research project on homelessness in an urban environment in order to understand and describe homelessness from the perspective of those experiencing it. Within the ethnographic project you might conduct a small field experiment to see how people respond to homeless men versus homeless women asking for spare change. The results might corroborate or otherwise augment what you observe and hear from participants in the field. Table 6.1 presents a summary of the different mixed methods designs.

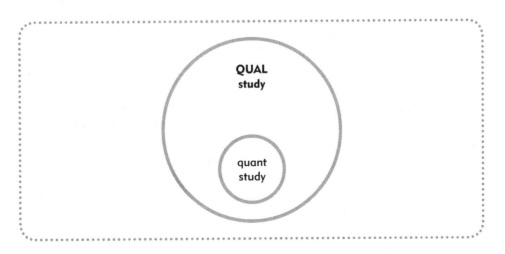

FIGURE 6.6. Quantitative nested in qualitative designs. Adapted from Hesse-Biber and Leavy (2011, p. 283). Copyright © 2011 Sage Publications, Inc. Adapted by permission.

TABLE 6.1. Mixed Methods Designs

Design	Procedures	Type of integration
Explanatory sequential	Quantitative method is followed by qualitative method in order to explain the quantitative findings	Explaining the data
Exploratory sequential	Explore a topic with a qualitative method and use the findings to develop and implement a quantitative instrument	Building the data
Convergent or concurrent	Quantitative and qualitative data are collected (simultaneously if concurrent), and the data are brought together and compared	Merging the data
Qualitative nested in quantitative	A secondary qualitative component is nested within the primary quantitative design	Embedding the data
Quantitative nested in qualitative	A secondary quantitative component is nested within the primary qualitative design	Embedding the data

 Ethics in Practice

Because MMR has become trendy in recent years, with more and more funding and publishing opportunities available for studies that combine quantitative and qualitative data, there are incentives to label work as *MMR*. If you're calling your study *mixed methods*, it's necessary to (1) make sure it truly meets the criteria for MMR (e.g., including an opened-ended "comment" question at the end of a survey does not make it a mixed methods study), and (2) develop competence in both qualitative and quantitative data collection and analysis (and seek the expertise of others as needed).

Now that we've reviewed MMR, let's look at a published example. Guy C. Jeanty and James Hibel (2011) conducted MMR to study adult family care home (AFCH) residents and informal caregivers. The mixed methods design was essential to successfully describe the experiences of this underresearched group. Through the mixed methods design, the researchers learned that participants preferred to live in an adult family care home versus a nursing home, the reasons why, and the impact on their informal caregivers once they had moved into an AFCH. The researchers summarize their findings in the following excerpt.

This study explored the experiences of AFCH residents and informal caregivers using a mixed methods approach. Through the use of a sequential exploratory design, emphasizing the qualitative method, insights about the experiences of AFCH residents and informal caregivers were gained. The findings revealed important insights about residents' preference for AFCHs and informal caregivers' emotional state after a family member became a resident of an AFCH. Residents in this study reported a preference to live in an AFCH rather than nursing homes or large adult facilities. Their preference was primarily associated with their perception of greater opportunities for meaningful social interaction in a household (e.g., being around children and participating/observing the routine events of daily life). Residents also perceived a greater ability to influence the social environment of the AFCH because of their immediate and frequent access to AFCH providers, in contrast to a nursing home where they might have little or no access to an administrator. Informal caregivers reported less emotional strain after a relative moved into an AFCH. They also reported a greater sense of "trust" of AFCH providers and perceived the providers as a surrogate family. (p. 650)

 REVIEW STOP 3

1. What is the basic idea of sequential designs?

   a. If a researcher wants to collect qualitative data in order to explain quantitative findings, what type of sequential design is appropriate?

   b. If a researcher conducts an MMR study with adult children who provide care to their aging/ill parent—an under researched population— and the researcher begins with in-depth interviews in order to learn about caregivers' perspectives and then designs a survey, what type of sequential design has he/she used?

   c. Several leading researchers suggest that sequential designs have a core and supplemental method. How is this relationship conveyed in our notation system?

2. If a researcher seeks to merge the quantitative and qualitative data to cross-validate or compare findings, what type of design is appropriate?

3. A researcher using a nested design seeks what form of integration?

   a. In nested designs are the data collected simultaneously or one set before the other?

☞ **Go to the end of the chapter to check your answers.**

Sampling and Participants

In which populations are you interested in learning? How will you access members of that population? Who will your participants be? What size samples will you draw for the quantitative and qualitative aspects of the study? If the qualitative sample is smaller, will it be drawn from the quantitative sample, or will you seek different participants for the two aspects of the study? How will your sampling strategies maximize the reliability and generalizability or transferability of your findings?

First, identify the **population** about which you are interested in later making claims. Next, identify the **study population,** the group of elements from which you will actually draw your sample(s). You also need to determine the **size** of your samples. Typically, quantitative research relies on large samples and qualitative relies on smaller samples. In some instances, mixed methods researchers use equally sized samples for both phases; however, given the time and expense associated with large qualitative samples, this format is not the norm. When equally sized samples are used, they are most common in convergent designs when the goal is to merge the two datasets (Creswell, 2015). Depending on what kind of mixed methods design you are employing, you may determine either the quantitative *or* qualitative participants at the outset. For example, in a sequential design, you may wait to carry out data collection and analysis with your first method and then determine the best sampling strategy for the second method. Conversely, in a convergent design, you will necessarily need to determine your samples upfront.

In MMR, **both quantitative and qualitative sampling strategies are employed.** As reviewed in Chapter 4, probability sampling is generally used in quantitative research, and as reviewed in Chapter 5, purposeful sampling is generally used in qualitative research. Consult Chapters 4 and 5 for a review of probability and purposeful sampling strategies and select particular strategies based on your specific research purpose and method.

Given that you need to follow sampling protocols per quantitative and qualitative practice, there is one special issue to consider: Will you draw the samples from the same study population? **Whether or not the samples are drawn from the same study population depends on the type of design.** Consult Table 6.2, which presents

---

TABLE 6.2. Samples in MMR

Explanatory sequential

Samples drawn from the same study population (quantitative sample drawn first; may ask for volunteers for the purposeful qualitative sample) (Creswell, 2015)

Exploratory sequential

Samples ideally drawn from the same study population but not mandatory (Creswell, 2015)

Convergent or concurrent

Samples drawn from the same study population (Creswell, 2015)

Qualitative nested in quantitative

Qualitative sample drawn from the quantitative sample

Quantitative nested in qualitative

Samples may be drawn from the same study population but not necessarily

common sampling protocols, bearing in mind there could be any number of reasons or constraints that force you to make other choices.

Data Analysis and Interpretation Strategies

Data analysis and interpretation are particularly challenging in MMR. First, you need to **prepare and organize both sets of data.** Quantitative data are entered it into a spreadsheet or statistical software program. Qualitative data may need to be transcribed, scanned, sorted, organized in a repository, and entered into a CAQDAS. Then continue to follow the protocols reviewed in Chapters 4 and 5 with respect to analyzing the quantitative and qualitative datasets. There are additional issues concerning the **relationship between the datasets.** At this point, you are thinking about how to use all of the data you have collected to address your research questions. Three issues to consider include (1) integration (2) comparability, and (3) data transformation.

Beginning with **integration,** Julia Brannen and Rebecca O'Connell (2015, p. 260) identify five possible frameworks for integration that occurs at the analysis phase:

1. *Corroboration:* One set of findings is confirmed by the other.

2. *Elaboration or expansion:* One type of data analysis contributes to the understanding gained by another.

3. *Initiation:* The use of the first method leads to new research questions or hypotheses, which are then investigated with the second method (in this case, the initial dataset is analyzed before the second method is implemented).

4. *Complementarity:* The quantitative and qualitative findings are juxtaposed to "generate complementary insights" and produce a more comprehensive understanding.

5. *Contradiction:* The quantitative and qualitative findings conflict with each other, and you explore the contradiction or juxtapose the two sets of findings for others to explore or privilege one set of findings over the other.

A second issue to consider is **comparability.** If your goal is to compare the quantitative and qualitative findings, you must consider the extent to which your sampling strategies allow for such comparisons. Further, what precisely are you comparing? What are the units of analysis in the quantitative aspect and the qualitative aspect? Are they comparable? **Data merging** occurs when "the same set of variables is created across quantitative and qualitative data sets" (Brannen & O'Connell, 2015, p. 261).

This brings us to the issue of **data transformation,** the term used when quantitative data are transformed into qualitative data, or vice versa—a **heuristic device** to assist in analysis (Brannen & O'Connell, 2015; Caracelli & Greene, 1993; Hesse-Biber & Leavy, 2005, 2011). A *heuristic device* is a tool that can help us to consider data in a new way. In MMR, data transformation is one analysis strategy for integrating datasets (Hesse-Biber & Leavy, 2005, 2011). There are two forms of data transformation: quantizing and qualitizing.

Quantizing is the process of transforming qualitative data into quantitative data (transforming qualitative codes into quantitative variables). CAQDAS programs can assist in the creation of variable data based on qualitative data, which can then be exported for statistical analysis (Hesse-Biber & Leavy, 2011; Sandelowski, Volis, & Kraft, 2009). For example, Sharlene Hesse-Biber (1996) conducted 55 in-depth interviews in a study about eating disorders. One of the variables she was interested in was whether having a parent, peer, or sibling critical of one's body influenced whether or not a young woman developed an eating disorder. After coding the qualitative data using CAQDAS, she converted the relevant qualitative codes (which represent interview data) into quantitative variables using a binary variable system (1 = the presence of a critical parent, peer, or sibling; 0 = the absence of a critical parent, peer, or sibling). By quantizing the data, she was able to compare the presence or absence of an eating disorder to the presence or absence or a critical parent, peer, or sibling. Tables 6.3 and 6.4 represent these results.

Qualitizing is the process of transforming quantitative data into qualitative data (transforming quantitative variables into qualitative codes) (Tashakkori & Teddlie, 1998). This process places quantitative data in a qualitative context and can provide you with a set of variables with which to sort the qualitative data (Hesse-Biber & Leavy, 2005, 2011). For example, Hesse-Biber (1996) also collected questionnaires (surveys) from the participants in her eating disorder study. She used this data to create an "eating typology." She then used the qualitative data from the interviews to provide a more detailed understanding of the typology (Hesse-Biber, 2010).

A **mixed data analysis design,** involving the transformation of data from one form into another, can make it possible to discern complex relationships in the data and identify patterns (Hesse-Biber & Leavy, 2005, 2011). However, this practice can create problems too, as treating qualitative codes like variables violates important measurement assumptions in quantitative research (Hesse-Biber & Leavy, 2005, 2011). Therefore, **measurement error** is a potential concern (Hesse-Biber & Leavy, 2011). When the intent is to merge or transform the data, advance planning

TABLE 6.3. Quantizing Data: Transforming Codes into Variables

	Interview No.															
	1	2	3	4	5	6	7	8	9	10	11	12	13	14	15	16
EATDIS 0 = no, 1= yes	0	0	1	1	0	1	1	0	0	1	1	0	0	0	0	1
PPSC 0 = no, 1= yes	0	1	1	1	1	1	0	1	0	0	0	1	0	0	0	1

Note. Only the first 16 cases of the study are shown as an illustration. From Hesse-Biber (2010, p. 95). Copyright © 2010 The Guilford Press. Reprinted by permission.

TABLE 6.4. Linking Qualitative and Quantitative Data in a Bivariate Table: The Relationship between Having an Eating Disorder and Growing Up with Parents, Peers, or Siblings "Critical" of One's Body and Eating Habits

	PPSC	
EATDIS	No	Yes
Yes	12.8 (5)	56.3 (9)
No	87.2 (34)	43.8 (7)
Total	100% (39)	100% (16)

Note. n = 55. From Hesse-Biber (2010, p. 96). Copyright © The Guilford Press. Reprinted by permission.

at the initial design stage is critical to success. Beginning with the same measures on the quantitative and qualitative instruments facilitates this kind of integration during data analysis (Creswell, 2015).

Representation

As with quantitative and qualitative research, in MMR the findings may be represented in any number of **formats,** including a journal article, conference presentation, monograph (book), and/or a popular form of writing such as a story or blog. **Identify the intended audience(s)** and how the format chosen allows you to reach that audience.

In MMR you need to decide how you will represent **three sets of findings: qualitative, quantitative, and mixed methods** (the latter being the additional insights gained by the mixed approach). The research purpose, questions, the design employed, and your goal with respect to linking the datasets all influence how you present the findings. You may describe each set of findings in **individual subsections** of the results. Or, you may create **side-by-side displays** of the qualitative and quantitative data through the use of tables, graphs, charts, or figures and then provide a mixed methods discussion.

Ethics in Practice

If the quantitative and qualitative datasets contradict each other, there may be a temptation to bury one set of results in favor of those results that support your hypothesis. Ethical practice requires an honest representation of the data. If you privilege one set of results over another—meaning, you give more credence to one set of results—note the disjuncture in results and explain why you think one dataset is more valid (e.g., perhaps there is reason to believe that the mixed results stem from a flaw in sampling or another design issue in one phase of the research).

Ethics Statement

An MMR ethics statement provides a **discussion of the ethical substructure** of your project, addressing your values system, ethical praxis, and reflexivity.

Begin by clarifying the **values system** guiding your research. Possible topics to address include (as applicable) the values or timeliness driving your topic selection; the use of underrepresented groups; special attention paid to language that is accessible and culturally sensitive during all interactions with participants and the representation of research findings; and intentions toward using the project to promote positive social change or impact public policy.

Next provide a detailed discussion of your attention to **ethical praxis.** Topics to address include (as applicable) the status of necessary IRB approvals; informed consent (explaining the risks and benefits of participation, the voluntary nature of participation, confidentiality, and participants' right to ask questions); permissions rights; relational ethics (what kinds of relationships you intend to develop with participants in qualitative research and how you will do so, including setting appropriate expectations); dealing with participants at the completion of data collection (debriefings, making findings and resources available); and the representation and dissemination of findings.

Finally, describe how you will practice **reflexivity.** Topics to address include (as applicable) your place in the research project (documenting your feelings, impressions, assumptions); your attention to power issues in the research process; and all efforts to reduce or eliminate the Hawthorne effect or testing effect.

✊ REVIEW STOP 4

1. What kinds of sampling strategies are used in MMR?

2. In addition to quantitative and qualitative data analysis protocols, what must mixed methods researchers consider?

   a. What are the two major issues in this regard?

3. _____ is the process of transforming qualitative data into quantitative data, which may be used purely as a heuristic device to assist in looking at the data in new way.

4. A researcher conducts an MMR study and then only reports the quantitative data because it confirmed his/her predictions, whereas the qualitative data did not. Is this ethical? Briefly explain why or why not.

☛ **Go to the end of the chapter to check your answers.**

References

See Chapter 4.

Appendices

Timeline

Present a proposed timeline for the project, noting the time period allotted for each phase of the research process. Things usually take longer than you anticipate, so bear that in mind so that you come up with a reasonable timetable and avoid undue stress.

Proposed Budget (If Applicable)

If the research is funded or you are seeking funding, you will need to include a detailed proposed budget. The budget may include the cost of equipment (data analysis software), payments to participants (including reimbursement for travel expenses), and any other anticipated expenses. In well-funded research, you may be hiring experts or assistants, such as consultants to help design a survey instrument, transcribers to transcribe interview data, or statisticians to analyze quantitative data; however, students and novices typically do this work themselves.

Recruitment Letter and Informed Consent Document

If you are working with research participants, include these documents.

Permissions

If you are working with textual/material data or a dataset created by others (e.g., in content analysis, document analysis, or secondary data analysis), include any necessary permissions with appropriate citations.

Instruments

Include copies of all instruments and protocols used in the study. In quantitative research, these may include a pretest, survey instrument (questionnaire), experimental intervention, measurement instrument, and, posttest; in qualitative research, these may include an interview guide.

Conclusion

As reviewed in this chapter, MMR is particularly useful for learning about a complex phenomenon and research problems through both deductive and inductive means. MMR allows us to provide a comprehensive understanding of the phenomenon under

> **Expert Tip**
>
> Dr. David Morgan, University Professor at Portland State University, notes the importance of integrating datasets, notwithstanding how challenging it is. He doesn't like the term *mixed methods* because it's like "tossed salad" and doesn't necessarily capture the integration of all components.

investigation by collecting and, in some way, integrating quantitative and qualitative data in a single project. This approach adopts a pragmatic stance, prioritizing the research problem and using methods and theories instrumentally, based on their applicability.

Here is a brief summary of the template for an MMR design proposal.

Title: Contains your main topic (including the central variables, if possible) and the mixed method design.

Abstract: This 150- to 200-word overview should be composed at the end. Includes the main problem or phenomenon, research purpose(s), and methods, including the mixed methods design, participants, and why an MMR study on the topic is needed.

Keywords: Provides five to six keywords a reader would Google to find your study, including the main phenomenon, the variables, and the concepts and theories guiding the study (as applicable).

The Topic under Investigation: Describes the phenomenon investigated in your study, including its dimensions, the values guiding the study, pragmatic issues, and timeliness (as applicable).

Research Purpose Statement: Outlines the primary objectives, the participants and setting, the quantitative and qualitative methods, the mixed methods design, the theoretical framework guiding the study (as applicable), and the primary rationale for carrying out the study.

Research Questions and Hypotheses (as applicable): Provides an integrated set of at least three research questions or research questions and hypotheses: the quantitative question or hypothesis, the qualitative question, and the mixed methods question. A quantitative hypothesis is a statement that clearly identifies the variables in your study and predicts how the independent variable affects the dependent variable (if any intervening variables are also under investigation, note these as well). A quantitative research question is the central deductive question your study seeks to answer. A qualitative question is the central inductive question your study seeks to answer. A mixed methods question addresses the relationship between the quantitative and qualitative data.

Philosophical Statement and Theoretical Perspective: Discusses the theoretical school(s) of thought and specific theories guiding design choices (as applicable).

Literature Review: Synthesizes the most relevant research on your topic, including previous qualitative, quantitative, and mixed methods research, and demonstrates how your project contributes to the literature. Includes relevant theories and their origins and conceptual frameworks (as applicable).

Design and Methods of Data Collection: Identifies the type of mixed methods design proposed, the quantitative and qualitative methods selected, and how the data will be integrated.

Sampling and Participants: Describes the population in which you are interested, your study population, and your sampling procedures for both the quantitative and qualitative samples.

Data Analysis and Interpretation Strategies: Describes in detail the strategies you will use to analyze and interpret both sets of data, including the use of computer software programs. Also discusses how you will make sense of the relationship between the datasets at this phase, including the integration framework adopted, comparability and merging the data (as applicable), and data transformation (as applicable), together with any issues that may arise, such as measurement error.

Representation: Identifies your intended audience(s) and a format to represent your findings to that audience. Also notes how you will present all three sets of findings—qualitative, quantitative, and mixed methods (the additional insights gained by the mixed approach)—such as back-to-back subsections in the report or side-by-side displays of the quantitative and qualitative findings, followed by a mixed methods discussion.

Ethics Statement: Discusses the ethical substructure of your project, addressing your values system, ethical praxis, and reflexivity.

References: Includes a full list of citations, properly crediting all those from whom you've borrowed ideas or quoted. Follow your university reference style guidelines (if applicable) or the norms within your discipline.

Appendices: Includes your proposed timeline, budget, copies of your recruitment letters and informed consent, permissions, and copies of all instruments (e.g., pretests, survey instruments [questionnaires], experimental interventions, measuring instruments, interview guides, posttests).

✓ REVIEW STOP ANSWER KEY

Review Stop 1

1. professors, peers, researchers, colleagues, associates at relevant organizations

2. The quantitative and qualitative components of the research are linked in some way.

   a. quantitative, qualitative, mixed methods

   b. the mixed methods nature of the study/what is learned by combining quantitative and qualitative data

3. whatever works in a particular research context/the utility of methods and theories

4. It draws on prior quantitative, qualitative, and MMR and may also include studies or theories outside of the researcher's discipline.

Review Stop 2

1. component

2. It leads you to the best design option.

3. merging the data, explaining the data, building the data, embedding the data

Review Stop 3

1. time order (either the quantitative or qualitative data collection phase precedes the other)

   a. explanatory sequential design

   b. exploratory sequential design

   c. Capital letters note the primary method, and lowercase letters denote the supplemental method.

2. convergent/concurrent

3. embedding the data

   a. could be either

Review Stop 4

1. both quantitative (probability) and qualitative (purposeful)

2. the relationship between the datasets

   a. integration and comparability

3. quantizing

4. No. The researcher needs to report both datasets, and if emphasizing one set as more valid, the researcher needs to say so and explain his/her rationale.

Further Engagement

1. Explain the five primary mixed methods designs (one paragraph each) and draw your own diagram for each one to represent the relationship between the quantitative and qualitative aspects of the design.

2. Select a research topic in which you are interested and design a "mock" mixed methods study.

   a. Conduct a short literature review to learn more about what research exists on the topic (six sources total: two quantitative studies, two qualitative, two mixed methods)

   b. Write the research purpose.

   c. Write an integrated set of three research questions (qualitative, quantitative, mixed methods).

   d. Determine which design to use and what methods to employ.

   e. Write a brief justification for your plan (one to two paragraphs).

3. As noted in this chapter, pragmatism developed at the start of the 20th century out of the work of Charles Sanders Peirce, William James, John Dewey, and George Hebert Mead. Select one of these thinkers and read one of their original works. Write a brief response about how what you read contributes to pragmatism today (one page).

Resources

Creswell, J. (2015). *A concise introduction to mixed methods research.* Thousand Oaks, CA: Sage.

Hesse-Biber, S., & Johnson, R. B. (Eds.). (2015). *The Oxford handbook of multimethod and mixed methods research inquiry.* New York: Oxford University Press.

Tashakkori, A., & Teddlie, C. (Eds.). (2010). *SAGE handbook of mixed methods in social and behavioral research* (2nd ed.). Thousand Oaks, CA: Sage.

Suggested Journals

International Journal of Multiple Research Approaches (Taylor & Francis)
www.tandfonline.com/toc/rmra20/current

Journal of Mixed Methods Research (SAGE)
http://mmr.sagepub.com

Notes

1. Scientific realism is perhaps the most popular alternative to pragmatism. Joseph Maxwell, one of scientific realism's most vocal proponents, describes this worldview as follows: "Realism provides a philosophical stance that is compatible with the essential characteristics of both qualitative and quantitative research, and can facilitate communication and cooperation between the two" (2004, p. 1). Consult his work for the major characteristics of this perspective.

2. Morse and Niehaus also suggest an additional type they call *emergent design,* in which, after the core method is underway or completed, the researcher thinks the results are inadequate and adds a supplemental component (2009, p. 17).

3. Some researchers use *quan* instead of *quant,* which is merely a personal preference.

4. Morse and Niehaus use the term *simultaneous* to denote studies in which the core and supplemental methods are used at the same time (2009, p. 16). However, this term is not as widely used in the literature, nor do all who use it assume that one method has priority over the other.

5. Creswell uses the term *single-phase design* to denote designs in which both kinds of data are collected at the same time (2015, p. 37).

CHAPTER 7

Arts-Based Research Design

Arts-based research (ABR)[1] involves adapting the tenets of the creative arts to social research projects. ABR values aesthetic understanding, evocation, and provocation. These approaches allow us to tap into the unique capabilities of the arts as a way of knowing. Methodologically, these practice-based approaches rely on generative processes in which the artistic practice itself may be the inquiry. These approaches are most commonly used when the aim is to explore, describe, evoke, provoke, or unsettle.

Structure of a Research Proposal

The arts-based paradigm is enormously diverse. Given the long list of artistic genres and specific arts practices, coupled with the multiplicity of theoretical frameworks ABR practitioners use in conjunction with different interpretations of ABR philosophy, the possibilities are innumerable. Added to these variations, art practice is highly individualistic. Further, a cornerstone of ABR practice is that it follows a generative and emergent process, open to the unexpected—to surprises, new insights, and bends in the road. So even when we have a plan for how a particular inquiry will proceed, in practice, it can and often *ought* to be a messy process. Therefore, the creation of any templates is highly problematic (more so than with the other approaches reviewed in prior chapters). However, it is important to have a model for students trying to get their thesis work approved, for researchers applying for social science grants, and so forth. In that spirit, consider Template 7.1 as one of many ways one might conceive of an ABR project. If you are a student seeking approval for a project, particularly in an institutional environment less familiar with ABR, this model contains the information gatekeepers are likely to require in a format that is not totally unfamiliar to them.

TEMPLATE 7.1

Title Abstract Keywords	Basic Introductory Information

The Topic under Investigation or the Theme
    Significance, Value, or Worth
    Literature Review
 Research Purpose or Goal Statement
 Research Questions (Optional)
	The Topic

Philosophical Statement Participants and/or Content Genres and Practices Representation and Audience Evaluation Criteria Ethics Statement References Appendices	The Research Plan

For the remainder of this chapter, I fill in Template 7.1.

Basic Introductory Information

Title

ABR titles should clearly state the main phenomenon or theme and the artistic practice being used.

Abstract

In ABR this 150- to 200-word overview of your project typically includes the phenomenon or theme you are studying, the research purpose or goal, and basic information about the genre and research practice (including any arts practices used, and why the project is worthwhile).

Keywords

Five to six keywords let readers know the main phenomenon or theme, the artistic practice, the participants (if applicable), and the primary theory guiding your research proposal (if applicable).

The Topic

The Topic under Investigation or the Theme

Clearly state the primary phenomenon or theme you are proposing to investigate. Although you will discuss the arts practice being used in more detail in the section on genres and practices, it is appropriate to state it briefly here because the arts practice is likely bound inextricably to the topic. It is also important to give readers a sense of how you came to your topic, including pragmatic issues. Here you can briefly share your **personal interest** in the topic; any **special skills** you have that have drawn you to this topic, including the **artistic skills** necessary to carry out the research; **funding opportunities** for working on this topic; and/or **how you are well positioned to gain access to the participants** (if applicable).

There are two additional issues to address when writing about your topic: (1) the significance, value, or worth of studying this topic; and (2) how your understanding of the topic is shaped by existing literature and how your study will contribute to that literature. In your proposal, you may discuss the significance of research on your topic as subsections of your section on "The Topic under Investigation or the Theme" or in separate sections of your proposal.

Significance, Value, or Worth

Outline the project's **underlying values system and any social justice or political imperatives.** For example, note if the research is intended to counter stereotyped images or cultural narratives that systematically disadvantage or exploit particular groups. If the rationale for the project is linked to raising public awareness or stimulating reflection about a timely issue or recent event, make these connections explicit. For example, if you are proposing a project that aims to evoke discussions about women's reproductive health at a time when Planned Parenthood funding is a national topic of debate, you should address the timeliness of the project and the uses to which it could be put (e.g., lobbying for/against federal funding).

Literature Review

An arts-based literature review should provide a solid foundation for readers to understand what is already known about your topic and what is yet to be studied. An arts-based literature review includes a review of how ABR, popular arts, and/ or fine arts practices within the arts genre you intend to use, have contributed to knowledge on the topic. For example, if you are planning a visual art installation and there have been noteworthy visual artworks in the fine arts field created on your topic, mention them. You may also include studies done with other designs, such as qualitative research. The literature review may also include relevant theories or conceptual frameworks (which may shape the research purpose statement and research questions), or you may review theoretical frameworks as a part of your philosophical statement later in the proposal.

Research Purpose or Goal Statement

Briefly state the purpose of the proposed inquiry by explaining the **primary focus or goals.** To do so, clearly state the main phenomenon or theme under investigation, the research/artistic genre and practice for generating and analyzing content, and the primary reason for initiating the project. With respect to your reason for carrying out the project, your primary purpose may be to explore, describe, evoke, provoke, or unsettle.

Research Questions (Optional)

ABR purpose statements may be followed by a list of **central questions** your research seeks to address. ABR questions are **inductive, emergent, and generative.** They often emphasize experiential knowledge, artistic practice, and an emergent, open-ended, evolving inquiry process. They may employ **nondirectional language that emphasizes emergence and/or the resistive nature of art,** including words and phrases such as *explore, create, play, emerge, express, trouble, subvert, generate, inquiry, stimulate, illuminate, unearth, yield,* and *seek to understand.*

> **Expert Tip**
>
> Dr. Bonnie Meekums, in the School of Healthcare at the University of Leeds, reminds us that design is a process. Your research question is vital, but your curiosity about something may not be clear or fixed upfront. You can even use an arts practice and your "embodied wisdom" to develop clarity.

 ## REVIEW STOP 1

1. Arts-based research involves what?
    a. What do these approaches allow researchers to access?
2. When research questions are used in ABR, they employ _____ _____ language?
    a. What does this kind of language emphasize?

☛ Go to the end of the chapter to check your answers.

The Research Plan

Philosophical Statement

ABR, or what some call *performative social science,* emerges out of a fusion between artistic practice and scientific or social scientific practice (Gergen & Gergen, 2011;

Jones, 2006, 2010, 2013). Inquiry practices are informed by the belief that the arts and humanities can facilitate social scientific goals (Jones, 2010). The philosophical statement provides a discussion of the arts-based paradigm and how it is specifically guiding the proposed project.

ABR is grounded in a **philosophy of arts-based research,** which Gerber et al. (2012, p. 41) suggest:

- Recognizes that art has been able to convey truth(s) or bring about awareness (both knowledge of the self and knowledge of others).
- Recognizes that the use of the arts is critical in achieving self/other knowledge.
- Values preverbal ways of knowing.
- Includes multiple ways of knowing, such as sensory, kinesthetic, and imaginary.

The philosophical beliefs form an "aesthetic intersubjective paradigm" (Chilton et al., 2015). **Aesthetics** draw on sensory, emotional, perceptual, kinesthetic, embodied, and imaginal ways of knowing (Chilton et al., 2015; Cooper et al., 1997; Dewey, 1934; Langer, 1953; Harris-Williams, 2010; Whitfield, 2005). ABR philosophy is also strongly influenced by philosophical understandings of "the body" and specifically, advances in embodiment theory and phenomenology. **Intersubjectivity** refers to the relational quality of arts as knowing, as we make meanings with others and with nature (Conrad & Beck, 2015).

Ethics in Practice

A philosophy of ABR values multiple ways of knowing and acknowledges that the arts are able to create knowledge. Words, images, and movement are all valuable. However, we still see a hierarchy between textual forms of representation and visual or embodied forms. For example, graduate students who engage in nontextual forms of ABR are often required to produce large texts to accompany or qualify their work. The same is often true for researchers publishing their ABR work. It is unethical to value some arts practices more than others. In your philosophical statement, focus on the ABR paradigm without qualifying it by comparing it to other, more "accepted" forms of research in order to help legitimate these ways of knowing.

Embodiment Theories

Over the past several decades **"the body"** has garnered considerable attention due to the advances of **feminist, postmodern, poststructural,** and **psychoanalytic theories of embodiment. Embodiment theory** explains that all social actors are *embodied* actors. We experience the world through our bodies, through our senses. Celeste Snowber (2012) reminds us that "we do not have bodies, we are bodies."

Elizabeth Grosz (1994) distinguishes between the "inscriptive" and the "lived body." The **inscribed body** serves as a site where social meanings are created and resisted. Influenced by the work of Michel Foucault (1976) and Susan Bordo (1989), Grosz writes, "The body is not outside of history, for it is produced through and in history" (1994, p. 148). We can conceptualize bodies themselves as interdisciplinary (or transdisciplinary). Beatrice Allegranti (2011) writes: "Bodies are quintessentially interdisciplinary; we are socially and biologically constructed. Moreover, bodies are not neutral: gender, sexuality, ethnicity and class are socio-political aspects that shape our mental, emotional and physical selves and inform our ethical values" (p. 487). The **lived body** refers to people's **experiential knowledge** (and is thus connected to phenomenology, reviewed in Chapter 5). The mind and body are interconnected and experience is embodied and sensory (Merleau-Ponty, 1962; Wiebe & Snowber, 2011).

With respect to the ABR paradigm, Charles R. Garoian eloquently writes, "Bodies make artworks just as artworks make bodies" (2013, p. 21). An arts-based philosophy takes embodiment into account, viewing experience holistically and the mind and body as interconnected. Working directly from this perspective, arts-based researchers may seek to access bodily knowledge. For example, Sean Wiebe and Celeste Snowber (2011) contend that "our memory is located in our senses" (p. 111). Consider the power of smell to evoke memories—a loved one's perfume, the smell of a favorite childhood place, aromas from a holiday meal cooking (Leavy, 2015).

Art–Science

It is important to note that not all arts-based researchers share precisely the same perspective on the nature of reality and what we can learn about it. Although arts-based researchers value the arts as a source of knowledge building, there are many perspectives one may hold. ABR occurs along an **art–science continuum** (see Figure 7.1). Some practitioners adopt more of an arts practice-based philosophy and are likely to prioritize the insights gained from the act of "doing," "making," or "experiencing" an arts practice. On this end of the continuum, the art-making process may be viewed as the method of content generation, analysis, *and* the final output. On the other far end of the continuum, practitioners may have a more scientistic view of the process, perhaps collecting and analyzing data (content) with traditional quantitative or qualitative methods and strategies, and then incorporating an arts

FIGURE 7.1. Art–science continuum.

practice into one phase of the process, such as representation. Philosophically, their worldview models a more qualitative (interpretive) understanding of the nature of social reality and how we might study it. There are many points in between on the art–science continuum from which a project might emerge.

The philosophical statement explains how the project is harnessing the unique strengths of the arts as a way of building knowledge, to what extent it is doing so, and under what philosophical basis. In other words, what assumptions about the arts practice being used are guiding the project? Is an art practice being used to tap experiential knowledge or emotional understanding otherwise out of reach? If so, how is the art form capable of doing so?

Additional Schools of Thought in Your Philosophical Statement

Finally, arts-based projects may also draw on interpretive, critical, or transformative theoretical schools of thought, and in those instances should be discussed (see Chapters 1, 5, and 8 for discussions of those theoretical schools). For example, in an ABR project grounded in a feminist theoretical framework, both the ABR paradigm and the specific feminist theories guiding the project warrant discussion.

Participants and/or Content

Regardless of the genre of ABR within which you are working, there are three primary approaches to ABR design that impact how participants are selected or how content is created.

First, there are projects in which **data are collected from research participants using traditional quantitative, qualitative, or mixed methods designs.** In these instances, sampling decisions occur based on the method or methods being used in conjunction with the research purpose and questions. (Appropriate sampling strategies are reviewed in Chapters 4–6.) Most frequently, researchers will collect qualitative data to analyze and/or represent using an arts-based approach. Accordingly, a strategy of purposeful sampling is generally employed.

Second, there are projects in which **participants make art, and the art pieces become the data.** In these instances, sampling decisions occur based on the research purpose and questions. Given the philosophical basis of ABR and particularly the value placed on multiple truths and multiple ways of knowing, a strategy of purposeful sampling is generally employed so that the "best" participants are selected— those with the most to offer in regards to the topic.

Finally, there are projects in which **the artistic practice is both the method of inquiry and the content.** In these instances, you create the art and there aren't any research participants.

Given the different ways in which meanings are generated in ABR, in some instances the word **data** is appropriate (e.g., when data are collected via other standard research methods). In other instances, the word **content** is appropriate (e.g., when artistic practice is both the method of inquiry and the content). Throughout this chapter, I use the words *data* and *content* as appropriate to the discussion at hand.

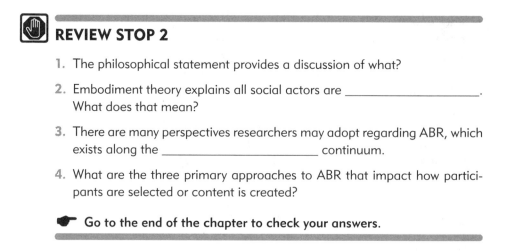

REVIEW STOP 2

1. The philosophical statement provides a discussion of what?

2. Embodiment theory explains all social actors are _____.
   What does that mean?

3. There are many perspectives researchers may adopt regarding ABR, which
   exists along the _____ continuum.

4. What are the three primary approaches to ABR that impact how participants are selected or content is created?

☛ **Go to the end of the chapter to check your answers.**

Genres and Practices

ABR is characterized by numerous research practices (consult Table 1.2 in Chapter
1). They cannot all be adequately covered in this text, so I review three genres and
a corresponding practice in each genre (for a broader review of available practices,
see Leavy, 2015).

Literary Genres and Fiction-Based Research

The following is an excerpt from my 2015 novel, *Low-Fat Love: Expanded Anni-
versary Edition* (Sense Publishers), which is grounded in interview research with
women about body image, relationships, identity, and self-esteem. Through the use
of a narrator's voice, coupled with interior dialogue, I was able to tap into how some
women consume and internalize the messages of commercial media aimed at them,
thereby offering a sociological critique of popular culture. Here is an excerpt:

> Remote in hand, she flipped between her usual stations and landed on *Access Hol-
> lywood*. They were featuring a story about Brad Pitt and Angelina Jolie. She always
> bought tabloids when they were on the cover. Although she despised the idea that
> they were mostly adored for their good looks, she was fascinated. Sometimes she
> fantasized about what Angelina's life was like. More than any other celebrity, Angelina
> seemed to have it all. She was ridiculously gorgeous, the kind of beauty that doesn't
> seem to go out of style or age. She had lived a wild life, and now she had a massive,
> multicultural family (that she probably never had to take care of with all her nannies,
> assistants, and so forth), a fabulous partner who undoubtedly worshipped her, and an
> amazing career. Somehow she had managed to be both an artist and a commercial
> success, or at least she could reasonably claim to be both. People admired her. People
> like Prilly. As Prilly watched the story she felt a familiar storm cloud of envy, longing,
> and self-loathing.

Access Hollywood was just the prelude to whatever "movie of the week" she could find. Tonight she was watching a Lifetime movie about a woman who worked as a newspaper reporter and, while reporting on a local crime, became the next target of a psychopath. As Prilly picked up each forkful of the vegetable stir-fry she made during the commercials, she couldn't help but think, *In some ways the reporter is lucky. At least her life is exciting.*

Prilly lived in between who she was and who she wanted to be. (p. 4)

Literary genres rely on written language to communicate and therefore most closely resemble the other approaches to research reviewed in this text (particularly qualitative approaches). **Fiction-based research (FBR), fiction as a research practice (FARP), or social fiction**[2] is an emergent practice with unique capabilities for creating engaging, evocative, and accessible research. FBR is well suited for portraying the complexity of lived experience because it allows for details, nuance, specificity, contexts, and texture. FBR is adept at cultivating empathy and self-reflection through relatable characters, and disrupting dominant narratives or stereotypes by showing and not telling (which can be used to build critical consciousness and raise awareness). Fiction is both a form of writing and a way of reading (Cohn, 2000), as readers approach fiction differently and immerse themselves in fictional worlds. The promotion of **empathy or empathic engagement** (de Freitas, 2003) in readers is a primary advantage of this practice. As readers engage with fiction and develop emotional connections with the characters, they are constructing intimate relationships with "the imagined other" (de Freitas, 2003, p. 5).

There are three primary approaches to FBR with respect to the generation of data or content: (1) data gathered by other methods (typically qualitative methods such as field research, interview, or autoethnography) are represented via fiction; (2) content from a literature review is represented via fiction; and (3) the writing of fiction is used as both the act of inquiry and analysis. To expand on the latter category, Elizabeth de Freitas (2004) explains that reflexive writing is her methodology, and Rishma Dunlop (2001) creates an assemblage of "facts" and imagination, drawing on literary traditions, in her practice. Typically, there is slippage between these three categories because they all require drawing on the imaginative to varying degrees. Further, projects often combine data from qualitative research (at times, cumulative impressions of data collected over a substantial part of a researcher's career) with content from a literature review and imaginative data.

Regardless of how content is generated, there are design features to execute. These features can be broken down into four categories: structural, stylistic, characterization, and literary (Leavy, 2013, 2015).

There are several **structural features** in FBR. First, you need to determine an appropriate **format**, which might be a short story, novella, or novel. How much space do you need to convey your content? Is there one narrative or intertwining narratives? Next, you need to determine your plot and storyline. A work of fiction is a narrative about something (your topical or thematic coverage). You need to determine the narrative. The **plot** is the overall structure of your narrative, and the **storyline** is the sequence of events within the plot (Saldaña, 2003). At times, researchers employ a **master plot or master narrative,** which is a story that has been told over and over again within a culture (Abbott, 2008). For example, the classic rags-to-riches story is a master plot that has been reimagined many times. Master plots are useful tools because they resonate; they tap into deeply held values and "carry enormous emotional capital" that researchers can utilize to stimulate new learning (Abbott, 2008, p. 59). As you develop the plot and storyline, you need to carefully consider the **ending** of the narrative. Will you provide closure or resolution? What are readers' expectations likely to be and will you satisfy or subvert them? For example, you can adopt a "Cinderella story" master plot but then subvert the conventional story by having the female protagonist end up without a romantic partner.

As you outline the plot and storyline, consider the placement of gaps in the narrative. Fictional narratives are incomplete and leave space for readers' interpretations and imagination. Authors often intentionally include **interpretive gaps** (Abbott, 2008; de Freitas, 2003).

Finally, with respect to structure, once you have your narrative structure, consider the basic methods for writing fiction: scenes and narrative (Leavy, 2013). You will likely use some combination of the two. **Scenes** are a dramatic approach to writing in which the action is unfolding before the reader's eyes. Well-done scenes offer a high degree of realism (Caulley, 2008; Gutkind, 1997). The writing of scenes often involves active verbs (Caulley, 2008). **Narrative** writing is a means of summarizing and providing information or commentary that is not in the scenes. Narrative writing can be an important tool for incorporating voices from a literature review, theory, and/or the researcher's voice as narrator. Narrative writing often employs third-person narration and passive verbs. Table 7.1 presents a comparison of scenic and narrative writing (the excerpts are from my 2016 novel, *Blue*).

Stylistic elements give FBR its feeling and include genre, themes and motifs, tone, and style (Leavy, 2013). **Genres** are "recurrent literary form[s]" (Abbott, 2008, p. 49) that are thematically based. Examples include suspense, action, chicklit, romance, and the like. Genres are selected in accord with the research purpose, topic, and intended audiences (and to what you anticipate those audiences will respond). Also consider **themes and motifs,** which are linked to each other. The former is a central idea and the latter is a recurrent idea, subject, or symbol (Leavy, 2013). When considering the content of the work, the **tone** is also important in communicating the desired content accurately and effectively. For example, is the final fictional work meant to be humorous, joyful, melancholic, tragic, ironic, or sarcastic? These decisions are linked to both the most effective delivery of the content (the topic, purpose, genre) and the author's own strengths and style. Each researcher brings his/her own **style or fingerprint** to bear on fictional writing (which relies largely on how he/she combines other design features, including literary tools).

In addition to structural and stylistic features, characters are central to the practice of FBR. **Characters** are the individuals that people your story, and

TABLE 7.1. Comparison of Scenic and Narrative Writing		
Writing methods	Description	Excerpts from *Blue*

Scenes	Dramatic way of writing, with continuous action unfolding before the reader's eyes	He smiled and waved his arm, to indicate she should pass by. With only a few aisles in the small store, moments later Tash bumped into him again in the produce section.
		    "Should I even ask what that's about?" she said while giggling, looking at the twenty or more coconuts in his hand basket.
		    "Oh these are for a party I'm deejaying for a couple of friends over at NYU."
		    "They're serving whole coconuts?" she asked, mystified.
		    He laughed. "People try to get them open. It's like a drinking game kind of thing. It's pretty funny." (pp. 8–9)

Narrative	Summarizing and offering readers information beyond what is evident in scenes	As she crossed over into the Village, the restaurants and corner cafés were already bustling with people clamoring to sit outside. After a brutal winter New Yorkers were ready to enjoy outdoor eating. Waiters turned on heat lamps and uncorked wine bottles amid casual conversation and bubbling laughter. (p. 6)

characterization is the process of developing those characters. As you develop characters, avoid stereotypes and represent people sensitively, multidimensionally, and in their complexity. Depending on how you have garnered the data or content, characters may be composites meant to represent themes from the data. Developing character profiles assists in the characterization process. Here are some features to consider: a robust physical description (including relevant status characteristics), activities (how the character spends his/her time), personality (including his/her values, motivations, and how he/she makes others feel), and name (which may carry additional meanings, such as nationality, age, etc.) (Leavy, 2013).

Characters are also shown engaged in **dialogue and interaction** with others. Consider their use of language, gestures, mannerisms, the tone of conversations, and how dialogue and interaction reveal information about the relationship among characters. Fiction also offers us unique access into **interiority** by representing **interior dialogue** (what a character is thinking). This is a central feature of FBR that differs from the other practices and methods reviewed in this text. Fiction allows us to access the inner lives of characters, which can cultivate empathy in readers, often a research goal.

Ethics in Practice

It is vital to represent multidimensional characters in order to avoid reinforcing stereotypes. Take the time to go beneath the surface of characters and represent their complexity. Consider issues such as gender, sexuality, race, ethnicity, religion, and other status characteristics carefully, and seek input from others as appropriate.

Finally, FBR design and execution require the careful use of **literary tools. Language** is the only tool of a writer and must be used skillfully. Paying rigorous attention to craft and artistry enables us to successfully execute FBR (de Freitas, 2004; Leavy, 2013). Consider using **metaphors and similes** to enhance the aesthetic quality of the work, help create macro–micro connections, create subtext, or jar readers into questioning commonly held assumptions. Metaphors and similes can be a new conceptual frame through which readers are asked to explore an issue. An implicit goal in all FBR is the creation of realistic or believable worlds that mirror social realities or give readers an alternative way to imagine a particular social reality. Creative writing also requires **specificity of language** for aesthetic power and to create believable worlds for readers to enter. **Verisimilitude** refers to the creation of realistic, authentic, and lifelike portrayals and is a benchmark of success in FBR (Leavy, 2013). Techniques to help us achieve verisimilitude include incorporating details and descriptions. Draw on the senses to paint scenes. Descriptions and details written in a work of FBR can be considered "data" or content (Iser, 1997). Table 7.2 summarizes the design features in FBR.

Once you have a complete draft, you will need to engage in **cycles of editing, revising, and rewriting.** It's advisable to stick your draft in a drawer for a week when you first complete it to get some distance from it. Then do a first read-through, looking for global changes that may be needed (e.g., filling unintentional gaps in the plot, restructuring the storyline, reordering the scenes). On the next read-through, take a sharp eye and red pen and edit ruthlessly, line by line. Reading aloud is a useful strategy that can reveal issues with flow and language that sticks, thus disrupting the flow. The goal is to achieve clarity in your writing. In FBR, **rewriting is an act of analysis.** It is also important to **solicit feedback.** You may share the writing with peers (other students or researchers), in a writing group (check your local library if you're looking to join one), or research participants (if you have gathered data with another research method). You can solicit general feedback and/or present readers with specific questions to respond to in order to see the extent to which you are communicating what you intend to communicate. For example: "What is your impression of character *x*? What pivotal situation did he [she] find himself [herself] in? What did you learn about those circumstances?" This process reveals any interpretive problems that still need to be addressed.

TABLE 7.2. Design Features of Fiction-Based Research

Structural features

Format
Plot
Storyline
Master plot or master narrative
Ending
Interpretive gaps
Scenes
Narrative

Stylistic elements

Genres
Themes and motifs
Tone
Style or fingerprint

Characters

Characterization
Dialogue and interaction
Interiority/interior dialogue

Literary tools

Language
Metaphors and similes
Specificity (descriptions and details)

 REVIEW STOP 3

1. In fiction-based research (FBR), the _____ is the overall structure of the narrative and the _____ is the sequence of events there within.

2. Define a master plot or master narrative.
   a. Why are master plots useful tools?

3. Most FBR combines two basic methods for writing fiction: scenes and narrative. Define each.

4. In addition to showing characters engaged in dialogue and interaction, fictions offers unique access into what a character is thinking (his/her inner life) by representing _____.

5. _____ refers to the creation of realistic, authentic, and lifelike portrayals and is a benchmark of success in FBR.

6. Cycles of editing, revising, and rewriting are important in FBR. Rewriting is considered an act of _____.

☛ **Go to the end of the chapter to check your answers.**

Performative Genres

The following is an excerpt from Tara Goldstein's 2013 play *Zero Tolerance,* which is based on a 595-page report about school safety titled *The Road to Health.* The report was compiled in response to the killing of 15-year-old Toronto high school student, Jordan Manners.

Scene 1

TARA GOLDSTEIN: *(to the audience)* What do you think of when you hear the words *zero tolerance*? What comes to mind? When I asked a group of my students that question, this is what they said:

TEACHER 1: Bullying.

TEACHER 2: Fighting.

TEACHER 3: Weapons.

TEACHER 4: Suspension.

TEACHER 5: Expulsion.

TEACHER 2: No second chances.

TEACHER 4: Discipline.

TEACHER 5: Safety.

TARA GOLDSTEIN: *(to the audience, walking from downstage left, to downstage centre, to downstage right)* Is that what you were thinking? Today, I am going to tell you a story about zero tolerance for bad behaviour in schools. And how a zero tolerance approach to discipline has not protected students from violence in their schools. My story includes the story of a fifteen-year-old boy named Jordan Manners who was shot in his school during the school day in May 2007.

Dramatic or theatre arts are able to access and present rich, textured, descriptive, situated, contextual experiences and multiple meanings from the perspectives of research participants. Moreover, theatre arts allow researchers to explore the dimensionality, tonality, and multisensory experiences that occur within the field in ways not enabled by traditional textual representation.

Ethnodrama and ethnotheatre are widely used performance-based research practices, first used in anthropology (Ackroyd & O'Toole, 2010). **Ethnodrama** refers to the writing up of research findings in dramatic or script form and may or may not be performed. **Ethnotheatre** is a live, performance-based practice. These practices rely on using qualitative data garnered from ethnography, interviews, public documents, autoethnography, and other qualitative research methods, and then analyzing, interpreting, and representing the data via dramatic arts. **Health theatre** is one area into which ethnotheatre is rapidly expanding, due to its ability to sensitively portray multiple perspectives and engage public audiences. Whereas ethnodrama is a genre of writing, the styles within that genre include realist (most commonly used), musical, and performance collage or revue (Saldaña, 2011a, p. 146). Ethnodramas may also be written in alternative formats, such as screenplays (Saldaña, 2011a).

In ethnodrama and ethnotheatre, **data are collected from research participants using qualitative methods** (see chapter 5). The process by which you code and thus **prepare the data** for ethnodramatic writing is an important first step in moving from qualitative data to an ethnodramatic work. Johnny Saldaña (2011a) advocates for the use of *in vivo* **coding,** in which the participants' own words are used as coding labels during the analytic process, because such categories may later assist the researcher to determine which passages should be used for dialogue and monologues. Grounded theory and other inductive analysis strategies are appropriate. As noted in Chapter 5, **grounded theory** involves an inductive coding process in which data are analyzed, typically line by line, and code categories emerge directly out of the data (see Charmaz, 2008). The categories and themes that emerge during this process may eventually become scenes in the play (Saldaña, 1999, p. 61). Once you have your analyzed data, as with FBR, there are structural design features to consider: characters, dialogue/monologues, plotting, structures, scenography, and costuming (for live theatre there are additional issues such as directing, staging, and acting) (Saldaña, 1999).

Much of what was reviewed in the FBR section on characters and characterization applies here as well, so I will not repeat the basics. However, in ethnodrama there are issues relating to the number of characters and the sources of data from which one develops characters. Saldaña (1999, 2003) proposes that the number of research participants whose stories stand out during a review of the data become the number of characters in the script. Characters may be **composites,** so that the themes that emerged during data collection can be used to create character "types." The **number of characters** and their **relations to one another** affect the plot and structure, which need to be considered as well. For example, the play may unfold from the perspective of a central character (the protagonist), two characters in conflict (protagonist and antagonist), two flawed characters that guide each other to greater understanding, multiple characters in vignettes, or other standard formats (Saldaña, 1999).

Saldaña (1999, p. 62) provides sources researchers can utilize to create three-dimensional portrayals:

1. From interviews: what the participant reveals about his/her perceptions.
2. From field notes, journal entries, or memoranda: what the researcher observes, infers, and interprets from the participant in action.

3. From observations or interviews with other participants connected to the primary case study: perspectives about the primary participant.

4. From the research literature: what other scholars and theorists offer about the phenomena under study.

Dialogue and monologue are also central to characterization. Dialogue or monologue may be extracted directly from the raw data (e.g., an excerpt from an interview transcript), or the researcher could construct the text during the interpretive process. Saldaña (1999, 2011a) notes that dialogue can reveal how characters react to one another. Well-done monologues can offer social insight (which may include the researcher's voice or voices from the literature review or theory) and can also foster emotional responses in the audience (Saldaña, 1999, pp. 63–66). Monologues can be conceptualized as "portraits in miniature" that may reveal the essentials of a character, such as his/her motivations or obstacles (Saldaña, 2011a, p. 66). In the case of composite characters, Saldaña (1999, p. 64) offers the following guidelines for interweaving participant voices from two or more interviews:

1. Offer triangulation through their supporting statements.

2. Highlight disconfirming evidence from their contrast and juxtaposition.

3. Exhibit collective story creation through the multiplicity of perspectives.

As the researcher, you must consider **your own role within the script.** Your place within the process, part of your philosophical grounding, becomes explicit as you decide how to write yourself into the script, if at all. Saldaña (1999, p. 66) proposes the following role options (not intended as an exhaustive list) for how a researcher might appear in his/her ethnodramatic text:

1. A leading role

2. An extra not commenting, just reacting

3. A servant

4. The lead's best friend

5. An offstage voice heard on speakers

6. A character cut from the play in an earlier draft

Decisions should be made based on what is necessary for the promotion of audience understanding and what aligns with your philosophical worldview (Leavy, 2015; Saldaña, 1999).

Plot, storyline, and structure are also central in ethnodramatic writing (much of which was reviewed in the section on FBR). In the construction of ethnodramas, **plotting and creating the storyline** begin as distinct processes but eventually become interlinked (Saldaña, 2003, p. 220). Saldaña (2005) notes that *plotting* is the "conceptual framework of ethnodrama" (p. 15). In addition to plot and storyline, the **structures** that frame the play also communicate meaning. Typically called

units in theatre, traditional structures include **acts, scenes, and vignettes** that may be arranged in a **linear or episodic sequence** (Saldaña, 2003). How the story unfolds will depend on the analytic process the data have undergone and the range of meanings you intend to convey.

Ethnotheatre also has a **visual dimension** that allows us to capture and communicate the visual components of social life, which are indistinguishable from human experience and our study of it. **Sceneography** communicates information about the time, place, and social climate. **Costumes and makeup** help establish "the look" of the characters and the show (Saldaña, 2003, p. 228). In addition to scenic elements and costumes, it is important to consider the **performance venue, lighting, media technology, and sound/music** (Saldaña, 2011a). Finally, issues including **casting, acting, directing, and staging** also come to bear on live performance. To assign/ tackle these roles well, learn as much as possible about theatre arts and seek out the expertise of professionals.

✋ REVIEW STOP 4

1. What is ethnodrama?
   a. How does ethnotheatre differ?

2. How are data collected for ethnodrama and ethnotheatre?

3. _____ coding involves using the participants' own words as coding labels during analysis.

4. _____ and monologue are central to characterization.
   a. A monologue may reveal what?

5. When developing the plot and storyline, researchers must consider units in theatre. These structures commonly include _____.
   a. These units may be arranged in a linear or _____ sequence.

☛ **Go to the end of the chapter to check your answers.**

Visual Art Genres: Photography, Photovoice, and Collage

Donna Davis (2008) created the collage depicted in Figure 7.2 as a part of a research project on body image and eating disorders. The image was inspired by a testimonial from an anorexic teenager and Hilde Bruch's (1978) *The Golden Cage*, about the emergence of anorexia. Davis draws heavily on the power of symbolism in this piece.

Visual art genres rely on visual images. Visual arts research practices draw

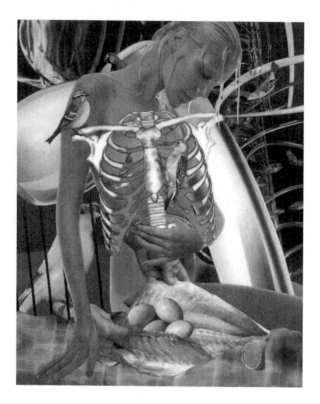

FIGURE 7.2. "The Gold Standard" by Donna Davis. From Davis (2008, p. 255). Copyright © 2008 LEARN. Reprinted by permission.

on the power of visual art to provoke, evoke, and express nonverbal or preverbal knowledge; to jar people into seeing and thinking differently; and to challenge stereotypes. Visual art has the capacity to promote **defamiliarization,** which is why it is a powerful tool for prompting people to look at something in a new way—a great appeal for social researchers. In this respect, visual art has a **resistive and transformational capability.**

In *Art on My Mind: Visual Politics* (1995), the cultural critic bell hooks conceptualizes art as a medium for conveying political ideas, concepts, beliefs, and other information about the culture in which it was produced, including dominant views of race, class, and gender. She suggests that art can function as a site of exclusion but also carries a transformative power that can resist and dislodge stereotypical ways of thinking. hooks offers a methodological strategy of **"aesthetic intervention"** for researching the capability of art to jolt people into seeing differently.

This genre of ABR is extremely diverse methodologically, with many research practices grounded in various arts practices. I review three of those practices: photography, photovoice, and participant-made collage and art journals. I chose these because they are widely used and also tend to be less intimidating to researchers without formal art training (most of us have some experience with photography and collage making from daily life/childhood).

In visual arts research practices, the generation of data or content may occur via **researcher-made art, participant-made art, or a combination of the two.** Visual art practices allow us to broaden the scope of those with whom we may collaborate because language barriers are not a concern. Therefore, in participatory designs that involve participant art making, we can work with participants who are often excluded from research, such as those with whom we have difficulty communicating due to age or disability, indigenous populations, or those from other cultures (e.g., within cross-cultural or transnational studies).

Photography

Photography is widely used in research across the disciplines. With the proliferation of digital cameras and smartphone cameras, these practices are increasing, partly because they are becoming inexpensive to carry out. Photography can be used for a variety of research purposes, including those that involve chronicling; documenting; eliciting data; engaging marginalized groups; and addressing hard-to-get-at, highly conceptual, or metaphorical topics (Holm, 2014). Photographic surveys can be used to study changes in people, places, and processes over time (Holm, 2014; Rieger, 2011). When using photography, the data (photographs) may be preexisting, researcher-created, or participant-created. In all of these instances, **document the context of production** to the extent to which you are able.

You also need to plan how to deal with particular ethical issues. **Access, informed consent, and confidentiality** can become complex with photographic data (Holm, 2014). First, decide whether photos will be edited (e.g., by blurring faces in the case of children or people in the background who could not give informed consent). Second, there may be questions of **ownership and copyright** that should be negotiated and agreed upon upfront (e.g., if participants take the photos themselves, who owns them?) (Holm, 2014; Pink, 2007). If participants are taking photographs, you need to provide them with instructions. The guidelines you provide might be very specific or open, depending on the research purpose and questions. Think about the kind of photographic data sought and consider to what extent you will provide instructions/restrictions on the following:

- Time (when photos are taken)
- How many photographs
- Content of photographs
- Whether participants are allowed to edit the photographs

Photovoice is a specific practice that merges photography with participatory methods. Some refer to this as a method for conducting **arts-based action research** (Chilton & Leavy, 2014). Participants are given cameras and asked to photograph their environment and circumstances. Of course, research goals and instructions to participants vary greatly, but generally, participants are documenting their circumstances as they relate to a larger goal, such as improving their community, affecting particular public policy, or increasing self- and social awareness on a specific topic. For example, the "Witness to Hunger Project" involves low-income mothers in Philadelphia taking photos and recording their stories in order to influence social welfare policy (Chilton, Rabinowich, Council, & Breaux, 2009; see also *www.witnesstohunger.org*). Photovoice can also be used in multimethod or mixed methods research and has become popular in public health research, where the data are used to advocate for community improvement (see Berg, 2007; Holm, 2008).

In terms of research design in photovoice, consider the following general guidelines (Wang, 2005, as quoted in Holm, 2008, p. 330):

- Conceptualizing the problem
- Defining broader goals and objectives
- Recruiting policymakers as the audience for photovoice findings
- Training the trainers
- Conducting photovoice training
- Devising the initial theme/s for taking pictures
- Taking pictures
- Facilitating group discussion
- Critical reflection and dialogue
- Selecting photographs for discussion
- Contextualizing and storytelling
- Codifying issues, themes, and theories
- Documenting the stories
- Conducting the formative evaluation
- Reaching policymakers, donors, media, researchers, and others who may be mobilized to create change

Participant-Made Collage and Visual Journals

Collage is a widely used practice across the disciplines. The researcher and/or participants can create the collages; here I focus on participant-made art. Gioia Chilton and Victoria Scotti (2013) note that collage is popular because materials are accessible and people are generally not intimidated by the prospect of participating in collage making. Collage can therefore be used inclusively with a range of participants, including those often left out of the research process due to age, disability, or language differences.

Collages are made by **selecting images** from magazines, newspapers, textured papers, or other sources, and then **cutting, placing, and attaching** them (often with glue) to a surface such as a piece of paper or cardboard (Chilton & Scotti, 2013). Nontraditional materials may be used as well. For example, Lisa Kay (2009) developed a method of "bead collage" that involves the use of beads and found objects.

By transforming the different bits into something new, which is greater than the sum of its parts, new ideas may emerge (Chilton & Scotti, 2013). Collages often **bring disparate elements together** and can be a powerful way of jarring people into thinking and seeing differently, performing cultural critique, producing connections that would otherwise remain out of reach, inferring new associations, or refining or enhancing meanings (Chilton & Scotti, 2013; Diaz, 2002; Vaughan, 2008). Collage may also include images and text in an attempt to create a reality and find meaning (Diaz, 2002). The **juxtaposition of words and images** opens up new meanings that would not otherwise be possible.

There are some practical considerations for engaging participants in collage making. First, determine the **materials you will provide,** such as a surface material (typically paper, cardboard, or poster board); sources of images (e.g., magazines, photo albums, newspapers); pre-cut sources (e.g., magazine or newspaper clippings); writing, drawing, or painting instruments (e.g., pens, pencils, colored pencils, crayons, magic markers, paint and brushes, ink blotter); additional papers; adhesive (e.g., glue, tape, stapler); and nontraditional objects (e.g., dried flowers, beads, glitter, stickers).

Second, consider what, if any, **materials you will ask participants to provide** (e.g., photographs, diaries, personal mementos).

Third, **create a set of instructions** for the participants. Instructions may range from very general to highly specific, depending on your research purpose or goal. Instructions are intended to help elicit the kind of collages you are interested in and to make the participants comfortable by clarifying guidelines and expectations. Instructions should be clear, concise, and directly linked to the research purpose or goal as well as the research questions, if applicable. For example, you might ask participants to create a collage that responds to a statement, vignette, topic, image, or question you provide. Or you could ask them to create a series of collages illustrating a particular experience or time in their lives. Consider what time frame you are imposing as well. These are just examples. Formulate the instructions based on the specifics of the project.

Art journaling is a method in which **participants create visual journals** that may include text and images, such as magazine clippings or drawings (Chilton & Leavy, 2014) similar to collage making. For example, art education researchers Lisa LaJevic and Stephanie Spriggay (2008) had student teachers create visual journals to reflect on their experiences. Once again, the instructions given to participants may range from quite open to highly specific with respect to the prompts for journaling (topics, questions), materials, and frequency of journaling.

✋ REVIEW STOP 5

1. bell hooks offers a methodological strategy of "aesthetic intervention" for what purpose?

2. In visual arts research practices, the generation of data or content may occur in what ways?

3. What ethical issues may emerge when using photography as a method?

4. Define photovoice.

5. In collage, bringing disparate elements together or juxtaposing words and images can do what?

6. What are three practical considerations for engaging participants in collage making?

7. Name the method that involves participants creating visual journals that may include text and images.

☛ **Go to the end of the chapter to check your answers.**

Representation and Audience

In ABR you are thinking about representation and audience from the outset, as the inquiry process itself generates the artwork. The form of the representation is vital to the delivery of the content because people consume a painting differently than a play or a novel. The medium should be selected for its ability to generate and represent the content and speak to the audience(s) of interest. Two overarching issues to consider are the quality of the artistic representation and how to reach audiences.

A strength of ABR centers on the potential to develop **holistic or synergistic** approaches to research (Blumenfeld-Jones, 2008; Cole & Knowles, 2008). Several concepts can be applied in judging the holistic or synergistic quality of a final project. As discussed in Chapter 5 on qualitative research, **thoroughness** refers to the comprehensiveness of the approach. **Coherence** (Barone & Eisner, 2012), **congruence** (Leavy, 2011b), or **internal consistency** (Cole & Knowles, 2008) refers to how well the components of the project, including the final representation, fit together. In other words, these terms refer to the **strength of the form** (Barone & Eisner, 2012).

- Does it tell a story?
- Does it make sense?
- Does it have a beginning, middle, and end?
- Does it follow the norms of the medium (or innovate in a way that makes sense?

Arts-based works may be judged based on their **truthfulness and trustworthiness.** Truthfulness and trustworthiness in ABR may be thought of in conjunction with the concept of **resonance.** Guiding questions are thus:

- Does it ring true?
- Is it believable?
- Does it feel authentic?
- Does the work resonate?

Aesthetic quality, aesthetic power, or artfulness is central in the execution and later evaluation of ABR (Barone & Eisner, 2012; Chilton & Leavy, 2014; Faulkner, 2009; Leavy, 2009; Patton, 2002). How one achieves artfulness varies from genre to genre, but there are some overarching guidelines. Aesthetic power is created through the **incisiveness, concision, and coherence** of the final artistic output (Barone & Eisner, 2012; Chilton & Leavy, 2014). In other words, an artistic rendering must get to the heart of the issue and present that essence in a coherent form in order to achieve aesthetic power.

All arts practices are **crafts**, and therefore there are no cookie-cutter models; rather, each practitioner brings him/herself to the project. The **personal fingerprint of the artist** may be used to assess ABR (Banks, 2008; Barone & Eisner 1997, 2012). Artistic works have a **voice**. This research practice is about finding and expressing your voice.

You must also **identify potential audiences** for the work and consider how to reach them. For example, if you are creating an ethnodrama, will it be published and/or performed? If it will be performed, what venues are best suited to access the "right" audiences (i.e., those whom you think will benefit from the research)? In addition to identifying audiences and venues, consider **the presentation of the artwork.** How will you label the artwork? For example, in the case of FBR, will you label the work a novel, a research-informed novel, or something else? Will you include a preface, foreword, and/or afterword explaining the process by which the fiction was created and clarifying what parts are "fictional" and the sources of any "nonfictional" material?

Audience response is another marker of success. ABR has the potential to be emotional, evocative, provocative, illuminating, educational, and transformative. It may also be employed to unsettle or disrupt stereotypes or commonly held assumptions, bridge differences, challenge dominant ideologies, present resistive narratives or possibilities, prompt social reflection, and stimulate self-awareness. Therefore, it may be necessary to evaluate how well a piece of ABR has accomplished those ends, as applicable to the project goals.

> **Expert Tip**
>
> Dr. Sandra Faulkner, in the Communication Department at Bowling Green State University, reminds us that it is important to learn the craft of your art form and suggests the following practical options: Take an art class online or in your community; join or start an art or writing group; articulate who your favorite artists, writers, or arts-based researchers are and why; mimic your favorite artists/writers as a form of practice; and read and participate in art widely.

Ethics in Practice

People can have visceral and deeply emotional responses to artworks in any form. Although harnessing this potential is one of the primary advantages of ABR, it also creates an ethical responsibility. As you determine how to present artworks to audiences, consider if there should be content warnings about sensitive subject matter. Also, consider how to prepare for audience responses. You may hold debriefing sessions, offer response cards or questionnaires, and provide resources for those impacted by the topic. For example, if you are hosting an art show for works created about body image and eating disorders, you may provide viewers with pamphlets detailing local eating disorder support groups.

Evaluation Criteria

Although you rarely write directly about evaluation in your research proposal, how you will address criteria appropriate to your project will be a part of the discussion of your research genre and practice (the methodological discussion). I am separating these discussions for instructive purposes.

There are lists of evaluation criteria for different genres of ABR that you can consult depending on your project (e.g., see Faulkner, 2009, for poetic criteria). Ultimately, each genre needs to be evaluated based on standards that fit the specific approach within the genre. With that said, there are general criteria that can be used to assess ABR (see Leavy, 2015). As I have noted in earlier work, although I separate these criteria out for instructive purposes, in practice, there is overlap as they are often interconnected. For instance, a few of the criteria I present are aesthetics, methodology, usefulness, and audience response. In actuality, aesthetics may be intertwined with methodological practice and usefulness. In artistic practice, a sound methodology includes attention to craft, and the aesthetic power of the piece impacts audience response and thus usefulness. It's a messy terrain.

There are various strategies of **data analysis** one might employ in an arts-based project, and the act of doing so can serve as another evaluative criterion. First, you can **solicit feedback from peers, have an external dialogue, or employ data analysis cycles** (Tenni et al., 2003). You can use a team approach to external dialogue as occurs in **reflective teams** (Jones, 2003). It can also be useful to solicit feedback specifically from artists/practitioners in the artistic field within which you are working. **Cross-pollination** can strengthen your artistic practice if your original training is in another field.

Second, researchers are also advised to be in tune with their emotional, carnal, psychological, and intellectual indicators. Tenni and colleagues (2003) refer to this as engaging in an **internal dialogue.** Keeping a diary is one strategy for consistently noting where one is located within the research process (Tenni et al., 2003).

Third, you can **explicitly use theory during data analysis** to open up the data to new interpretations and alternate meanings (Tenni et al., 2003). Similarly, you can examine how literature was used as data or to interpret, frame, and contextualize findings.

In ABR we are often moving from one form to another, which involves a process of **translation.** For example, we may be moving from text to visual images or from poetry to prose, and so forth. Another framework for thinking about translation in ABR is to consider **adaptation theory,** which focuses on adaptations from one genre to another (Ackroyd & O'Toole, 2010). Different genres require a different treatment of the source material (Ackroyd & O'Toole, 2010).

As noted in Chapter 5 on qualitative research, **transparency or explicitness** refers to a clear demonstration of the process by which the research occurred. This factor has been deemed an important evaluative criterion by some arts-based scholars (Butler-Kisber, 2010; Rolling, 2013), although be mindful that some practitioners value "the mystery" of art over explicitness.

Usefulness, significance, or the substantive contribution of the research is an important evaluative criterion. Research is intended to advance knowledge in a given area (Cole & Knowles, 2008; Richardson, 2001) or result in improved life conditions (Butler-Kisber, 2010; Mishler, 1990). Research should illuminate, educate, transform, or emancipate. Lynn Butler-Kisber writes, "There needs to be an upfront and continuous questioning of the 'so what' or utility of our work. Does our work make a difference, and if so for whom, and how and why?" (2010, p. 150). The knowledge produced by the research experience is necessarily *about something* and *for something.* Arts-based approaches are employed because they enable our research goals, and therefore one evaluative criterion is the social significance of the research purpose and how well that purpose has been realized. In ABR the final product may prompt intellectual and/or emotional growth in the viewers or bring them to understand a particular topic differently (Norris, 2011). The work may also be politically motivated to varying degrees (Denzin, 2003), and at one end of the continuum may be used to shape public policy. In these circumstances the work can also be evaluated based on its effectiveness in achieving its policy-related goals. With respect to considering usefulness as an evaluative criterion, it is important to shy away from questions such as "Is it a good piece of art?" and rather ask "What is this piece of art good for?" (Chilton & Leavy, 2014; Leavy, 2010, 2011a, 2015).

A great advantage of ABR is the ability to make research **accessible to broad audiences,** including those beyond the academy, and contribute to **public scholarship** (Cahnmann-Taylor & Siegesmund, 2008; Leavy, 2009, 2011a, 2013). ABR can be judged based on its accessibility in two ways. First, it should be **jargon free,** and in that regard accessible to diverse audiences. Second, it should be **disseminated via appropriate channels to relevant stakeholders,** including nonacademic stakeholders. As noted earlier, issues of **audience** are thus paramount, with the need both to identify relevant audiences *and* find ways to reach them. In ABR, **multiple meanings** may emerge. Therefore, **ambiguity** can be seen as a strength of ABR in certain cases (e.g., narrative gaps in a film or fiction in which readers or viewers can insert their own critical thinking).

Whereas all research must meet general ethical standards (reviewed in Chapter 2), there are a few particular standards for ABR that also serve as evaluative criteria. First, it is vital to **sensitively portray** human experience through **multidimensional portrayals** (Cole & Knowles, 2001).

Second, arts-based practitioners need to be cognizant of **protecting audience members** during public performances or showings. For example, sensitive topics may require content warnings.[3] "Post-performance forum sessions" can be used to analyze audience responses to the performance in order to assess the show's impact (Mienczakowski, Smith, & Morgan, 2002, p. 49).

Third, ABR may involve **participatory work,** such as partnerships between academic researchers and artists or community participants. In cases of joint art making or situations in which participants are imaged in art (e.g., photography), issues of **ownership and copyright** may arise (Holm, 2014). It is best to set clear expectations with participants or co-creators. Likewise, participatory arts-based approaches often demand developing meaningful relationships with co-creators (Ackroyd & O'Toole, 2010; Lather, 2000).

Fourth, consider **artistic license.** There may be tension between our obligation to represent the data truthfully and our use of artistry in order to produce quality art (Saldaña, 2011a). How the artistic rendering is contextualized and framed for audiences, including what information is given about the construction of the artistic work, is also linked to ethical practice.

Finally, practitioners need to practice **reflexivity.** One way of exhibiting reflexive practice is through memo or diary writing about their choices and practices.

Table 7.3 combines the criteria for a strong representation and these additional evaluation criteria.

Ethics Statement

An arts-based ethics statement provides a **discussion of the ethical substructure** of your project addressing your values system, ethical praxis, and reflexivity.

Begin by clarifying the **values system** guiding your research. Possible topics to address include (as applicable) the moral or social justice imperative driving your topic selection; the exploration of stereotypes, presentation of new ways of seeing/thinking, or inclusion of underrepresented groups; and intentions toward using the project to promote positive social change, social awareness, and self-reflection or to impact public policy.

Next provide a detailed discussion of your attention to **ethical praxis.** Topics to address include (as applicable) the status of necessary IRB approvals; informed consent (if participants are involved, discuss); relational ethics (if participants are involved, discuss what kinds of relationships you intend to develop with them, how you will do so, and if participatory work is involved); and the representation and dissemination of findings (format, sensitive and multidimensional portrayals, protecting audience members with content warnings, sharing with participants, sharing with research communities, efforts toward public scholarship, how you are addressing artistic license, and ownership and copyright issues).

Finally, describe how you will practice **reflexivity.** Given the immediacy and visceral nature of art for potential audiences, it is important to step back and

TABLE 7.3. Arts-Based Evaluation Criteria

Strength of form
Components of project fit together and form a comprehensive whole

Solicit feedback from peers
External dialogue, data analysis cycles, or reflective teams

Internal dialogue
Used diary or other strategy to keep a record of self in the project

Literature or theory
Data viewed using literature or a theoretical lens on a different level (micro ↔ macro)

Transparency or explicitness
Methodology disclosed (including translation process)

Usefulness
Makes a substantive contribution

Resonance
Final representation feels truthful and trustworthy

Accessible/contributes to public scholarship
Jargon free and disseminated to relevant stakeholders

Audience response
Extent to which desired audience response was achieved

Multiple meanings
Strategic use of ambiguity

Aesthetic power
Aesthetic quality and artfulness achieved through incisiveness, concision, and coherence

Personal fingerprint
Presence of researcher's voice/style

Ethics
Sensitive and multidimensional portrayals, protection of audience members, ownership of artistic output agreed upon, artistic license balanced with truthfulness, and demonstrated reflexivity

examine your process and final representation. Practicing reflexivity can be particularly challenging in ABR due to the personal nature of art. Topics to address include (as applicable) your place in the research project (documenting your feelings, impressions, assumptions, artistic practices); and your attention to the issue of power in the research process (how participatory work is carried out, strategies for ensuring sensitive and multidimensional portrayals, how your voice and others' voices are represented in the final representation, decisions regarding artistic license, and adherence to the data or content).

 REVIEW STOP 6

1. In ABR, "strength of form" or how well the components of a project fit together is an important evaluative criterion. What's one of the three terms that addresses this?

2. All arts practices are crafts, and there are no cookie-cutter models. Each researcher brings what to his/her projects?

3. How might an arts-based researcher solicit feedback after staging an ethnotheatre?

   a. If the project is on a sensitive topic such as sexual assault, researchers should do what two things for audiences (before and after the performance)?

4. Soliciting feedback from peers, having an internal dialogue, and using theory are all strategies of _____.

5. ABR has the potential to contribute to public scholarship. What are two ways of making ABR accessible?

6. What three dimensions does an ABR ethics statement address?

☛ **Go to the end of the chapter to check your answers.**

References

See Chapter 4.

Appendices

Timeline

Present a proposed timeline for your project, noting the time period allotted for each phase of the research process. Although it can be difficult to preplan artistic practice, discipline is key, and one strategy is to set goals (e.g., drafting a scene, writing a chapter, or creating a visual work in *x* amount of a time).

Proposed Budget (If Applicable)

If your research is funded or you are seeking funding, include a detailed proposed budget. The budget may include the cost of materials (art supplies, pens/paper, costumes, props); equipment (audio recorders, tapes, computers or tablets, digital cameras, digital programs such as Photoshop); payments to participants (including reimbursement for travel expenses); rental fees (theater space, gallery space, film screening room); publishing costs for self-published work; and any other anticipated expenses.

Recruitment Letter and Informed Consent (If Applicable)

If you are working with participants, include these documents.

Instruments (If Applicable)

If you are working with data collected via another method (interview, survey), include the data collection instrument (interview guide, questionnaire).

Artist–Researcher Statement

Many artists include a statement explaining, describing, or contextualizing their work for audiences. Include such a statement, as appropriate to your artistic genre, if you plan to create one to accompany the final representation.

Sample Art and/or Image from the Art-Making Process

Include examples of the art (e.g., clips, links, images, excerpted drafts) and/or images from the art-making process (e.g., a sample of work at various stages, from planning to drafts).

Conclusion

As reviewed in this chapter, ABR is useful for tapping into issues that are otherwise out of reach. ABR allows us to produce engaging, evocative, and widely accessible research outcomes by harnessing the unique capabilities of the art to create self-knowledge and prompt social reflection. This is an emergent and generative approach to inquiry that values aesthetic, preverbal, and multiple ways of knowing. The inquiry process itself may be viewed as a form of data generation, analysis, and representation.

Here is a brief summary of the template for an arts-based research design proposal.

Title: Contains keywords and the art practice.

Abstract: This 150- to 200-word overview should be composed at the end. Includes the phenomenon or theme you are studying, the research purpose or goal, basic information about the genre and research practice (including noting any arts practices used), and why the project is worthwhile.

Keywords: Provides five to six words a reader would Google to find your project, including the main phenomenon or theme, the artistic practice, the participants (if applicable), and the primary theory guiding your research proposal (if applicable).

The Topic under Investigation or the Theme: Discusses the phenomenon or theme to be investigated; the arts practice to be used; personal and pragmatic reasons for the research; and the significance, value, or worth of the project.

Literature Review: Synthesizes the most relevant research, popular art, and fine art on your topic, demonstrating how your project contributes to the literature.

Research Purpose or Goal Statement: Outlines the primary focus or goals of your project, the research/artistic genre and practice, and the rationale.

Research Questions (optional): Provides one to three open-ended, emergent, or generative questions to which your projects aims to respond.

Philosophical Statement: Discusses how the arts-based paradigm is guiding the proposed project and where the project is positioned on the art–science continuum.

Participants and/or Content: Describes your desired participants (demographics and particular experiences) and the sampling strategy that will be used, or describes how your artistic practice is both the method of inquiry and the content.

Genres and Practices: Describes in detail the strategies you will use to collect data or generate content, making note of how you will address the primary issues associated with the practice you are employing.

Representation and Audience: Describes your attention to the quality of the artistic representation and plans for reaching relevant audiences (see evaluation criteria).

Evaluation Criteria: Explains the rationale for your process, including how it is holistic, steps taken to achieve thoroughness and strength of form; data analysis strategies; the usefulness of the project; accessibility to broad audiences and strategies for gauging their responses; your attention to resonance, artfulness, and your personal fingerprint; and your attention to ABR ethical standards (if applicable).

Ethics Statement: Discusses the ethical substructure of your project, addressing your values system, ethical praxis, and reflexivity.

References: Includes a full list of citations, properly crediting all those from whom you've borrowed ideas or quoted. Follow your university reference style guidelines (if applicable) or the norms within your discipline.

Appendices: Includes your proposed timeline; budget; and copies of your recruitment letter, informed consent, any instruments, your artist–researcher statement, sample art, and/or images from the art-making process (if applicable).

☑ REVIEW STOP ANSWER KEY

Review Stop 1

1. adapting the tenets of the creative arts in social research
   a. the unique capabilities of the arts as a way of knowing
2. nondirectional
   a. emergence and/or the resistive nature of art

Review Stop 2

1. the arts-based paradigm and how it is guiding the proposed project
2. embodied, which means that we experience the world through our bodies/senses
3. art–science
4. Data are collected from research participants using traditional quantitative, qualitative, or mixed methods designs; participants make art, which becomes the data; the artistic practice is both the method of inquiry and the content.

Review Stop 3

1. plot, storyline
2. a story that has been told repeatedly in the culture
   a. because they resonate/tap into deeply held values/carry emotional capital
3. Scenes contain dramatic elements in which the action unfolds before the reader's eyes; narrative is a means of summarizing and providing information/commentary that is not in the scenes.
4. interiority or interior dialogue
5. verisimilitude
6. analysis

Review Stop 4

1. writing up research findings in dramatic or script forms
   a. Ethnotheatre is necessarily performed.

2. from research participants using qualitative methods

3. *in vivo*

4. dialogue

   a. the essentials of a character (motivations/obstacles)

5. acts, scenes, vignettes

   a. episodic

Review Stop 5

1. researching the capability of art to jolt people into seeing differently

2. researcher-made art, participant-made art, a combination of the two

3. access, informed consent, confidentiality, ownership, copyright

4. a method wherein participants are given cameras and asked to photograph their environment/circumstances

5. jar people into thinking/seeing differently and open up new ideas/meanings

6. materials you will provide; materials you will ask them to provide; creating a set of instructions

7. art journaling

Review Stop 6

1. coherence, congruence, or internal consistency

2. his/her personal fingerprint or voice

3. debriefing sessions with the audience, providing response cards or questionnaires

   a. provide content warning and resources

4. data analysis

5. jargon free; disseminate via appropriate channels to relevant stakeholders

6. values system, ethical practice, reflexivity

Further Engagement

1. If you have conducted research with participants, such as interviews or field research, develop a character profile, based on one of your participants, which could be used in an FBR or ethnodrama (if you don't have your own data, go online to an oral history database [there are many], and select an interview transcript to use for this exercise). Think about how you would describe the character in terms of his/her major values or motivations, challenges, and relationships with others (e.g., family and friends) (one to two pages). Go a step further and write a sample monologue for the character, in which we learn what motivates him/her (at least one paragraph).

2. Take a primary concept or term from your literature review and create a collage to represent the concept using both words and images. What does the collage tell you about the concept (one paragraph)? How does it enhance your thinking, if at all? What do the juxtaposition of words and images do (one paragraph)?

3. Read a book from the *Social Fictions* series of Sense Publishers (which publishes literary forms of ABR, including novels, plays, poetry, and creative nonfiction). What did you learn from the book (one page)? What did you think about the writing style and format (one page)? For example, how did it make the topic more or less interesting to you? Did it create an emotional response, and if so, what kind of a response? There are "free previews" of each book available for download on the publisher's website: *www.sensepublishers.com/catalogs/bookseries/social-fictions-series*

Resources

Barone, T., & Eisner, E. W. (2012). *Arts-based research*. Thousand Oaks, CA: SAGE.
Harris, A., & Holman Jones, S. (2016). *Writing for performance*. Rotterdam, The Netherlands: Sense Publishers.
Leavy, P. (2015). *Method meets art: Arts-based research practice* (2nd ed.). New York: Guilford Press.
Social Fictions book series, Sense Publishers
www.sensepublishers.com/catalogs/bookseries/social-fictions-series

Suggested Journals

Art/Research International: A Transdisciplinary Journal (ARI) (University of Alberta)
https://ejournals.library.ualberta.ca/index.php/ari

Etudes: An Online Theatre and Performance Studies Journal for Emerging Scholars
www.etudesonline.com/cfp.html

UNESCO Observatory Multidisciplinary Journal in the Arts (University of Melbourne)
http://education.unimelb.edu.au/about_us/specialist_areas/arts_education/melbourne_unesco_observatory_of_arts_education/the_e-journal

Notes

1. There are many terms in the literature that refer to ABR. Some commonly used examples include *arts-based educational research* (ABER), *arts-informed inquiry*, and, *a/r/tography*. Please see Chilton and Leavy (2014) for a list of terms.
2. I coined the terms *fiction-based research* (FBR) and *fiction as a research practice* (FARP) in 2013 and the term *social fiction* in 2010.
3. Some researchers use the term *trigger warnings* instead of *content warnings*; however, the use of the word *trigger* has been the subject of some critique, so I recommend the more neutral term *content warning*.

CHAPTER 8

Community-Based Participatory Research Design

Community-based participatory research (CBPR)—also commonly referred to as *community-based research* (CBR), *participatory action research* (PAR), *community-based participatory action research* (CBPAR), *social action research,* among other terms[1]—involves forming research partnerships with nonacademic stakeholders to develop and execute a research project based on a particular community-identified problem or issue. CBPR values collaboration, power sharing, and different kinds of knowledge (scientific, lay, experiential). CBPR develops projects from the ground up, with those whose lives are most impacted by the problem at hand, in an effort to create needed changed. Methodologically, these are problem-centered or problem-driven approaches to research that require flexibility. These approaches are generally used when the aim is to promote community change or action, and may also be used simultaneously to explore, describe, evaluate, evoke and unsettle (or any combination thereof).

It is important to note that in most research methods texts, CBPR is placed within chapters on qualitative research. Although many qualitatively inclined researchers engage in this work, from a research *design perspective,* there are a host of specific goals and issues relating to CBPR that go beyond the qualitative research design guidelines. Many are predisposed *not* to consider quantitative methods in relation to CBPR; however, it was community self-surveys (a quantitative method) in the 1940s and 1950s that helped lay the foundation for what became community-based or participatory action research (Torre & Fine, 2011). Experts consider community self-surveys, which represented a "radical inclusion" of community members in the research process, as a predecessor to CBPR (Torre & Fine, 2011, p. 110). CBPR is not within the purview of qualitative researchers alone, although they have advanced the field greatly. Further, quantitative, qualitative, mixed methods, and arts-based practices may be used in any given CBPR project (which is why it is placed as the last chapter).

Structure of a Research Proposal

CBPR projects are highly individualized in relation to the particular problem, community, and resources at play. Additionally, CBPR often follows responsive designs in which the methodology is revised during the research process in accord with new learning and the changing needs of stakeholders. Therefore, templates are highly problematic. Every research proposal will look somewhat different, just as each project will follow a different plan. With this said, research proposals typically include some discussion of what I suggest in the following template. The template can be altered significantly to suit your specific project, but bear in mind these components.

TEMPLATE 8.1	
Title Abstract Keywords	Basic Introductory Information
The Problem or Issue Literature Review Research Purpose Statement Research Questions	The Topic
Philosophical Statement Setting(s) and Participants Design and Methods Data Analysis and Interpretation Representation and Dissemination Ethics Statement References Appendices	The Research Plan

For the remainder of this chapter, I fill in Template 8.1.

Basic Introductory Information

Title

CBPR titles should clearly state the main problem or issue and the community of interest.

Abstract

In CBPR these 150- to 200-word overviews typically include the problem or issue driving the research, the relevant stakeholders, community partners, setting and participants, the research purpose and questions, basic information about the methods, and what social action agenda is driving the research.

Keywords

Five to six keywords identify the main problem or issue, the community and stakeholders, and the CBPR design.

The Topic

The Problem or Issue

Determining the problem or issue involves a process of initially starting with a general topic, identifying key stakeholders and community partners, collaboratively identifying the problem or issue, conducting a literature review, and then collaboratively crafting a problem or issue statement. Although not all projects follow this model for a host of reasons (e.g., community partners may locate you and bring you into an ongoing project; the project is less collaborative upfront), this process signifies key phases in problem formulation that can be adjusted to meet your needs.

CBPR occurs in all research areas on general topics in research domains that include (but are not limited to) environmental studies, development, urbanization, health care, prisons and criminal justice, immigration studies, and worker health and safety. Any number of factors might lead you to your general **topic**, including your **disciplinary background, personal interests, and prior research or professional experiences.** With respect to prior research or professional experiences, skills you have acquired come to bear. For example, if the topic involves working with Spanish-speaking migrant workers, the ability to speak Spanish may be a factor in whether or not you pursue the topic. Your **professional network** may also lead you to a topic. A professional network may include professors, peers, researchers, and colleagues or associates at nonprofits or other relevant organizations. People in your network may be able to connect you to possible community-based organizations, collaborators, and/or participants. **Funding opportunities** may also drive initial topic selection. Searching for available grants or contacting people in your network to see if they are working on any grant proposals in which you could be included are two strategies. Finally, **timeliness** may impact your topic selection. If you are aware of a particular local issue or problem (from newspaper accounts, word of mouth, etc.), you may investigate to see if it is a researchable topic. Funding opportunities and timeliness are often interconnected in CBPR, as funding often becomes available to study a topic of national concern in local hotspots.

Identifying relevant stakeholders and community partners is a vital part of moving from a general idea to a researchable problem. Stakeholders are those parties who have a vested interest in your topic. For example, in a project about bullying in schools, stakeholders may include individuals from the following categories:

- Teachers
- Students
- Parents
- Guidance counselors
- Social workers
- School administrators
- After-school programming staff
- School bus drivers
- Local leaders
- Law enforcement
- Researchers in sociology and psychology

A project about diabetes prevention may include the following stakeholders:

- Lay citizens in high-risk groups
- Physicians
- Nurses
- Psychologists
- Nutritionists
- Researchers in public health

A project about programming in prisons to reduce recidivism (repeat offenses) may include the following stakeholders:

- Prisoners
- Prison guards
- Law enforcement
- Psychologists
- Social workers
- Researchers in education, criminology, criminal justice, and sociology

There are countless examples depending on the particular topic. In addition to identifying stakeholders, finding **collaborators/coinvestigators/community partners** is essential. Your professional network may assist as you locate possible partners and begin to develop working relationships. Depending on the topic, there may be an established **community-based organization (CBO)** or CBOs with which you can try to forge a partnership. For example, Rogerio Pinto (2009) conducted HIV prevention research with 10 CBOs; five provided primarily medical HIV-related services, and the other five provided primarily social services related to HIV (e.g., counseling and prevention workshops). The CBOs he worked with collaborated with academics, public health experts, psychologists, and social workers and provided services to lay citizens.

Regardless of how many people are on the formal research team, you may establish a **community advisory board (CAB)** to incorporate community perspectives into the project (Israel, Eng, Schultz & Parker, 2005; Letiecq & Schmalzbauer, 2012). Soliciting formal input from differently positioned members of the community can be essential as you seek to formulate the problem and develop a **culturally competent** approach to investigating it. Members of advisory boards may "serve as cultural guides, bridges to the most marginalized community members, research consultants, and sources of critical feedback" (Letiecq & Schmalzbauer, 2012, p. 248).

Once you have a team in place, **identification and formulation of the problem or issue** begin. Two major issues come to bear: (1) the social value of the project and (2) accounting for multiple stakeholders' needs and perspectives.

CBPR is necessarily **social justice driven.** Researchers engage in CBPR and related approaches to research to address inequality, include marginalized people and perspectives in all phases of the research, empower disenfranchised groups, and democratize knowledge production and dissemination. Questions to consider include:

- What is the moral or ethical imperative for basing a project around this problem?

- What area of inequality or exclusion does the project address?

- Whose voices, perspectives, and needs are shaping the project?

- What is the social, cultural, or political value of studying this problem?

- What are the real-world applications? Whom might these applications benefit?

Multiplicity is also an active characteristic of problem identification. Everyone comes to the project with different perspectives, experiences, and skills, all of which must be valued. It's often useful to take an inventory of where each person is coming from, including his/her stake in the topic and personal hopes and expectations with respect to what will come from the research. This process helps home in on how to conceptualize the problem or issue so that the project is beneficial for all participants and takes proper advantage of the different skill sets and knowledge people bring to the table.

Concept maps (reviewed in Chapter 3) are often useful in this process. Begin with the primary topic and visually show how the different stakeholders relate to it, including the knowledge, perspectives, and skills they bring to the project. Different relationships or synergies may be denoted by linking words with lines or arrows or by overlapping circles (i.e., Venn diagrams) (Ahloranta & Ahlberg, 2004; Umoquit et al., 2013). Concept or literature maps may also be helpful in compiling the literature review.

Literature Review

In CBPR a **literature review** is **problem-centered and interdisciplinary (or trans-disciplinary)**, often drawing on literature from numerous disciplines and research traditions in order to present a holistic review of the current and landmark research related to the central problem. The process of compiling and synthesizing the review is much more complicated in a CBPR project because you are seeking literature in multiple relevant fields. Researchers must immerse themselves in those literatures, learning their language, and seeking the expertise of others as needed. As literature is pulled from numerous disciplines, the process of taking an **inventory** of the relevant literature alone can be a long process, and ample time must be given to building this framework (Darbellay, Cockell, Billotte, & Waldvogel, 2008). Take inventories of what is just beyond the scope of each relevant discipline and determining where synergies can be found or forged (Darbellay et al., 2008). In an earlier work, I presented a version of the following steps for conducting this kind of literature review (Leavy, 2011a, p. 64):

1. Determining relevant disciplinary bodies of knowledge

2. Locating and summarizing relevant literature (current and landmark studies) from each discipline or area

3. Determining what is just beyond the scope of each discipline or area

4. Locating existing synergies between different resources

5. Locating and creating possible/new synergies between different resources

6. Synthesizing the literature in order to build a conceptual framework

This process may involve extensive negotiations between differently positioned research partners (Leavy, 2011a). In addition to different disciplinary or other areas of expertise, **culturally sensitive** definitions must be sought (as relevant to the project). Terms used to build the conceptual framework and any data collection instruments must be relevant to the communities the research serves—to **community understandings** of relevant concepts. This is even more challenging in transcultural or transnational research, in which various cultural perspectives are also brought to bear.

An excellent example comes from a 10-year cross-cultural project, conducted in eight developing countries, called "The Household, Gender, and Age Project." A primary challenge during the first year was developing a definition of "the household" that worked across disciplines and in the eight different cultural contexts. The researchers worked together and came to view the term

> from an economic point of view in terms of income; from a sociological point of view in terms of numbers of members of the household; from a psychological perspective in terms of interrelations within the family; from a historical point of view in terms of changes in the household; and from an anthropological point of view in terms of co-residence. (Masini, 2000, p. 122)

With respect to how cultural understandings of "the household" differ across contexts, the team considered the conventional Western notion of the household (co-residence) and other cultural understandings, such as kinship and obligations of nonresident "household" members to resident members (e.g., financial or child care obligations) (Masini, 1991).

Balancing different bodies of literature as well as the perspectives of the different players involved can be taxing, but when done with care, the effort can result in the creation of appropriate and highly effective concepts. It is highly unlikely you're working on a 10-year, eight-country project, or anything near that scope, but it's important to be sensitive to the complexity of defining a term like "the household" that most of us take for granted. Building a CBPR project—from the problem to the literature review—requires reflexivity about that which you take for granted—the skills and perspectives you bring to the table as well as the biases and assumptions that may not be shared.

At this point the research team reconvenes and formulates the problem or issue at the center of the research project.

Note that although I chronologically reviewed the topic, the stakeholders and collaborators, the problem or issue, and the literature review, in practice there is likely overlap during these phases of research design (i.e., they may occur simultaneously). Figure 8.1 depicts the general process I have outlined (note that the bubbles around *Topic* indicate the different factors reviewed that might initially steer you in that direction).

As discussed later in the section on design and methods, once data collection begins, there may be periods of cycling back and refining the problem or issue statement based on new learning.

 Ethics in Practice

The problem or issue at the heart of any CBPR project is social justice driven, so it is vital that the selection of a topic, and the entire process by which it is selected, reflects good ethical practice. An inclusive and collaborative process is most likely to result in a worthwhile, mutually beneficial, and culturally sensitive approach.

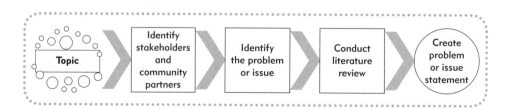

FIGURE 8.1. From topic to problem statement.

✋ REVIEW STOP 1

1. Who are relevant stakeholders?
   a. In addition to identifying stakeholders, in CBPR researchers must find
      _____ with whom to work.

2. In order to incorporate community perspectives into the project, researchers may establish a _____.
   a. Soliciting input from differently positioned members of the community
      can be essential in what two ways?

3. Why is the process of completing a literature review more complicated in
   CBPR?

👉 **Go to the end of the chapter to check your answers.**

Research Purpose Statement

The research team collectively moves from the general topic to the specific problem or issue and ultimately to the research purpose. Briefly state the purpose of the proposed study, focusing on the **primary focus or goals.** To do so, clearly state the main problem or issue, the stakeholders, the setting and participants, the methodology (data collection methods, how the methods will be employed, and the philosophical framework and any theories guiding the study), and the primary reason for conducting the research. It is possible that there will be **multiple phases or levels** to the research purpose. For example, the first phase may involve creating knowledge about the central problem with community participation, and the second phase may involve lobbying to change public policy. It is also possible that the research purpose will **evolve.** When employing a recursive design that allows cycling back to accommodate new learning (discussed in the methods section), you may modify any phase of the project, including refining or expanding the purpose. In general, your primary purpose in carrying out the project is to promote a specific community change or action and may also be used simultaneously to explore, describe, evaluate, evoke, and unsettle (or any combination thereof).

Research Questions

The research team collectively generates the **central questions** the research seeks to answer. This process optimally involves bringing members of the community of interest into the development process to create "community-generated research questions" (Stoeker, 2008, p. 50). There are typically one to three primary questions that may have additional subquestions, but that number is not carved into stone. As with the research purpose, the research questions may also evolve over the course of the project. The design of specific questions is linked to the approach employed within a particular study (if quantitative, qualitative, mixed and/or arts-based methods and practices are used). With that said, CBPR questions are generally **inductive, change-oriented, and inclusive.** They may employ words and phrases such as *co-create, collaborate, participatory, empower, emancipate, promote, foster, describe,* and *seek to understand from the perspective of various stakeholders.*

The Research Plan

Philosophical Statement

CBPR emerges out of a social justice and action-oriented transformative paradigm. Inquiry practices are informed by the belief that social research has an ethical mandate to serve community interests, and those interests are best identified by the communities themselves. CBPR philosophy developed in, and draws on, multiple disciplines, area studies, and theoretical schools of thought, including (but not limited to) sociology, psychology, critical pedagogy within education, feminism, critical race theory, and indigenous studies. Although the transformative paradigm, discussed shortly, is relatively new, the cross-disciplinary seeds of this orientation to research have been planted at various times for over a century. Here's a cursory look at some of those seeds.

Notably, feminist sociologist and activist Jane Addams (1860–1953) engaged in what would now be considered community-based research with immigrant women in Chicago (Boyd, 2014). In the 1800s **critical theorists** Karl Marx and Friedrich Engels demonstrated the principles of community-based research in their efforts to raise the consciousness of workers exploited under capitalism. Feminist and critical theories serve as theoretical frames for many CBPR projects today. **Education reformers** John Dewey (1859–1952) and Paulo Freire (1921–1997) also directly influenced the philosophy of CBPR. Freire founded **critical pedagogy,** a cornerstone of CBPR, which posits that education must be used to liberate the poor from oppression, who are active leaders in their own liberation (Boyd, 2014). In the 1940s Kurt Lewins challenged the borders between research, theory, and action in psychology and is widely credited with beginning "action research" in the United States (Fine et al., 2003).

The **social justice movements** (discussed in Chapter 2)—the women's, civil rights, labor, and gay rights movements—all influenced the development of CBPR philosophical principles. A common effect from the social justice movements was a thorough reexamination of **power** dynamics within social research, which led to the kind of power sharing that characterizes CBPR. Further, these movements cumulatively prompted a renegotiation of why we undertake research, what we believe about who should be included in research, what topics are valuable to study, and the uses to which social research might be put. **Feminist, critical race, and indigenous theories** are all influential. Feminism and critical race theories have been discussed in earlier chapters; here I briefly expand on indigenous theories.

Critical approaches to indigenous inquiry emerged in the 1990s prompted by the theoretical approaches born from the social justice movements coupled with the effects of globalization. These perspectives place "indigenous knowledges, voices, and experiences" at the center of research practices (Tuhiwai Smith, 2005, p. 87). Norman Denzin and Yvonna Lincoln (2008) write, "Critical indigenous inquiry begins with the concerns of indigenous people. It is assessed in terms of the benefits it creates for them" (p. 2). These approaches aim to access the subjugated knowledge of indigenous people for social justice purposes, determined—at least partly—by research participants (and non-Western researchers). Critical indigenous inquiry "embraces the commitment by indigenous scholars to decolonize Western methodologies, to criticize and demystify the ways in which Western science and the modern academy have been part of the colonial apparatus" (Denzin & Lincoln, 2008, p. 2).

Together, what these different perspectives and practices—critical theory, critical pedagogy, action research, feminism, critical race theory, indigenous theory—bring to research is a focus on action, community participation, and the transformational possibilities of research, which are the foundation of the transformative paradigm (see Figure 8.2).

Donna Mertens (2005, 2009) has pioneered the development of the transformative paradigm (which she formerly called the *emancipatory paradigm*). The **transformative paradigm** is a human rights and social justice approach to research in which those historically forced to the margins of the research process are actively included in the entire process (Mertens, 2009; see Figure 8.3). Inclusion extends

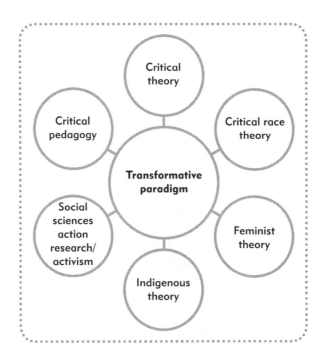

FIGURE 8.2. Theoretical influences on the transformative paradigm.

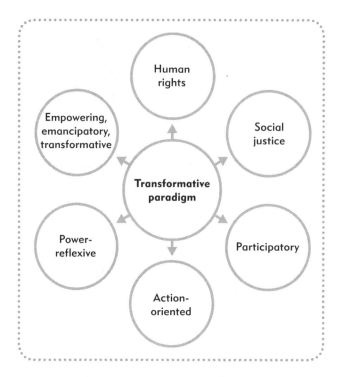

FIGURE 8.3. The transformative paradigm.

far beyond serving as "the subjects" of research, but rather, *partners* within the research endeavor. Mertens writes: "The transformative paradigm provides a metaphysical umbrella with which to explore similarities in the basic beliefs that underlie research and evaluation approaches that have been labeled critical theory, feminist theory, critical race theory, participatory, inclusive, human-rights based, democratic, and culturally responsive" (2009, p. 13). Under this perspective, research partners should include those who face discrimination and oppression on any basis (Mertens, 2005, 2009). For example, women, people of color, the poor, people with disabilities, indigenous peoples, and others confronting structural inequalities and exclusion are sought out for research partnerships, their concerns and perspectives brought to the forefront. By forming research partnerships with those marginalized persons or groups, for whom the research matters on practical levels, research is understood to be **participatory and action-oriented.** Further, this is a **power-reflexive or power-sensitive** approach to research (Haraway, 1991; Pfohl, 1992). This philosophy posits that research should be **empowering, emancipatory, and transformative** (in whatever ways are possible).

The philosophical statement explains **how your project is situated within the transformative paradigm** and may also involve a discussion of **specific theories** employed (which may stem from any number of disciplines, area studies, or critical theoretical schools of thought).

Setting(s) and Participants

Where does the research take place? The setting or settings in CBPR drives the selection of research participants (and vice versa) as well as other design and methods choices. CBPR necessarily involves leaving the research academy. Research may occur in **formal or informal community settings.** For example, formal community settings may include CBOs, nonprofits, and community centers. Parks and participants' homes are examples of informal community settings. Often, CBPR occurs in multiple settings, including a mix of formal and informal environments.

In order to gain access to the settings of interest, you need to develop trusting relationships through the means discussed earlier (rapport building, demonstrating care). As was discussed in Chapter 5 with respect to qualitative field research, there can be both formal and informal **gatekeepers.** Formal gatekeepers are people working in the CBOs, nonprofits, schools, prisons, or other institutionalized settings to which you seek access. However, even if you gain entrance into those settings, which can be particularly long processes in some cases (e.g., prisons and schools), every setting has informal gatekeepers. Each person in the setting in which you are conducting your research can decide whether or not he/she will participate. Community buy-in and accessing different stakeholders' viewpoints is vital in CBPR, so bear this in mind as you develop relationships.

Your research partners/collaborators/co-investigators, may be the research participants. For example, in a study of a particular CBO, there may not be any research participants beyond those who work at and use the services of the CBO, who you may

> ### Expert Tip
>
> Dr. Meredith Minkler, at the School of Public Health, Community Health and Human Development at the University of California, Berkeley, reminds us that community organizations are often "middlemen" between researchers and communities. They can help you gain access to community members, but they can also act as gatekeepers in relation to who is invited into the research process and how the research findings are used.

define as your research partners. In other projects, there may be a research team and also a sample of **traditional research participants.** In these instances, how will your community partners (whether co-investigators and/or a community advisory board) assist in the location of good participants?

Although the kinds of sampling strategies used varies depending on the particular methods employed, often CBPR relies on **purposeful sampling,** which, as noted in Chapter 3, is based on the premise that seeking out the best cases for the study produces the best data (Patton, 2015). Given the nature of CBPR, **snowball sampling** is a popular strategy. This is an approach whereby each participant leads to another participant via referral (Adler & Clark, 2011; Patton, 2015). As you meet people in the community of interest and develop relationships, members of the community may suggest additional participants or you may directly ask them to suggest other possible participants (Babbie, 2013). For example, if a participant is a particularly good source of information about one subgroup within the larger community (representing one set of stakeholder interests), you may ask him/her to suggest others who share similar experiences and perspectives.

✋ REVIEW STOP 2

1. In CBPR, what is the primary research purpose?

2. Numerous theoretical perspectives inform the _____ paradigm that guides CBPR.

   a. Identify the six foci of this paradigm.

3. Does every setting have formal or informal gatekeepers?

4. CBPR often relies on what kind of sampling?

   a. Given the nature of CBPR, what is a popular sampling strategy?

☛ **Go to the end of the chapter to check your answers.**

Design and Methods

The following is an excerpt explaining the research design for a project in women's prisons in New York that investigated the impact of college on female prisoners both within the prison environment and after their release (Fine et al., 2003).

> The design of the research called for both qualitative and quantitative methods. The research questions required that a quantitative analysis be undertaken to assess the extent to which college, in fact, reduced recidivism and disciplinary incidents; and a qualitative analysis to determine the psychosocial effects of college on the women, the prison environment, their children, and the women's lives postrelease. (p. 180)

CBPR is an **orientation** to research, not a particular set of methods (Boyd, 2014; Reason & Bradbury, 2008). In other words, CBPR is a way of approaching research that shapes *how* we use methods. Often multimethod, mixed method, or multiphase designs are employed. A project may involve multiple phases of interview research, field research combined with surveys, focus groups, document analysis, and so on. There are innumerable possibilities. Because CBPR can involve any of the methods/practices reviewed in this text, and in any number of combinations, each project will look different. Consult previous chapters for instruction on particular methods you may be using in your project. However, there are core principles in CBPR that are applicable to every design: a problem-centered orientation, collaboration, cultural sensitivity, social action and social justice, recruitment and retention, trust and rapport, multiplicity, flexibility and innovation. Note that in CBPR, **evaluation** is linked to how well you have executed these core principles *as well as* meeting the evaluation criteria for the particular methods/strategies employed (consult appropriate chapters).

CBPR is **problem-centered or problem-driven,** and research design choices flow from that principle. Methods, strategies, and approaches are selected for their ability to best address the research problem. Some CBPR projects favor a responsive approach to design. **Responsive designs** follow the principle of **recursiveness,** which in this context refers to an iterative research process, whereby the team cycles back and repeats steps, checking data, and adapting to new insights (Pohl & Hadorn, 2007). This approach builds recurring communication and evaluation into the process (Krimsky, 2000). The best way to build a project around the problem at hand will be determined by the research team, ideally comprised of relevant stakeholders. Figure 8.4 illustrates a responsive design.

Collaboration is at the heart of CBPR. Collaboration between all research partners—academic researchers and nonacademic stakeholders—ideally occurs during all phases of the research process, including problem identification, conceptualization and planning, data collection and interpretation, and the representation and dissemination of the research findings. This does not mean that all research partners must be equally involved in each phase (e.g., not every research partner

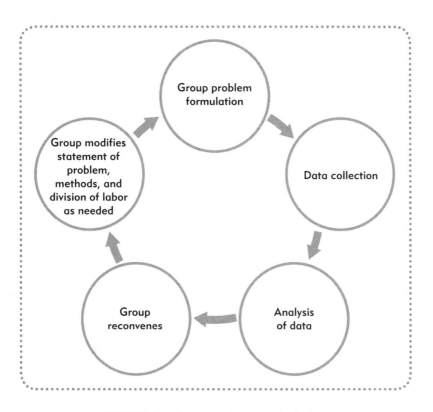

FIGURE 8.4. A responsive research design.

needs to coauthor the resulting publications, or coauthor "equal" amounts). However, each partner should be actively involved in making these determinations. In-depth collaboration requires clearly determining, dividing, and balancing roles, responsibilities, and resources (Pinto, 2009). Collaboratively delineate a clear **division of labor** that serves each stakeholder's interests and abilities. When doing so, consider "mundane" and time-consuming tasks, so that no one unwittingly gets overburdened with these jobs. When working with a CBO or any kind of nonprofit, bear in mind that it may already be understaffed and overburdened, running on a shoestring budget. It is important to avoid overburdening staff or draining resources (e.g., consider costs of tasks such as photocopying). The goal is to achieve "partnership synergy" (Lasker, Weiss, & Miller, 2001). Participation in the research should be **mutually beneficial** for all parties. Community needs must be identified collaboratively to avoid the power imbalances that often occur when academic researchers go into communities to conduct research. Many practitioners regard **power sharing** to be a core principle (Boyd, 2014). Different stakeholders should be given **leadership roles** in the various stages of the research process to avoid research that occurs within communities, but not *with* communities (Minkler, 2004; Montoya & Kent, 2014) (see Figure 8.5).

Notwithstanding the preference for highly participatory and collaborative designs, there are a host of reasons why a particular CBPR project may fall under the leadership of the principal researcher—including the time and effort it takes to see the research to completion. Although there is a preference for research partnerships, there are instances of lone researchers working with community input in the form of an advisory board. Figure 8.6 illustrates the two different forms collaboration might take: a principal researcher as leader with community input and a full research partnership.

Collaborative efforts help ensure attention to **cultural sensitivity.** Research must be sensitive to the community's cultural definitions and understandings of key terms, as well as to the interventions and strategies that are most likely to be effective with the relevant population. The customs, norms, and values of the group or groups with which you're working need to be understood, valued, and respected. Here are a few examples of areas that may differ considerably: gestures used in a group that denote particular meanings (e.g., snaps in a drama class instead of clapping), slang words or phrases with common understandings, shared insider knowledge about how things "really work" in a setting (e.g., an office, university, public program), food preferences within a group, experiences with microaggressions that are taken as common within a group (e.g., racism/racial privilege, sexual

Researcher driven ⟷ Fully collaborative

FIGURE 8.5. Continuum of collaboration.

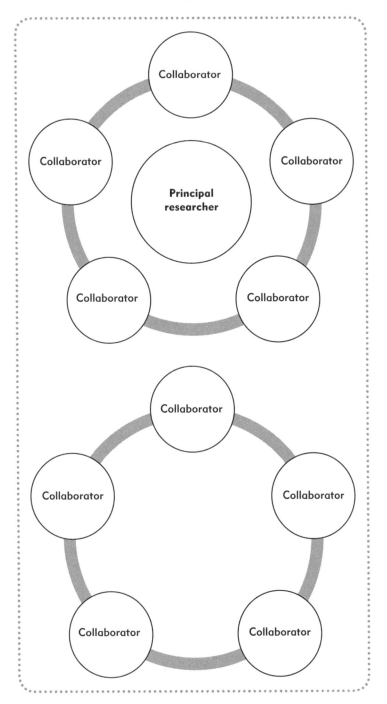

FIGURE 8.6. Community input versus community partnership.

harassment). Different groups with which you work are likely to have any number of norms and values they take for granted that you must learn and respect. Understanding the norms, values, and common understandings within a group assists in the development of data collection instruments or intervention strategies, regardless of the particular methods employed. For example, with respect to **data collection instruments,** cultural understandings shape the kinds of questions asked in a survey or interview (content and language). The goal is to be *effective* in addressing the problem at hand, thereby maximizing the benefits to the community. **Intervention strategies** must also be culturally competent (Montoya & Kent, 2014). Here's an example in the field of public health research.

Loftin et al. (2005) conducted multiple CBPR projects on diabetes prevention in rural African American communities. The first study was a feasibility study that addressed creating a dietary self-management intervention so that people could improve their own health through their eating habits. The dietary self-management intervention consisted of three sequenced components: (1) four dietary education classes lasting 90 minutes each, (2) two monthly discussion groups lasting 60 minutes each, and (3) nurse case manager follow-up by weekly telephone calls and one home visit. In order for their dietary self-management intervention to be effective, it needed to be culturally appropriate.

> Culturally competent characteristics of the intervention reflect the beliefs, values, customs, food patterns, language, and health care practices of Southern, rural African-Americans and seek to integrate these values into healthy dietary strategies. First, the intervention focused on the most meaningful and relevant topic reported by African-Americans in previous research, dietary education. Meals or snacks of typical ethnic food preferences were served at each screening and intervention session to integrate black cultural traditions associated with food. Participation of family members was encouraged to capitalize on the value of family and to provide transportation. Experiential learning approaches, such as participation in a cooking class, were used because they are the primary mode of learning for this population. Peer-professional discussion groups facilitated cultural translation of contents and culturally competent learning methods, such as story-telling. (Loftin et al., 2005, p. 253)

Creating an effective program that has the potential to facilitate successful outcomes depends on community participation.

CBPR has a real-world goal beyond creating knowledge for the sake of knowledge such that the **social action and social justice** imperatives driving the research must remain in focus. Randy Stoeker writes: "The ideal research project is one that serves community-identified needs, is sensitive to the cultural understandings of the community, and supports action around some community-identified issue" (2008, p. 50). Projects are "designed in the context of knowledge application" in some area (Chopyak & Levesque, 2002, p. 205). In this regard, research findings are considered "active," not passive (Cammarota & Fine, 2008). Research findings are "launching pads for ideas, actions, plans, and strategies to initiate social change" (Cammarota & Fine, 2008, p. 6).

Recruitment and retention often prove challenging in CBPR (getting appropriate people to participate for the duration of the project). If seeking funding for the project, address these issues in your grant proposal because they may require both time and funds (Loftin et al., 2005). Multiple recruitment strategies may be needed (Loftin et al., 2005). Recruiting and retaining interested participants are directly linked to how effectively research teams have incorporated and collaborated with relevant stakeholders within the community. Community understandings, norms, and values should permeate the conceptualization process, helping you to determine **culturally competent strategies** for recruiting your desired participants (Leavy, 2011a; Loftin et al., 2005). As noted, CBPR is reliant on community buy-in.

It is important to build **trust and rapport** with community members, research partners, and participants. CBPR is a "relational" approach to research, and therefore relationship building is essential (Boyd, 2014). One challenge is that the idea of *research* may be poorly received by members of some communities, particularly disenfranchised or marginalized populations, or those with histories of exploitive research conducted on them (Meade, Menard, Luque, Martinez-Tyson, & Gwede, 2009). Collaboration, egalitarianism, and power sharing go a long way toward building positive relationships. The more community members shape the potential outcomes and benefits of the research, the greater value they will place on the project and more trust they will develop toward "outsiders" (researchers). **Insider-outsider status** certainly comes to bear. Remember, you are not an organic member of the community, nor are you the "expert" on the community's inner workings or needs. Negotiating insider–outsider statuses requires building genuine relationships by engaging in mutual sharing. Show why and how you care.

A CBPR design is imbued with a commitment to power sharing and respecting multiple kinds of knowledge. This level of commitment requires an honest examination of one's own position in the research, including educational privilege (often a factor) and an acknowledgment of how much you have to learn about the activities and norms within the community. Research partners come to CBPR projects with different experiences, skills, kinds of knowledge, assumptions, and perspectives, which, when harnessed, become a core strength of CBPR. **Multiple and different forms of knowledge**—experiential, scientific, and lay—are valued.

CBPR designs also require **flexibility and innovation** as multiple resources and viewpoints are brought together in a problem-centered capacity. Things do not always go according to plan with these kinds of projects, and it's necessary to adapt to circumstances as they emerge (Leavy, 2011a). The need for flexibility and innovation, however, must be balanced against the need for structure. These projects create a paradox; they require both openness and structure (Leavy, 2011a). Although all partners must be open to adaptation, roles and responsibilities must

> **Expert Tip**
>
> Dr. Leonard A. Jason, at the Center for Community Research at DePaul University, says that you must rely on your intuition because it's not always a rational process. Trust your gut and "allow the voices that call to us to be honored."

also be clearly delineated or mayhem may ensue. As new situations emerge that may change the division of labor, partners should consult one another and come to a new arrangement based on these developments.

Finally, CBPR requires researchers to expand. In addition to research skills and learning how to work with the methods best suited to the problem, researchers need to develop **organizational, relational, and facilitation skills** to work effectively with community partners (Boyd, 2014). Table 8.1 provides a summary of CBPR design principles.

TABLE 8.1. Summary of CBPR Design Principles

Problem-centered

Methodological strategies that best suit the research problem; often responsive designs that follow a recursive process

Collaboration

Deep collaboration between all research partners, clearly delineated division of labor, power sharing, and mutually beneficial outcomes

Cultural sensitivity

Community cultural definitions, understandings, norms, and values are included and respected

Social action and social justice

Research is geared toward a community-identified need and will be used to create or initiate positive social change

Recruitment and retention

Good community buy-in is elicited and retained for the duration of the project by using culturally competent recruiting strategies

Trust and rapport

Trusting and egalitarian relationships built through power sharing, attention to insider–outsider statuses, and demonstrating genuine caring/concern

Multiplicity

Different forms of knowledge—experiential, scientific, lay—are included and validated

Flexibility and innovation

Adaptation to emerging circumstances fostered by balancing structure and openness

Researcher skills

Development of researcher's organizational, facilitation, and relational skills

Ethics in Practice

The research design phase is a time to plan ahead—who will do what, how long things will take, and so forth. At no time is this more important than in CBPR. In order to create a collaborative, mutually beneficial, nonexploitive project that values multiplicity and maintains participants' investment in the project, build ample time into the design for planning, negotiating, debating, and cycling back to check in with each other, and adapt to new learning or to evolving needs or expectations. These phases of the design, as well as the ability to be flexible, are a part of ethical praxis.

REVIEW STOP 3

1. CBPR is problem-centered and often follows responsive designs. What is a responsive design?

2. Collaboration is at the heart of CBPR and helps ensure attention to cultural sensitivity. Why is this important?

3. CBPR values multiplicity and what three forms of knowledge?

☞ **Go to the end of the chapter to check your answers.**

Data Analysis and Interpretation

Data analysis and interpretation strategies are selected based on the methods or practices, which differ from project to project. Consult Chapters 4–7 for appropriate strategies for your methodology. Whereas the strategies selected depend on the methods used, there are a few components that permeate most projects: collaboration, theoretical frameworks, and transferability.

Like other phases of CBPR, the analysis and interpretation processes involve **collaboration** among research partners. These processes should follow an inclusive, participatory, and collaborative model. What this looks like in practice depends on the particulars of the study. For example, if survey research was used, it may be that the academic researchers or hired consultants are left to do the initial statistical analysis. How will the rest of the research partners be brought into the interpretation process? Perhaps they will be asked what they think the raw findings mean, which will help lead to theoretical frames by which to make sense of the data. In a qualitative interview and field research project, research partners and participants may be given their interview transcripts at various stages of analysis for feedback, discussion, and revision, as well as to negotiate the meanings drawn from the data. These are just examples. It is important that the findings are **credible** to all of the constituents involved.

Data are generally interpreted inductively through the lens of one or more **theoretical**

frameworks. Depending on the particulars of the study, theories may be brought in from any number of disciplines or area studies (e.g., feminist theories in psychology, critical race theories in sociology). In some cases, **theoretical triangulation** is used, which, as noted in Chapter 5, considers the data through more than one theoretical lens in order to allow different interpretations to emerge (Hesse-Biber & Leavy, 2011, p. 51).

Finally, although CBPR is intended to promote action or change in a specific context, often research teams have additional aspirations to use the research findings in other, similar contexts. **Transferability**—the ability to transfer research findings from one context to another—may therefore be a goal (Lincoln & Guba, 1985). As noted in Chapter 5, the extent to which you can transfer findings from one context to another depends on the similarity, or what Lincoln and Guba (1985) termed the "**fittingness,**" of the two contexts. The more similar the contexts are, the greater the extent to which you can transfer your findings from one to another, necessitating detailed, thick, vivid descriptions of the case at hand.

Representation and Dissemination

Because the interconnected issues of representation and dissemination are central to CBPR, the proposal should include a robust discussion. There are three main issues to consider, which, like other aspects of CBPR, overlap in practice: audience(s), accessibility, and authorship.

Because issues of **audience and accessibility** are intertwined, I review them together. CBPR typically has **multiple audiences,** which need to be identified. First, there is the community in which the research occurred. Optimally the research findings can be used to positively impact that community—a goal in CBPR. Second, there are multiple other possible audiences, depending on the nature of the project. These audiences may include adjacent communities, the public (or some segments of the public), and policymakers. CBPR is meant to produce **public scholarship** that is **useful** in one or more settings, and in one or more social or political conversations. Finally, there are academic audiences. Although academic audiences should not be the primary beneficiaries of CBPR, it is important to share research projects within the academy so that others may learn about the substantive knowledge gained as well as the methodology. You may write one or more peer-reviewed research articles out of the project to speak to academic audiences, but traditional academic writing is of little value to anyone outside of academia, so other formats are needed.

In order to benefit the relevant stakeholders—the audiences for your project—accessibility is paramount. Two aspects of research findings must be accessible: their content and their distribution (Leavy, 2011a). First, the findings need to be **understandable.** Prohibitive language and academic jargon should be avoided. Second, the findings need to be **distributed** through channels to which identified audiences (stakeholders) have access. These channels may include (Leavy, 2011a, p. 98):

- Local organizations, business, schools, religious centers, art galleries, or CBOs
- Radio

- The Internet
- Local and/or national newspapers
- Presentations at public meetings or in community locations
- Other venues likely to reach the target audiences

The importance of disseminating research findings in appropriate venues is evident in a 1986 Chicago-based fair housing project in which the team presented preliminary findings at a local conference that they organized and to which they invited many nonacademic stakeholders. Additionally, the team held a press conference during which they presented their findings to the media and public (Lukehart, 1997). Given the group's desire to impact public policy regarding fair housing and segregation, and to include the public in its own development process, inviting the media into the process was vital. In this regard, the press conference had the double effect of educating the public and putting pressure on local government to promote positive social change.

Because CBPR likely has multiple audiences, the research findings may be represented in **multiple and alternative formats** (alternative formats are those other than traditional research articles or scholarly book chapters) (Leavy, 2011a, pp. 98–99), such as:

- Pamphlets, newsletters, brochures, community board postings
- Podcasts
- Blogs, online articles or essays, photoblogs
- Op-eds
- Performances (theatre, music, dance)
- Poetry or spoken word readings
- Documentary films
- Visual art or photography
- Other forms

The issue of multiple formats or outcomes is interconnected with **authorship.** In CBPR the community (theoretically) may ethically "own" the results (Strand et al., 2003). Depending on the particular project, findings may have the potential to impact the community's development process, health care opportunities, or access to educational services. There may be public policy implications as well. Questions to consider:

- Who gets to represent the findings?
- How many representations will there be? Over what period of time?
- Who gets to disseminate the results?

Group research efforts carry many challenges in this regard, and it's imperative to come to understandings about these issues early in the process. Each partner's expectations should be discussed and an agreed-upon plan put in place. Questions to consider include:

- What are the expected coauthored outcomes of the project?
- Where will coauthored outcomes be disseminated?
- How will the writing and editing process occur in ways that are inclusive and fair to all partners?
- What rights do the various research participants have to represent and/or disseminate research results?
- How will issues of "the team" be dealt with/noted with respect to credit for the research?
- What expectations does each partner have?
- How will issues of informed consent, confidentiality, and anonymity be addressed, particularly when researchers from different disciplines and CBO partners may hold different norms regarding these issues?

Given the out-of-the-box thinking that is often required to best represent and disseminate CBPR findings, an example is provided. The Tampa Bay Community Cancer Network (TBCCN) was established to study cancer disparities in Florida and create effective health interventions in multiethnic, medically underserved communities. The TBCCN partnered with local organizations and piloted several studies. One study, conducted by Meade et al. (2009), addressed the issue of providing early screening for prostate cancer, which is the second leading kind of cancer afflicting African American men, who have both a higher incidence and mortality rate than any other group (Meade et al., 2009). The study involved the development of a research initiative and an outreach component.

Researchers identified the need to create cancer awareness materials that could be easily accessed and understood by the target population. They wrote: "Cancer awareness materials such as brochures, booklets, and fact sheets are valuable tools used to disseminate information to the community; however, many materials are not always culturally and literacy appropriate nor easily accessible to all population groups" (Meade et al., 2009, p. 5). Therefore, they decided to construct a three-part study. In the first phase of the project, the researchers aimed to develop customized cancer awareness materials that would be accessible and understandable to the relevant community. The research team partnered with local barbers in order to develop the materials and a protocol for distributing them. The researchers elected to carry out the project at barber shops because they were known to attract large numbers of African American men in the participating communities. Preliminary research also showed this venue to be a "trustworthy" site within the community, with trust being previously identified as a major hurdle when conducting health research with this population. In the second phase of the research, the team developed a "lay health advisor training curriculum" to prepare the barbers to distribute the materials. During this phase of the research, the curriculum was put into practice and the participating barbers were trained. The final phase of the research consisted of an assessment regarding the feasibility of using barbers to distribute health information and whether or not that would lead to discussions about cancer screening options with the participants' health care providers (Meade et al., 2009). This pilot project also propelled additional efforts: for example, creating a "Barbershop Advisory Council" and taking steps to maintain the availability of the cancer awareness materials and "information stations in the barber shops" (Meade et al., 2009).

 Ethics in Practice

The representation and dissemination stage is critical to ethical practice, given the social justice imperatives driving CBPR as well as the mandate to democratize the knowledge-building process. There are a host of questions you can consider. Have you contemplated issues of audience, identifying the most relevant potential audiences for the research? Are the findings accessible to those audiences? Are the findings understandable and available in appropriate venues? Have you engaged with multiple and appropriate formats as warranted by the project? Has the project contributed to public scholarship by being useful in one or more settings beyond the academy? Have issues of authorship, credit, and ownership of the findings been addressed equitably?

Public Policy

Public policies are plans of action that may carry widespread consequences for the communities that they impact (Wedel, Shore, Feldman, & Lathrop, 2005). As policies are often politically motivated, the public they most affect is often left out of the process. Policies typically deal with how the state relates to local populations/communities (Wedel et al., 2005), making the need for community involvement obvious. In order to participate in policy-making processes, the public needs to be engaged in shaping the policy agenda (McTeer, 2005). CBPR is an avenue for doing so. Impacting the policy-making process is difficult; however, it is an important extension of many CBPR practices. CBPR can generate data that can be used to lobby for changes in current policies. Bear in mind that "policy makers create and implement policy out of or along with, *already existing* programmes" (Carlsson, 2000, p. 202). CBPR projects can therefore be designed to examine the impact of current policies on particular communities and how those policies could be improved for the public good. For example, policies regarding public school lunches have received considerable media attention in recent years as a result of dramatic increases in childhood obesity. CBPR projects, such as the development and subsequent testing of a culturally competent food intervention in rural African American communities, can yield important insights into how to best create policies that serve local populations.

Let's look at the landmark 1986 CBPR study on community development and segregation in Chicago briefly referred to earlier. The research goals were "to document progress made in fair housing work, evaluate ongoing fair housing programs, and identify factors related to the persistence of segregation in some areas. The goal was to further the development of fair housing as an integral part of healthy communities" (Lukehart, 1997, p. 48.). The research team included the Leadership Council for Metropolitan Open Communities (a Chicago-based fair housing organization that began in the 1960s) as well as 12 academic researchers and several members of the Chicago Area Fair Housing Alliance (CAFHA) (Lukehart, 1997, p. 47). The team of CBO professionals, activists, academic researchers, and community members was actively involved during all phases of the research. Initially the large team participated in a series of meetings to discuss issues and identify research needs (Lukehart, 1997). This process led to the development of nine research projects. Due to the impressive and diverse group of people brought into the project, the research received considerable funding (Lukehart, 1997). The large group broke down into subgroups, each comprised of academic and community stakeholders that organized around each of the nine projects (Lukehart, 1997). Each team identified their research issue and determined an appropriate plan of action; however, the larger group was used as a "sounding board" throughout the process (Lukehart, 1997, p. 48). Research teams relied on a variety of quantitative and qualitative methods, including census data, policy analysis, structured interviews, unstructured interviews, document analysis, and participatory evaluation research (Lukehart, 1997). In order to continue the process of rich collaboration and multiplicity, each research team drafted a report about their findings, which was distributed to the entire team for feedback (Lukehart, 1997). The group then held a conference at the University of Chicago and invited additional stakeholders, such as members of government, community leaders, and activists, to offer feedback (Lukehart, 1997). This responsive process of feedback loops led to writing the final reports. Ultimately, the project was used to positively impact public policy regarding fair housing in Chicago—the primary goal of the project.

Ethics Statement

CBPR necessarily has a moral, social justice, and social action imperative. As such, the ethics statement provides a **robust discussion of the ethical substructure** of the project, addressing your values system, ethical praxis, and reflexivity.

Begin by clarifying the **values system** guiding your research. Possible topics to address include (as applicable) the social justice imperative driving topic selection and problem formulation; the principles of collaboration driving problem formulation and all other phases of the project (how community needs have been identified and remained central); the differently positioned community stakeholders involved in the project; attention to whose interests are served by the research; a focus on underrepresented groups and/or marginalized groups facing systemic inequality; attention to cultural competence; attention to power sharing; and how the project is being used to promote positive social change and/or impact public policy.

Next provide a detailed discussion of your attention to **ethical praxis.** Topics to address include (as applicable) the status of necessary IRB approvals; informed consent (explaining the risks and benefits of participation, the voluntary nature of participation, confidentiality, and participants' right to ask questions); relational ethics (involving collaborative, respectful, power-sharing relationships based on mutual concern around a central problem and commitment to the project); and the representation and dissemination of findings (multiple and accessible formats and venues of distribution, coauthorship, efforts toward public scholarship, and efforts to impact public policy).

Finally, describe how you will practice **reflexivity.** Topics to address include (as applicable) your attention to power and power-sharing issues in the research process (via attempts to structure collaborative, nonhierarchical relationships with research partners and participants); attention to issues of privilege and insider–outsider statuses; and efforts to avoid colonizing or exploiting research partners or participants (i.e., the researcher is not the authoritative voice; avoids "drive-by" scholarship; avoids voyeurism of disenfranchised communities; and works sensitively with vulnerable populations).

 REVIEW STOP 4

1. In order to make certain the research findings are credible to all of the constituents involved, the analysis and interpretation processes should follow what kind of model?

2. CBPR is meant to produce public scholarship and therefore must be *accessible* in which two aspects?

3. How can CBPR be used to engage people in policy-making processes?

4. A CBPR ethics statement addresses the researcher's values system, ethical practice, and reflexivity. Identify two of the topics that might be addressed in the section on reflexivity.

☛ **Go to the end of the chapter to check your answers.**

References

See Chapter 4.

Appendices

Proposed Budget (If Applicable)

If the research is funded or you are seeking funding, include a detailed proposed budget. The budget may include the cost of equipment (audio recorders, tapes, pens/

paper, computer-assisted quantitative and/or qualitative data analysis software); payments to participants (including reimbursement for travel expenses); the cost of reproducing documents; and any other anticipated expenses. In well-funded research, you may be hiring experts or assistants, such as transcribers to transcribe interview data or consultants to analyze survey data; however, students and novices typically do this work themselves.

Recruitment Letter and Informed Consent Document

If you are working with participants, include these documents.

Instruments (If Applicable)

If you have created any data collection instruments (e.g., interview guide, experimental intervention, survey), include them.

Conclusion

As reviewed in this chapter, CBPR is used to promote community-driven change or action. CBPR involves forming research partnerships with nonacademic stakeholders around a community-identified problem or issue. CBPR values collaboration, power sharing, and different kinds of knowledge. This is a problem-centered approach that emphasizes community participation, collaboration, and the democratization of knowledge-building processes.

Here is a brief summary of the template for a CBPR design.

Title: Includes the phenomenon and the community of interest.

Abstract: This 150- to 200-word overview should be composed at the end. Includes the main problem or issue, the stakeholders, community partners, participants and setting, the research purpose and questions, basic information about the methods, and the social action agenda.

Keywords: Provides five to six words a reader would Google to find your study, including the main problem or issue, the community and stakeholders, and the CBPR design.

The Problem or Issue: Identifies the problem or issue at the center of the research, as agreed upon by the research team and determined with ample community input.

Literature Review: Provides a problem-centered interdisciplinary or transdisciplinary synthesis of the most relevant research on your topic, looking for or creating synergies across different bodies of knowledge in order to facilitate problem development.

Research Purpose Statement: Outlines the primary purpose or goals of your study as well as the stakeholders, participants, setting, methodology, and rationale. The research purpose may involve phases and may make room for evolution and adaptation as the project progresses.

Research Questions: Provides one to three collectively generated open-ended and change-oriented questions your project aims to address. There may be additional subquestions.

Philosophical Statement: Discusses how the project is situated in the transformative paradigm as well as any particular theoretical school of thought guiding the project.

Setting(s) and Participants: Discusses where the research will occur (formal and informal community settings). Describes the relevant stakeholders, the research team, and traditional participants (each as applicable). When describing the participants, include their demographics and membership in the "community," as you define it, and the sampling strategy that will be used to locate them.

Design and Methods: Describes in detail the strategies you will use to collect or generate data, making note of how you will address the primary issues associated with the method you are employing. Also describes how you will adhere to the major principles of CBPR, which include a problem-centered orientation, collaboration, cultural sensitivity, social action and social justice, recruitment and retention, trust and rapport, multiplicity, and flexibility and innovation.

Data Analysis and Interpretation: Describes in detail the strategies you will use to analyze and interpret your data, employing the principle of collaboration and the use of theoretical frameworks (as applicable).

Representation and Dissemination: Identifies your intended audiences and the selected formats and venues of distribution that are accessible to those audiences. Notes any efforts at public scholarship and impacting public policy (as applicable).

Ethics Statement: Discusses the ethical substructure of your project, addressing your values system, ethical praxis, and reflexivity.

References: Includes a full list of citations, properly crediting all those from whom you've borrowed ideas or quoted. Follow your university reference style guidelines (if applicable) or the norms within your discipline.

Appendices: Includes your proposed timeline, budget, and copies of your recruitment letter, informed consent, and copies of any instruments (e.g., interview guide, experimental intervention, survey) (if applicable).

☑ REVIEW STOP ANSWER KEY

Review Stop 1

1. those parties who have a vested interest in the topic
   a. collaborators/coinvestigators/community partners
2. community advisory board (CAB)
   a. formulating the problem and developing a culturally competent approach to investigating it
3. because you are seeking literature in multiple fields (must immerse yourself in these literatures, seek expertise as needed, and take an inventory of the relevant inter- or transdisciplinary literature).

Review Stop 2

1. to promote a specific community change or action
2. transformative
   a. human rights, social justice, participatory, action-oriented, power-reflexive, empowering/emancipatory/transformative
3. informal
4. purposeful
   a. snowball sampling

Review Stop 3

1. a design that follows the principle of recursiveness, whereby the team cycles back, repeats steps, and adapts to new insights
2. Research must be sensitive to the community's cultural definitions and understandings as well as to the intervention strategies that are likely to be effective with the relevant population.
3. experiential, scientific, lay

Review Stop 4

1. inclusive, participatory, and collaborative
2. content (understandable, no prohibitive language or jargon) and distribution (appropriate channels to which identified audiences/stakeholders have access)
3. by generating data that can be used to lobby for changes in current policies (studying the impact of current policies on particular communities and how those policies might be improved)

4. attention to power and power sharing; attention to privilege and insider–outsider statuses; avoiding colonizing or exploiting research partners or participants

Further Engagement

1. Select a research topic in which you are interested and do the following:

a. Identify all of the relevant stakeholders.

b. Identify the relevant bodies of literature (disciplines/subject areas).

c. Identify potential community partners.

Although you aren't carrying out this research, just identifying the stakeholders, the bodies of literature, and the potential community partners will give you a sense of the complexity of initial topic formulation.

2. Get a peer-reviewed published CBPR study and evaluate the methodology based on:

a. The nine core principles of CBPR (two to three sentences on each)

b. The evaluation criteria for the specific methods used in the study (one to two paragraphs)

c. What worked well and what could be improved upon (one to two paragraphs)

3. Practice writing a blog or op-ed (common forms of public scholarship). The goal of this exercise is to get you in the habit of writing accessibly, not to publish your piece. If you have conducted research, using any research method, write a piece intended for popular audiences about your research. If you have not conducted research, select a current event of interest. The topic doesn't matter. This exercise is about writing accessibly. Op-eds are ideally 600–800 words. I suggest a four-paragraph format: The opening paragraph introduces the topic with a hook or something catchy, the second and third paragraphs present the information or arguments, and the fourth paragraph recaps the piece with a final, strong statement with which to leave the reader. Don't forget to give your piece a catchy title.

Resources

Caine, V., & Mill, J. (2015). *Essentials of community-based research*. Walnut Creek, CA: Left Coast Press/Routledge.

Hacker, K. (2013). *Community-based participatory research*. Thousand Oaks, CA: Sage.

Leavy, P. (2011). *Essentials of transdisciplinary research.* Walnut Creek, CA: Left Coast Press/Routledge.

Tuhiwai Smith, L. (2012). *Decolonizing methodologies: Research and indigenous peoples* (2nd ed.). Chicago: Zed Books.

Suggested Journals

Action Research (SAGE)
http://arj.sagepub.com

Health Education & Behavior (SAGE)
http://heb.sagepub.com

Progress in Community Health Partnerships: Research, Education, and Action (Johns Hopkins University Press)
www.press.jhu.edu/journals/progress_in_community_health_partnerships

Note

1. Although these terms carry slight differences in how they are used, with different researchers preferring different terms and definitions, the terms all signify a general set of beliefs and practices. See Boyd (2014) for a full list of terms used to refer to CBPR, or something like it.

GLOSSARY

Abstract	150- to 200-word overview of the study.
Aesthetic intervention	A methodological strategy created by bell hooks (1995) for researching the capability of art to jolt people into seeing differently.
Aesthetic power	An arts-based evaluation criterion that is created through the incisiveness, concision, and coherence of the final artistic output (Barone & Eisner, 2012; Chilton & Leavy, 2014).
Art journaling	A visual arts practice in which participants create visual journals that may include text and images such as magazine clippings or drawings (Chilton & Leavy, 2014).
Artificial setting	A research setting in which the participants and researcher would not otherwise be at that time (e.g., a lab, the researcher's office, a private room in a public library, the participant's home).
Aesthetic intersubjective paradigm	A philosophical belief system, developed at the intersection of the arts and sciences, that proposed the ability of the arts to access that which is otherwise out of reach; values preverbal ways of knowing, including sensory, emotional, perceptual, kinesthetic, and imaginal forms of knowledge (Chilton et al., 2015; Conrad & Beck, 2015; Cooper et al., 1997; Dewey, 1934; Langer, 1953; Harris-Williams, 2010; Whitfield, 2005).
Arts-based research (ABR)	An approach to research that adapts the tenets of the creative arts in a social research project to address social research questions in holistic and engaged ways; a generative approach that places the inquiry process at the center and values aesthetic understanding, evocation, and provocation.
Audience(s)	Those who read or consume the research findings.
Authorities or experts	Sources from whom we gain knowledge in daily life, including individuals we know personally such as our parents or guardians, friends, and teachers.

Autoethnography	A method whereby the researcher uses his/her personal experience as data and connects these experiences to larger cultural contexts.
Bar and line graphs	A visual way of illustrating one or more categorical variables that are the independent variables and one continuous variable that is the dependent variable. Typically, the independent variable(s) are on the x-axis (horizontal) and the dependent variable is on the y-axis (vertical) (Fallon, 2016).
CAQDAS	Computer-assisted qualitative data analysis. There are numerous programs, including NVivo, MAXQDA, ATLAS.ti, Deedoose, Ethnograph, Qualrus, HyperRESEARCH, and NUD*IST.
Coding	In qualitative research, a process of analysis that allows for the reduction and classification of the generated data. Coding is the process of assigning a word or phrase to segments of data. The code selected should summarize or capture the essence of that segment of data (Saldaña, 2009). Coding may be done by hand or using computer-assisted software (CAQDAS).
• Categorizing	The process of grouping similar or seemingly related codes together (Saldaña, 2014).
• Descriptive coding	A strategy that mainly uses nouns to summarize segments of data (Saldaña, 2014).
• *In vivo* coding	A strategy that relies on using participants' exact language to generate codes (Strauss, 1987).
• Memo writing	Thinking and systematically writing about the coded and categorized data; memos form a link between coding and interpretation (Hesse-Biber & Leavy, 2005, 2011).
• Values coding	A strategy that focuses on conflicts, struggles, and power issues (Saldaña, 2014).
Collage	A visual arts practice made by selecting images from magazines, newspapers, textured papers, or other sources and then cutting, placing, and attaching them (often with glue) to a surface, such as a piece of paper or cardboard (Chilton & Scotti, 2013).
Community advisory board (CAB)	Composed of members of the community whose perspectives are incorporated into a CBPR project (Israel et al., 2005; Letiecq & Schmalzbauer, 2012).
Community-based participatory research (CBPR)	Involves collaborative partnerships between researchers and nonacademic stakeholders, which may include established community-based organizations (CBOs); community involvement characterizes every aspect of the research process from the identification of a problem to the distribution of research findings; a highly collaborative and problem-centered approach to research requiring power-sharing.
• Settings	Research may occur in formal or informal community settings. Formal community settings may include CBOs, nonprofits, and community centers. Parks and participants' homes are examples

of informal community settings. CBPR often occurs in multiple settings.

Community change or action	Research conducted with the aim of prompting community change, social action, or a community intervention (a purpose for social research).
Content analysis or document analysis	A method for systematically investigating texts/studying documented human communications (Adler & Clark, 2011; Babbie, 2013). Content analysis relies on nonliving data, which means noninteractive data that exist independent of the research and are thus considered naturalistic (Reinharz, 1992, pp. 147–148).
Context of discovery	A discussion in which the researcher accounts for his/her own role as a researcher in the research process.
Context of justification	An explanation and justification of the research design procedures and the methods employed.
Covert research	Research that employs deception in order to access a hard-to-reach group or subculture engaged in illicit activities.
Critical paradigm	A philosophical belief system that developed in interdisciplinary contexts, including areas studies and other fields forged in critique (e.g., women's studies, African American studies), and that politicizes research and emphasizes power-rich contexts, dominant discourses, and social justice (Hesse-Biber & Leavy, 2011; Klein, 2000; Leavy, 2011a). Includes several theoretical perspectives: feminist, critical race, queer, indigenous, postmodernism, and poststructuralism.
Cultural beliefs	A source from which we gain knowledge in daily life based on social–historical conditions.
Cultural competence	When conducting research on or with individuals with whom the researcher shares social or cultural differences, such as race, ethnicity, religion, social class or education, he/she is mindful of different cultural understandings or experiences and commonly used expressions and other ways of communicating, and uses nonoffensive and mutually understandable language.
Cultural sensitivity	In CBPR, researchers must be sensitive to the community's cultural definitions and understandings of key terms, as well as to creating interventions and strategies that are most likely to be effective with the relevant population.
Data analysis	"Summarizing and organizing data" (Trent & Cho, 2014, p. 652).
Debriefing	A phase of research in which the researcher garners feedback from the participants about their experience (Babbie, 2013).
Description (or descriptive research)	Describes individuals, groups, activities, events, or situations (a purpose for social research).

Descriptive statistics	Describe and summarize the data (Babbie, 2013; Fallon, 2016). There are three kinds of descriptive statistics: frequencies, measures of central tendency (mean, median, mode), and measures of dispersion (the standard deviation is the most commonly used measure of dispersion) (Fallon, 2016, pp. 16–18).
Dissemination	The sharing or distribution of the final representation of the research findings.
Element	The kind of person, group, or nonliving item in which the researcher is interested.
Elements of research	The building blocks of a research project, including the paradigm, ontology, epistemology, genre/design, methods/practices, theory, methodology, and ethics.
Epistemology	A philosophical belief system about how research proceeds, how one embodies the role of researcher, and how one understands the relationship between the researcher and the research participants (Guba & Lincoln, 1998; Harding, 1987; Hesse-Biber & Leavy, 2004, 2011).
Ethical substructure	Impacts every aspect of the research process (Hesse-Biber & Leavy, 2011; Leavy, 2011a) and contains dimensions on three levels: philosophical, praxis, and reflexivity. The philosophical dimension of ethics is based on each person's values system and addresses the question "What do you believe?" The praxis dimension of ethics addresses the question "What do you do?" The reflexivity dimension of ethics combines the philosophical and praxis and addresses the question "How does power come to bear?"
Ethics	Philosophical and praxis levels of research that include values, ethics, and reflexivity. Comes from the Greek word *ethos,* which means *character,* and incorporates morality, integrity, fairness, and truthfulness.
● Code of ethics	Discipline-specific ethical considerations provided by professional organizations.
● Conflicts of interest	Pressure or monetary gain to derive certain outcomes or research findings.
● First, do no harm	Adapted from the biomedical community, the primary principle governing the protection of research participants stating that no harm should come to research participants or, by extension, the research setting.
● Principle of mutuality	Research should benefit both the researchers and participants (Loftin et al., 2005).
● Relational ethics	Ethical issues that center on the interpersonal relationships between the researcher and participants (Ellis, 2007); refers to an "ethics of care" (Ellis, 2007, p. 4).

• **Risks and benefits**	The possible risks (physical, mental, emotional) and benefits associated with participation in the research, which are explained to participants ahead of time.
• **Situational ethics**	"Ethics in practice" (Ellis, 2007, p. 4).
Ethnodrama	Writing up research findings in dramatic or script form, which may or may not be performed.
Ethnography	A written text about culture.
Ethnotheatre	A performance-based practice in which an ethnodrama is performed for an audience.
Evaluation	To assess the effectiveness or impact of a program or policy; can also be considered a type of explanation (a purpose for social research).
Evaluation (qualitative)	Criteria used to assess a qualitative study or project, which should be applied as they relate to the study at hand.
• **Congruence**	How the various components of the project fit together (Whittemore et al., 2001).
• **Craft**	How the project has been conceived, designed, and executed (Leavy, 2011b, p. 155).
• **Explicitness**	Clear accounting of the methodological strategies employed (Leavy, 2011b; Whittemore et al., 2001).
• **Thoroughness**	The comprehensiveness of the project, including sampling, data collection, and representation (Whittemore et al., 2001).
• **Vividness**	Providing detailed and rich descriptions, highlighting the particulars of the data (Whittemore et al., 2001).
Evoke, provoke, or unsettle	To jar specified audiences (groups of people) into thinking about or seeing something differently; to promote new learning or create an awareness campaign (a purpose for social research).
Experimental research	The oldest form of quantitative research; a research method that relies on hypothesis testing, in which a test is created to see, in a controlled and systematic manner, if the predicted outcome occurs.
• **Control groups**	Used in experiments to mitigate against the effect of the experiment itself. Members of a control group are similar to those in the experimental group in all relevant factors, but they do not receive the experimental intervention (in some cases, they may receive a placebo).
• **Double-blind experiments**	Neither the subjects nor the researcher know which subjects are in the experimental group and which are in the control group.
• **Experimental groups**	Groups that receive the experimental intervention (also called the *experimental stimulus*).
• **Field experiments**	Occur in natural environments.

259

Experimental research (*continued*)

- Matching

  The process of creating pairs of research subjects who are similar based on a list of predetermined characteristics or on their scores on a pretest. Pairs of similar subjects are then split into different groups (one member of a pair is placed in the experimental group and one in the control group).

- Preexperimental designs

  Based on studying a single group that is given the experimental intervention (experimental groups only). Campbell and Stanley (1963) identify three types of preexperiments: the one-shot case study, one-group pretest–posttest design, and the static group comparison.

- Pretest

  Determines a subject's baseline measure in some area prior to introducing the experimental intervention.

- Posttest

  Given after the experimental intervention to assess its impact.

- Quasi-experimental designs

  Utilization of natural settings or groups, and thus subjects are not randomly assigned. Campbell and Stanley (1963) identify 10 types of quasi-experiments, three of which are the time-series experiment, the multiple time-series experiment, and the nonequivalent control group design.

- Randomization

  Randomly assigning subjects to the experimental and control groups.

- True experimental designs (or "classical experiments")

  Experiments based on randomization, with research subjects randomly assigned to experimental and control groups. Campbell and Stanley (1963) identify three types of true experiments: the pretest–posttest control group design, the Solomon four-group design, and the posttest-only control group design.

Explanation (or explanatory research)

To explain causes and effects, correlations, or why things are the way they are (a purpose for social research).

Exploration (or exploratory research)

To learn about a new or underresearched topic (a purpose for social research).

Fiction-based research (FBR), fiction as a research practice (FARP) or social fiction

A literary method of arts-based research in which one writes fiction as a process of inquiry or based on data collected with another research method. Within this practice, rewriting is an act of analysis.

Field research

The oldest qualitative genre, with roots in cultural anthropology. Research that occurs in natural settings, referred to as "the field." The result of field research is an ethnography.

- Ethnography—field notes

  The written or recorded notes of field observations. Types of field notes include on-the-fly notes, thick descriptions, summary notes, reflexivity notes, conversation and interview notes, and interpretation notes (Bailey, 1996, 2007; Hesse-Biber & Leavy, 2005, 2011).

- Ethnography—gatekeepers

  Enable or prevent the researcher from accessing the site and may be both formal and informal.

• Ethnography—insider–outsider status	Status characteristics that the researcher either shares in common, or does not share in common, with the participants.
• Ethnography—key informants	Participants who share not only their own experiences but also introduce the researcher to other possible participants and/or provide an overview of people and activities in the setting.
• Ethnography—memo notes	Extended notes in which researchers develop ideas about the data (field notes), synthesize the data, integrate ideas, and discern relationships within the data (Hesse-Biber & Leavy, 2005, 2011).
• Ethnography—nonparticipatory observation	The researcher observes the participants in the setting, typically over a long period of time, without engaging in the same activities as the participants.
• Ethnography—participatory observation	Requires the researcher to engage in the activities of those he or she is researching, typically over a long period of time, and to record systematic observations.
Genres or designs	Overarching categories of different ways of approaching research (Saldaña, 2011b).
Grounded theory	An inductive coding process in which data are analyzed, typically line by line, and code categories emerge directly out of the data (Charmaz, 2008).
Hawthorne effect	The effect on research subjects of their awareness that they are participating in a study.
Histograms	A visual way of relaying distributions for a single variable (Fallon, 2016).
Hypothesis	A statement predicting how variables relate to each other that can be tested through research.
• Directional hypothesis	Relies on prior research to make a prediction that there is a specific difference between two groups with respect to the variable being tested.
• Nondirectional hypothesis	Predicts a difference between two groups with respect to the variable being tested, but does not predict what that specific difference will be.
• Null hypothesis	Predicts no significant difference between two groups with respect to the variable being tested.
Indicators	On a survey, these are questions designed to assess each dimension of the variable under investigation.
Inferential statistics	Test the research questions or hypotheses and make inferences about the population from which the sample was selected (Adler & Clark, 2011).

261

Informed consent	Written consent from participants acknowledging that they understand the possible risks and benefits associated with participation in the research, that their participation is voluntary and confidential, and that they freely agree to participate.
● **Process consent**	Reaffirms consent from participants at multiple points during a lengthy study, including the voluntary nature of the study and participants' right to withdraw (Adams et al., 2015).
Institutional review board (IRB)	Established in universities to ensure that ethical standards are upheld and that human subjects are protected. Prior to contacting potential research participants or beginning any data collection, researchers must obtain IRB permission.
Integration	The incorporation of both quantitative and qualitative datasets in mixed methods research.
● **In mixed methods research— building the data**	The qualitative findings are used to build the quantitative phase of the study (Creswell, 2015, p. 83).
● **In mixed methods research— embedding the data**	One set of data is used to augment or support the other set of data (Creswell, 2015, p. 83).
● **In mixed methods research— explaining the data**	The qualitative data are used to explain the results of the quantitative data (Creswell, 2015, p. 83).
● **In mixed methods research— merging the data**	The quantitative and qualitative results are brought together and compared (Creswell, 2015, p. 83).
Interpretation	"Finding or making meaning" from the data (Trent & Cho, 2014, p. 652).
Interpretive or constructivist paradigm	A philosophical belief system that developed in disciplinary contexts and examines how people engage in processes of constructing and reconstructing meanings through daily interactions. The major theoretical schools of thought are symbolic interactionism, phenomenology, ethnomethodology, and dramaturgy.
Interview	A commonly used research genre across disciplines in which conversation is used as a data generation tool. Interview methods available to qualitative researchers include in-depth, semistructured, oral history or life history, biographic minimalist, and focus group formats.
● **In-depth interviews**	Inductive or open-ended interviews that range from unstructured to semistructured.
● **Levels of structure**	Interviews may range from unstructured to semistructured to highly structured.

Invitation letter or recruitment letter	A letter outlining the basics of the study and inviting individuals to participate (a first step toward obtaining informed consent).
Keywords	Five to six words or phrases one would Google if researching your topic online.
Landmark study	A research study/article that is considered pivotal in the field and should be included in a literature review. (If you find several research articles that all cite one earlier study, it is likely a landmark study.)
Literature map or concept map	Visual illustration of how all of the literature or concepts in a study are connected.
Literature review	"The process of searching for, reading, summarizing, and synthesizing existing work on a topic or the resulting written summary of the search" (Adler & Clark, 2011, p. 89).
Mean	The average value.
Median	The "middle" value.
Methodology	A plan for how research will proceed—how the researcher will combine the different elements of research into a plan that indicates, step by stop, how the specific research project will be carried out (merges theory and methods).
Mixed data analysis design	Involves the transformation of data from one form into another; can make it possible to discern complex relationships in the data and identify patterns (Hesse-Biber & Leavy, 2005, 2011).
Mixed methods research (MMR)	Involves collecting, analyzing, and integrating quantitative and qualitative data in a single project, resulting in a comprehensive understanding of the phenomenon under investigation.
Mixed methods research designs	There are four types: convergent or concurrent, explanatory sequential, exploratory sequential, and nested.
• **Convergent or concurrent**	Involves collecting both quantitative and qualitative data, analyzing both datasets, and then integrating the two sets of analyses in order to cross-validate or compare the findings (Creswell, 2015).
• **Explanatory sequential**	Begins with quantitative methods, which are followed by qualitative methods designed to explain the quantitative findings in-depth (Creswell, 2015).
• **Exploratory sequential**	Begins with exploring a topic through qualitative methods and then using the findings to develop a quantitative instrument and phase of the research study (Creswell, 2015).
• **Nested (also called intervention)**	One method is used as the primary method, and additional data are collected using the other, secondary method (Creswell, 2003; Hesse-Biber & Leavy, 2011). *Qualitative nested in quantitative designs* involve using a quantitative method, such as an experiment, as the primary method and nesting a qualitative component in the design. *Quantitative nested in qualitative designs* involve using a qualitative method, such as field research, as the primary method and nesting a quantitative component in the design.

Mixed sampling strategies	A two-phase sampling procedure, either combining two purposeful sampling strategies or combining probability and purposeful samples (Patton, 2015).
Mode	The most frequent value in the sample.
Natural setting	A research setting in which participants are in the setting regardless of whether or not research is occurring.
Null hypothesis significant testing (NHST)	A commonly used inferential statistics test.
Ontology	A philosophical belief system about the nature of the social world.
Operational definition	A definition of a variable as conceived in a study, including its constituent dimensions.
Paradigm	A worldview or framework through which knowledge is filtered (Kuhn, 1962; Lincoln et al., 2011).
Personal and sensory experiences	A source of knowledge in daily life based on one's own personal experiences, including what one sees, hears, smells, tastes, and touches.
Philosophical substructure	Comprised of paradigm, ontology, and epistemology and addresses the question "What do we believe?"
Philosophy of arts-based research	Recognizes art as able to convey truth(s) or bring about awareness (both knowledge of the self and of others); recognizes that the use of the arts is critical in achieving self/other knowledge; values preverbal ways of knowing; and includes multiple ways of knowing such as sensory, kinesthetic, and imaginary (Gerber et al., 2012, p. 41).
Photography	A widely used visual practice for chronicling, documenting, and eliciting data; engaging marginalized groups; and addressing hard-to-get-at, highly conceptual or metaphorical topics (Holm, 2014).
Photovoice	A practice that merges photography with participatory methods in which participants are given cameras and asked to photograph their environment and circumstances. Some refer to this as a method for conducting arts-based action research (Chilton & Leavy, 2014).
Pilot test	A complete run-through of the study.
Plot	The overall structure of a narrative in fiction or ethnodrama (Saldaña, 2003).
Population	A group of elements about which the researcher might later make claims.

Postpositivist paradigm	A philosophical belief system that originally developed in the natural sciences and espouses an objective, patterned, and knowable reality.
Power sharing	A core principle in CBPR used to maximize collaboration among all research partners and ensure that the research is mutually beneficial (Boyd, 2014).
Pragmatic paradigm	A philosophical belief system that developed at the start of the 20th century out of the work of Charles Sanders Peirce, William James, John Dewey, and George Hebert Mead (Hesse-Biber, 2015; Patton, 2015), which holds no allegiance to a particular set of rules or theories but rather suggests that different tools may be useful in different research contexts.
Praxis	Comprised of genre/design, methods/practices, theory, and methodology and addresses the question "What do we do?"
Probability sampling	The use of any strategy in which samples are selected in a way that every element in the population has a known and nonzero chance of being selected.
● Cluster sampling	A multistage sampling strategy. First, preexisting clusters are randomly selected from a population. Next, elements in each cluster are sampled (in some cases, all elements in each cluster are included in the sample).
● Simple random sampling (SRS)	A sampling strategy in which every element in the study population has an equal chance of being selected.
● Stratified random sampling	A sampling strategy in which elements in the study population are divided into two or more groups based on a shared characteristic (these groups are called *strata*). Then simple random, systematic, or cluster sampling are conducted on each strata.
● Systematic sampling	A sampling strategy in which the first element in the study population is selected randomly and then every *k*th element, after the first element, is selected.
Public policies	Plans of action that may carry widespread consequences for the communities that they impact (Wedel et al., 2005).
Public scholarship	Research that is accessible to relevant audiences outside of the academy.
Purposeful sampling (or purposive or judgment sampling)	A strategic approach to sampling involving the use of any strategy, based on the premise that seeking out the best cases for the study produces the best data, and that research results are a direct result of the cases sampled (Morse, 2010; Patton, 2015).
● Convenience sampling	A sampling strategy in which the researcher identifies participants based on their accessibility to him/her (Hesse-Biber & Leavy, 2011). Some suggest that this is not a true purposeful sampling strategy.
● Exemplar of the phenomenon of interest	A sampling strategy in which a single significant case is selected because it can provide a wealth of rich data that speak directly to the research purpose and questions (Patton, 2015, p. 266).

Purposeful sampling (*continued*)

- **Homogeneous sampling** — A sampling strategy in which cases are sought out because they share a common characteristic (Patton, 2015).

- **Heterogeneity sampling** — A sampling strategy in which cases are sought out because they differ on key characteristics (Patton, 2015).

- **Quota sampling** — A sampling strategy whereby the relevant characteristics of the population of interest and their overall presence in the population are identified. Then cases (participants) are selected to represent each of the relevant characteristics in the same proportion in which they are represented in the population.

- **Single significant case based on self-study** — A sampling strategy used in autoethnography, whereby the researcher makes him/herself the case under investigation (Patton, 2015).

- **Single significant case that is an exemplar** — A sampling strategy whereby a particularly robust case that promises to yield rich data is identified (Patton, 2015).

- **Snowball sampling (or chain sampling)** — A sampling strategy in which one case organically leads to another (Babbie, 2013; Patton, 2015).

Qualitative research — Generally characterized by inductive approaches to knowledge building aimed at generating meaning (Leavy, 2014); is used to learn about social phenomenon; robustly unpack the meanings people ascribe to activities, situations, events, people, or artifacts; or build a depth of understanding about some dimension of social life (Leavy, 2014). Results in a depth of understanding (detailed information from a small sample) and is generally appropriate when the primary purpose is to explore, describe, or explain.

Qualitizing — The process of transforming quantitative data into qualitative data (transforming quantitative variables into qualitative codes) in mixed methods research (Tashakkori & Teddlie, 1989). Used as a heuristic device only.

Quantitative research — Characterized by deductive approaches to the research process aimed at disproving or lending credence to existing theories; involves measuring variables and testing relationships between variables in order to reveal patterns, correlations, or causal relationships; results in statistical data (generally from a large sample).

Quantizing — The process of transforming qualitative data into quantitative data (transforming qualitative codes into quantitative variables) in mixed methods research. Used as a heuristic device only.

Rapport — The building of relationships with participants in field, interview, and CBPR research, through active listening and demonstrating care.

Reliability	The dependability/consistency of results.
● Interitem reliability	Consistency of results across multiple questions or indicators intended to measure a single variable.
● Interrater reliability	Consistency of results using two or more researchers/observers.
● Test–retest reliability	Consistency of results testing the measure with the same subjects twice.
Replication studies	Involve "the purposeful repetition of previous research to corroborate or disconfirm the previous results" (Makel & Plucker, 2014, p. 2).
● Conceptual replication	Different methods are used to study the hypothesis or theories (Makel & Plucker, 2014).
● Direct replication	The same methods are used to corroborate or disconfirm previous findings (Makel & Plucker, 2014).
Representation	The final presentation of research findings; may occur in multiple formats.
Research methods (or research practices)	Tools for data collection or generation (or content generation, respectively).
Research purpose statement	Specifically states the purpose or objective of the research project.
Research questions	Central questions that guide a research project.
● Arts-based research	These research questions are inductive, emergent, and generative. They often use words and phrases such as *explore, create, play, emerge, express, trouble, subvert, generate, inquire, stimulate, illuminate, unearth, yield*, and *seek to understand*.
● Community-based participatory research	These research questions are inductive, change-oriented, and inclusive. They often use words and phrases such as *co-create, collaborate, participatory, empower, emancipate, promote, foster, describe*, and *seek to understand from the perspective of various stakeholders*.
● Directional language	Uses words such as *cause, effect, determine, influence, relate, associate*, and *correlate*.
● Mixed methods research	An integrated set of research questions (Brannen & O'Connell, 2015; Yin, 2006), including at least one quantitative, qualitative, and mixed methods question. The mixed methods questions typically use relational language.
● Nondirectional language	Uses words and phrases such as *explore, describe, illuminate, unearth, unpack, generate, build meaning*, and *seek to understand*.
● Qualitative	These research questions are typically inductive and use nondirectional language.

Research questions (*continued*)

- **Quantitative**   These research questions are typically deductive and use directional language.

- **Relational language**   Uses words and phrases such as *synergistic, integration, connection, comprehensive, fuller understanding,* and *better understanding.*

Research topic (researchable topic)   A topic that can be studied via research.

Responsive designs   Follow the principle of recursiveness, which is an iterative research process whereby the team cycles back and repeats steps, checking data and adapting to new insights (Pohl & Hadorn, 2007).

Sample   The number of individual cases ultimately drawn and from whom data are generated.

Sampling   The process by which a number of individual cases are selected from a larger population, thereby determining who or what is in the study.

Sampling error   Occurs with a biased sample (a significant concern in survey research).

Saturation point   The point at which the researcher is not learning new information, and may even be losing clarity, by collecting additional data.

Scatterplots   A visual way of illustrating the relationship between two continuous variables (Fallon, 2016).

Significance, value, or worth   The relative importance or use of studying a particular topic (may include timeliness).

Social research   A systematic way of building knowledge about the social world and human experience.

Stakeholders   Those parties who have a vested interest in the research topic.

Storyline   The sequence of events within the plot in a work of fiction or ethnodrama (Saldaña, 2003).

Strength of the form   An arts-based evaluation criterion referring to how well the components of the project, including the final representation, fit together (Barone & Eisner, 2012).

Study population (or sampling frame)   The group of elements from which the sample is actually drawn.

Survey research	The most widely used quantitative design in the social sciences. Surveys rely on asking people standardized questions that can be analyzed statistically. They allow researchers to collect a breadth of data from large samples and generalize to the larger population from which the sample was drawn. Surveys are typically used for ascertaining individuals' attitudes, beliefs, opinions, or their reporting of their experiences and/or behaviors.
● Cross-sectional designs	One of two major methodological designs of surveys. They seek information from a sample at one point in time.
● Exhaustive	All of the possible responses a respondent might wish to select are available.
● Forced-choice or fixed-choice questions	Survey questions in which respondents are provided with a range of response options to select from.
● Longitudinal designs	One of two major methodological designs of surveys. They occur at multiple times in order to measure change over time. There are three types of longitudinal designs: repeated cross-sectional, fixed-sample panel design, and cohort study (Ruel et al., 2016).
● Mutually exclusive	There is no overlap in response items.
● Objective data	A term for "facts," because they can be ascertained from sources other than the particular respondent (Vogt et al., 2014).
● Respondent burden	Occurs to the degree that respondents experience their participation as too stressful and/or time consuming (Biemer & Lyberg, 2003; Ruel et al., 2016).
● Respondent fatigue	Is caused by respondent burden and leads to a higher nonresponse rate and lower quality responses (Ruel et al., 2016).
● Respondent inventory or respondent audit	Record to keep track of respondents and reduce the risk of multiple responses from one individual (Ruel et al., 2016). Each respondent can be assigned a number for anonymity.
● Response bias	The effect of nonresponses on the results.
● Questionnaires (or survey instrument)	The primary data collection tool in survey research.
● Subjective data	Can only be ascertained from the respondents (Vogt et al., 2014).
● Survey delivery	May be administered in person, online, by mail, or by telephone.
● Survey items	Questions in the questionnaire designed to help test the hypotheses or answer the research questions. The questions designed around each concept in the study serve to operationalize the variables, and the answers indicate whether a variable is or is not present.
● Two-column-table approach	A strategy for drafting survey questions.

Tables	A visual way of presenting data on any number of variables; can be used for descriptive or inferential statistics (Fallon, 2016).
Theory	An account of social reality that is grounded in data but extends beyond those data (Adler & Clark, 2011). Theories specify paradigms (Babbie, 2013).
Transferability	The ability to transfer research findings from one context to another (Lincoln & Guba, 1985). The extent to which findings from one context can be transferred to another depends on the similarity, or on what Lincoln and Guba (1985) termed the *fittingness* of the two contexts.
Transformative paradigm	A philosophical belief system that developed in transdisciplinary contexts and draws on critical theory, critical pedagogy, feminist, critical race, and indigenous theories. This worldview promotes a human rights, social justice, social-action-oriented, inclusive, participatory, and democratic approach to research (Mertens, 2009).
Translation	The process of moving from one form (medium) to another in arts-based research.
Triangulation	A commonly used strategy when multiple methods or sources of data are applied to address the same question (Greene, 2007; Greene et al., 1989; Hesse-Biber & Leavy, 2005, 2011).
• Data triangulation	Using multiple sources of data to examine an assertion (Hesse-Biber & Leavy, 2011, p. 51).
• Investigator triangulation	Having two or more researchers study the same topic and compare their findings (Hesse-Biber & Leavy, 2011, p. 51).
• Theoretical triangulation	Considering the data through more than one theoretical lens in order to allow different interpretations to emerge (Hesse-Biber & Leavy, 2011, p. 51).
Type I error	Occurs when the researcher infers that a relationship exists that *does not* exist (Adler & Clark, 2011).
Type II error	Occurs when the researcher does *not* infer a relationship that *does* exist.
Validation	A process of confidence building that occurs in community (Koro-Ljungberg, 2008) through the development of intersubjective judgment (Polkinghorne, 2007).
Validity	The extent to which a measure is actually tapping what the researcher thinks it is accessing.
• Face	A judgment call made by laypeople that the measure is tapping what it is intended to access.
• Construct	The measure is tapping into the concept and related concepts the researcher intends it to access, which requires the researcher to create highly specific operational definitions.

● Content	A judgment call made by experts that the measure is tapping what it is intended to access.
● Ecological	The findings are generalizable to a real-world setting.
● External	The findings have been generalized only to populations supported by the tests.
● Internal	Precautions have been taken to safeguard against the possibility that an extraneous variable influenced the results.
● Statistical	The statistical analysis chosen was appropriate and the conclusions drawn are consistent with the statistical analysis and the rules of statistical law.
Variable	A characteristic that can be different from one element to another or can change over time.
● Categorical variables	Variables whose categories have names and distinct classes.
● Continuous variables	Variables whose differences steadily progress and "preserve the magnitude of difference between values" (Fallon, 2016, p. 16).
● Covariates	Variables for which the researcher controls.
● Dependent variable	A variable that is affected or influenced by another variable.
● Extraneous variables	Variables that are not under investigation but may impact the data.
● Independent variable	A variable that likely affects or influences another variable.
● Intervening (or moderator or mediator) variable	A variable that can mediate the effect of the former on the latter.
Verisimilitude	The creation of realistic, authentic, and life-like portrayals.
Voice	An implicitly political term typically used to talk about the ability to speak and be heard (Hertz, 1997; Motzafi-Haller, 1997; Wyatt, 2006).

271

REFERENCES

Abbott, H. P. (2008). *The Cambridge introduction to narrative* (2nd ed.). Cambridge, UK: Cambridge University Press.

Ackroyd, J., & O'Toole, J. (2010). *Performing research: Tensions, triumphs and trade-offs of ethnodrama*. London: Institute of Education Press.

Adams, T. (2008). A review of narrative ethics. *Qualitative Inquiry, 14*(2), 175–194.

Adams, T. (2011). *Narrating the closet: An autoethnography of same-sex attraction*. Walnut Creek, CA: Left Coast Press/Routledge.

Adams, T., Holman Jones, S., & Ellis, C. (2015). *Autoethnography: Understanding qualitative research*. New York: Oxford University Press.

Adler, E. S., & Clark, R. (2011). *An invitation to social research: How it's done* (4th ed.). Belmont, CA: Wadsworth.

Agar, M. (1986). *Speaking of ethnography*. Beverly Hills, CA: SAGE.

Agar, M. (1996). *The professional stranger: An informational introduction to ethnography* (2nd ed.). New York: Academic Press.

Aguinaldo, J. P. (2004). Rethinking validity in qualitative research from a social constructionist perspective: From "is this valid research?" to "what is this research valid for?" *The Qualitative Report, 9*(1), 127–136.

Ahloranta, M., & Ahlberg, V. (2004, April). *What do concept maps reveal about pupils' learning and thinking?* Paper presented at the annual meeting of the National Association for Research in Science Teaching Annual Conference, Vancouver, British Columbia, Canada.

Allegranti, B. (2011). Ethics and body politics: Interdisciplinary possibilities for embodied psychotherapeutic practice and research. *British Journal of Guidance and Counseling, 39*(5), 487–500.

Babbie, E. (2013). *The practice of social research* (13th ed.). Belmont, CA: Wadsworth, Cengage Learning.

Bailey, C. A. (1996). *A guide to field research*. Thousand Oaks, CA: Pine Forge Press.

Bailey, C. A. (2007). *A guide to qualitative field research*. Thousand Oaks, CA: Pine Forge Press.

Banks, S. P. (2008). Writing as theory: In defense of fiction. In J. G. Knowles & A. L. Cole (Eds.), *Handbook of the arts in qualitative research* (pp. 155–164). Thousand Oaks, CA: SAGE.

Barone, T., & Eisner, E. (1997). Arts-based educational research. In R. M. Jaegar (Ed.), *Complementary methods for research in education* (Vol. 2, pp. 93–116). Washington, DC: American Educational Research Association.

Barone, T., & Eisner, E. (2012). *Arts based research*. Thousand Oaks, CA: SAGE.

Bengtson, V. L. (2000). *Longitudinal study of generations, 1971, 1985, 1988, 1991, 1994, 1997, 2000* [California] (ICPSR 22100-v2). Ann Arbor, MI: Inter-university Consortium for Political and Social Research.

Beren, S. E., Hayden, H. A., Wilfley, D. E., & Grilo, C. M. (1996). The influence of sexual orientation on body image in adult men and women. *International Journal of Eating Disorders, 20*(2), 135–141.

Berg, B. (2007). *Qualitative research methods for the social sciences.* New York: Pearson.

Biemer, P., & Lyberg, L. E. (2003). *Introduction to survey quality.* Hoboken, NJ: Wiley.

Biesta, G. J. J., & Burbules, N. C. (2003). *Pragmatism and educational research.* Lanham, MD: Rowman & Littlefield.

Blumenfeld-Jones, D. S. (2008). Dance, choreogrpahy, and social science research. In J. G. Knowles & A. L. Cole (Eds.), *Handbook of the arts in qualitative research: Perspectives, methodologies, examples, and issues* (pp. 175–184). Thousand Oaks, CA: SAGE.

Blumer, H. (1969). *Symbolic interactionism: Perspective and method.* Englewood Cliffs, NJ: Prentice Hall.

Bochner, A. P., & Riggs, N. (2014). Practicing narrative inquiry. In P. Leavy (Ed.), *The Oxford handbook of qualitative research* (pp. 195–222). New York: Oxford University Press.

Bolen, D. M. (2014). After dinners, in the garage, out of doors, and climbing on rocks. In J. Wyatt & T. E. Adams (Eds.), *On (writing) families: Autoethnographies of presence and absence, love and loss* (pp. 141–147). Rotterdam, The Netherlands: Sense Publishers.

Bordo, S. (1989). Feminism, postmodernism, and gender skepticism. In L. Nicholson (Ed.), *Feminism/postmodernism* (pp. 133–156). New York: Routledge.

Boyd, M. R. (2014). Community-based research: Understanding the principles, practices, challenges, and rationale. In P. Leavy (Ed.), *The Oxford handbook of qualitative research* (pp. 498–517). New York: Oxford University Press.

Brannen, J., & O'Connell, R. (2015). Data analysis: I. Overview of data analysis strategies. In S. Hesse-Biber & R. B. Johnson (Eds.), *The Oxford handbook of multimethod and mixed methods research inquiry* (pp. 257–274). New York: Oxford University Press.

Brinkmann, S. (2012). *Qualitative inquiry in everyday life: Working with everyday life materials.* London: SAGE.

Brinkmann, S. (2013). *Qualitative interviewing.* New York: Oxford University Press.

Bruch, H. (1978). *The golden cage: The enigma of anorexia nervosa.* Cambridge, MA: Harvard University Press.

Butler-Kisber, L. (2010). *Qualitative inquiry: Thematic, narrative and arts-informed perspectives.* Thousand Oaks, CA: SAGE.

Cahnmann-Taylor, M., & Siegesmund, R. (2008). *Arts-based research in education: Foundations for practice.* New York: Routledge.

Cammarota, J., & Fine, M. (2008). Youth participatory action research: A pedagogy for transformational resistance. In J. Cammarota (Ed.), *Revolutionizing education: Youth participatory action research in motion* (pp. 1–11). New York: Routledge.

Campbell, D. T., & Fiske, D. W. (1959). Convergent and discriminant validation by the multitrait–multimethod matrix. *Psychological Bulletin, 56*(2), 81–105.

Campbell, D. T., & Stanley, J. C. (1963). *Experimental and quasi-experimental designs for research.* Chicago: Rand McNally.

Caracelli, V. J., & Greene, J. (1993). Data analysis strategies for mixed-method evaluation designs. *Educational Evaluation and Policy Analysis, 15*(2), 195–207.

Carlsson, L. (2001). Non-hierarchical evaluation of policy. *Evaluation, 6*(2), 201–216.

Caulley, D. N. (2008). Making qualitative research reports less boring: The techniques of writing creative nonfiction. *Qualitative Inquiry 4*(3), 424–449.

Charmaz, K. (2008). Grounded theory as an emergent method. In S. N. Hesse-Biber & P. Leavy (Eds.), *Handbook of emergent methods* (pp. 155–170). New York: Guilford Press.

Chilton, G., Gerber, N., & Scotti, V. (2015). Towards an aesthetic intersubjective paradigm for arts based research: An art therapy perspective. *UNESCO Observatory Multidisciplinary Journal in the Arts, 5*(1). Available at *www.unescomelb.org/volume-5-issue-1-1/2015/9/14/06-chilton-towards-an-aesthetic-intersubjective-paradigm-for-arts-based-research-an-art-therapy-perspective*.

Chilton, G., & Leavy, P. (2014). Arts-based research practice: Merging social research and the creative arts. In P. Leavy (Ed.), *The Oxford handbook of qualitative research* (pp. 403–422). New York: Oxford University Press.

Chilton, G., & Scotti, V. (2013). Snipping, gluing, and writing: An exploration of collage as arts-based research practice. Available at *www.academia.edu/4356991/Snipping_Gluing_and_Meaning-making_Collage_as_Arts-Based_Research*.

Chilton, M., Rabinowich, J., Council, C., & Breaux, J. (2009). Witnesses to hunger: Participation through photovoice to ensure the right to food. *Health and Human Rights: An International Journal, 11*(1), 73–85. Available at *www.centerforhungerfreecommunities.org/sites/default/files/pdfs/Pub1_Witnesses_HHR.pdf*.

Chopyak, J., & Levesque, P. N. (2002). Community-based research and changes in the research landscape. *Bulletin of Science, Technology, and Society, 22*, 203–209.

Coffey, A. (1999). *The ethnographic self: Fieldwork and the representation of identity*. London: SAGE.

Cogan, J. C. (2001). Body norms in lesbian culture. *Gay and Lesbian Review Worldwide, 8*(4), 26–32.

Cohn, D. (2000). *The distinction of fiction*. Baltimore: Johns Hopkins University Press.

Cole, A. L., & Knowles, J. G. (2001). Qualities of inquiry: Process, form, and "goodness." In L. Nielsen, A. L. Cole, & J. G. Knowles (Eds.), *The art of writing inquiry* (pp. 211–229). Halifax, Nova Scotia, Canada: Backalong Books.

Cole, A. L., & Knowles, J. G. (2008). Arts-informed research. In J. G. Knowles & A. L. Cole (Eds.), *Handbook of the arts in qualitative research: Perspectives, methodologies, examples, and issues* (pp. 53–70). Thousand Oaks, CA: SAGE.

Conrad, D., & Beck, J. (2015). Toward articulating an arts-based research paradigm: Growing deeper. *UNESCO Observatory Multidisciplinary Journal in the Arts, 5*(1). Available at *www.unescomelb.org/volume-5-issue-1-1/2015/9/14/05-conrad-towards-articulating-an-arts-based-research-paradigm-growing-deeper*.

Cook, T. D., & Campbell, D. T. (1979). *Quasi-experimentation: Design and analysis issues for field settings*. Boston: Houghton Mifflin.

Cooper, D., Lamarque, P., & Sartwell, C. (1997). *Aesthetics: The classic readings*. New York: Wiley-Blackwell.

Crenshaw, K. (1989). Demarginalizing the intersection of race and sex: A black feminist critique of antidiscrimination doctrine, feminist theory, and antiracist politics. *University of Chicago Legal Forum, 140*, 139–167.

Creswell, J. W. (2003). *Research design: Qualitative and quantitative approaches* (2nd ed.). Thousand Oaks, CA: SAGE.

Creswell, J. W. (2014). *Research design: Qualitative, quantities, and mixed methods approaches* (4th ed.). Thousand Oaks, CA: SAGE.

Creswell, J. W. (2015). *A concise introduction to mixed methods research*. Thousand Oaks, CA: SAGE.

Creswell, J. W., & Plano Clark, V. (2011). *Designing and conducting mixed methods research*. Thousand Oaks, CA: SAGE.

Crotty, M. (1998). *The foundations of social research: Meaning and perspective in the research process*. Thousand Oaks, CA: SAGE.

Darbellay, I., Cockell, M., Billotte, J., & Waldvogel, F. (2008). Introduction: For a world knowledge dialogue. In I. Darbellay, M. Cockell, J. Billotte, & F. Waldvogel (Eds.), *A vision of transdisciplinarity: Laying foundations for a world knowledge dialogue* (pp. xix–xxix). Boca Raton, FL: CRC Press.

Datta, L. E. (1997). A pragmatic basis for mixed-methods designs. In J. C. Greene, & V. J. Caracelli (Eds.), Advances in mixed-methods evaluation: The challenges and benefits of integrating diverse paradigms. *New Directions for Evaluation, 74*, 33–46.

Davis, D. (2008). Collage inquiry: Creative and particular applications. *LEARNing Landscapes, 2*(1), 245–265.

De Freitas, E. (2003). Contested positions: How fiction informs empathetic research. *International Journal of Education and the Arts, 4*(7), 11–22. Available at *www.ijea.org/v4n7*.

De Freitas, E. (2004). Reclaiming rigour as trust: The playful process of writing fiction. In A. L. Cole, L. Neilsen, J. G. Knowles, & T. C. Luciani (Eds.), *Provoked by art: Theorizing arts-informed research* (pp. 262–272). Halifax, Nova Scotia, Canada: Backalong Books.

Denzin, N. K. (2003). Performing [auto]ethnography politically. *Review of Education, Pedagogy, and Curriculum Studies, 25*, 257–278.

Denzin, N. K., & Lincoln, Y. (2008). Introduction: Critical methodologies and indigenous inquiry. In N. Denzin, Y. Lincoln, & L. Tuhiwai Smith (Eds.), *Handbook of critical indigenous methodologies* (pp. 1–20). Thousand Oaks, CA: SAGE.

Derrida, J. (1966). The decentering event in social thought. In A. Bass (Trans.), *Writing and difference* (pp. 278–282). Chicago: University of Chicago Press.

Dewey, J. (1934). *Art as experience*. New York: Minton, Balch.

Diaz, G. (2002). Artistic inquiry: On Lighthouse Hill. In C. Bagley & M. B. Cancienne (Eds.), *Dancing the data* (pp. 147–161). New York: Peter Lang.

Dunlop, R. (2001). Excerpts from *Boundary Bay*: A novel as educational research. In L. Neilsen, A. L. Cole, & J. G. Knowles (Eds.), *The art of writing inquiry* (pp. 49–70). Halifax, Nova Scotia, Canada: Backalong Books.

Eberhardt, J. L., Davies, P. G., Purdie-Vaughns, V. J., & Johnson, S. L. (2006). Looking deathworthy: Perceived stereotypicality of Black defendants predicts capital-sentencing outcomes. *Psychological Science, 17*, 383–386.

Ellis, C. (2004). *The ethnographic I: The methodological novel about autoethnography*. New York: AltaMira Press.

Ellis, C. (2007). Telling secrets, revealing lives: Relational ethics in research with intimate others. *Qualitative Inquiry, 13*(1), 3–29.

Epel, E. S., Spanakos, A., Kasl-Godley, J., & Brownell, K. D. (1996). Body shape ideals across gender, sexual orientation, socioeconomic status, race, and age in personal advertisements. *International Journal of Eating Disorders, 19*(3), 265–273.

Etherington, K. (2007). Ethical research in reflexivity relationships. *Qualitative Inquiry, 13*(5), 599–616.

Fallon, M. (2016). *Writing quantitative research*. Rotterdam, The Netherlands: Sense Publishers.

Faulkner, S. L. (2009). *Poetry as method: Reporting research through verse*. Walnut Creek, CA: Left Coast Press.

Fine, M., Torre, M. E., Boudin, K., Bowen, I., Clark, J., Hylton, D., et al. (2003).

Participatory action research: From within and beyond prison bars. In P. Camic, J. E. Rhodes, & L. Yardley (Eds.), *Qualitative research in psychology: Expanding perspectives in methodology and design* (pp. 173–198). Washington, DC: American Psychological Association.

Ford, D. Y., & Toldson, I. (2015). American Educational Research Association "UnAREA" panel presentation, Chicago, IL.

Foucault, M. (1976). Power as knowledge. In R. Hurley (Trans.), *The history of sexuality: Vol. 1. An introduction* (pp. 92–102). New York: Vintage Books.

Fowler, F. J., Jr. (2009). *Survey research methods* (4th ed.). Thousand Oaks, CA: SAGE.

Fowler, F. J., Jr. (2014). *Survey research methods* (5th ed.). Thousand Oaks, CA: SAGE.

French, S. A., Story, M., Remafedi, G., Resnick, M. D., & Blum, R. W. (1996). Sexual orientation and prevalence of body dissatisfaction and eating disordered behaviors: A population-based study of adolescents. *International Journal of Eating Disorders, 19*(2), 119–126.

Funder, D. C., Levine, J. M., Mackie, D. M., Morf, C. C., Sansone, C., Zazire, S., et al. (2014). Improving the dependability of research in personality and social psychology: Recommendations for research and educational practice. *Personality and Social Psychology Review, 18*(1), 3–12.

Garfinkel, H. (1967). *Studies in ethnomethodology.* Englewood Cliffs, NJ: Prentice Hall.

Garoian, C. R. (2013). *The prosthetic pedagogy of art: Embodied research and practice.* Albany: State University of New York Press.

Geertz, C. (1973). *The interpretations of cultures.* New York: Basic Books.

Gerber, N., Templeton, E., Chilton, G., Cohen Liebman, M., Manders, E., & Shim, M. (2012). Art-based research as a pedagogical approach to studying intersubjectivity in the creative arts therapies. *Journal of Applied Arts and Health, 3*(1), 39–48.

Gergen, M. M., & Gergen, K. J. (2011). Performative social science and psychology. *Forum: Qualitative Social Research, 12*(1), Art II.

Gilgun, J. (2005). "Grab" and good science: Writing up the results of qualitative research. *Qualitative Health Research, 15*(2), 256–262.

Gilgun, J. (2014). Writing up qualitative research. In P. Leavy (Ed.), *The Oxford handbook of qualitative research* (pp. 658–676). New York: Oxford University Press.

Glaser, B. G., & Strauss, A. (1967). *The discovery of grounded theory: strategies for qualitative research.* New York: Aldine.

Goddard, T., Kahn, K. B., & Adkins, A. (2015). Racial bias in driver yielding behavior at crosswalks. *Transportation Research Part F: Traffic Psychology and Behaviour, 33*, 1–6.

Goffman, E. (1959). *The presentation of self in everyday life.* Edinburgh, Scotland: University of Edinburgh Social Sciences Research Centre.

Gramsci, A. (1929). Intellectuals and hegemony. In *Selections from the prison notebooks* (pp. 3–14). New York: International Publishers.

Gravetter, F. J., & Wallnau, L. B. (2013). *Statistics for the behavioral sciences* (9th ed.). Belmont, CA: Wadsworth.

Greene, J. C. (2007). *Mixed methods in social inquiry.* San Francisco: Jossey-Bass.

Greene, J. C., Caracelli, V. J., & Graham, W. F. (1989). Toward a conceptual framework for mixed-method evaluation designs. *Educational Evaluation and Policy Analysis, 11*, 255–274.

Greenwood, J. D. (1992). Realism, empiricism, and social constructionism. *Theory and Psychology, 2*, 131–151.

Grosz, E. (1994). *Volatile bodies: Toward a corporeal feminism.* Bloomington: Indiana University Press.

Guba, E. (1990). *The paradigm dialog.* Thousand Oaks, CA: SAGE.

Guba, E., & Lincoln, Y. (1998). Competing paradigms in qualitative research. In N. K. Denzin & Y. S. Lincoln (Eds.), *The landscape of qualitative research: Theories and issues* (pp. 195–220). Thousand Oaks, CA: SAGE.

Gutkind, L. (1997). *The art of creative nonfiction: Writing and selling the literature of reality.* New York: Wiley.

Haig, B. D. (2013). The philosophy of quantitative methods. In T. Little (Ed.). *The Oxford handbook of quantitative research methods: Vol. 1. Foundations* (pp. 7–31). New York: Oxford University Press.

Haney, C., Banks, C., & Zimbardo, P. (1973). Interpersonal dynamics in a simulated prison. *International Journal of Criminology and Penology, 1,* 69–97.

Haraway, D. (1991). *Simians, cyborgs, and women: The reinvention of nature.* New York: Routledge.

Harding, S. (1987). *Feminism and methodology.* Bloomington: Indiana University Press.

Harding, S. (1993). Rethinking standpoint epistemology: What is "strong objectivity"? In L. Alcoff & E. Potter (Eds.), *Feminist epistemologies* (pp. 49–82). New York: Routledge.

Harris, A. (2014). Ghost-child. In J. Wyatt & T. E. Adams (Eds.), *On (writing) families: Autoethnographies of presence and absence, love and loss* (pp. 69–75). Rotterdam, The Netherlands: Sense Publishers.

Harris-Williams, M. (2010). *The aesthetic development: The poetic spirit of psychoanalysis.* London: Karnac Books.

Heidegger, M. (1962). *Being and time* (J. Macquarrie & E. Robinson, Trans.). New York: Harper & Row. (Original work published 1927)

Heidegger, M. (1982). *The basic problems of phenomenology* (A. Hofstadter, Trans.). Bloomington: Indiana University Press. (Original work published 1927)

Hertz, R. (1997). *Reflexivity and voice.* London: SAGE.

Hesse-Biber, S. (1996). *Am I thin enough yet?: The cult of thinness and the commercialization of identity.* New York: Oxford University Press.

Hesse-Biber, S. (2010). *Mixed methods research: Merging theory with practice.* New York: Guilford Press.

Hesse-Biber, S. (2015). Introduction: Navigating a turbulent research landscape: Working the boundaries, tensions, diversity, and contradictions. In S. Hesse-Biber & R. B. Johnson (Eds.), *The Oxford handbook of multimethod and mixed methods research inquiry* (pp. xxxiii–liii). New York: Oxford University Press.

Hesse-Biber, S., & Johnson, R. B. (Eds.). (2015). *The Oxford handbook of multimethod and mixed methods research inquiry.* New York: Oxford University Press.

Hesse-Biber, S., & Leavy, P. (2004). *Approaches to qualitative research.* New York: Oxford University Press.

Hesse-Biber, S., & Leavy, P. (2005). *The practice of qualitative research.* Thousand Oaks, CA: SAGE.

Hesse-Biber, S., & Leavy, P. (Eds.). (2006). *Emergent methods in social research.* Thousand Oaks, CA: SAGE.

Hesse-Biber, S., & Leavy, P. (Eds.). (2008). *Handbook of emergent methods.* New York: Guilford Press.

Hesse-Biber, S., & Leavy, P. (2011). *The practice of qualitative research* (2nd ed.). Thousand Oaks, CA: SAGE.

Hill-Collins, P. (1990). Black feminist thought in the matrix of domination. In P. Collins (Ed.), *Black feminist thought: Knowledge, consciousness, and the politics of empowerment* (pp. 221–238). London: HarperCollins.

Ho, K. (2009). *Liquidated: An ethnography of Wall Street*. Durham, NC: Duke University Press.

Holm, G. (2008). Visual research methods: Where are we and where are we going? In S. N. Hesse-Biber & P. Leavy (Eds.), *Handbook of emergent methods* (pp. 325–342). New York: Guilford Press.

Holm, G. (2014). Photography as a research method. In P. Leavy (Ed.), *The Oxford handbook of qualitative research* (pp. 380–402). New York: Oxford University Press.

Holman Jones, S., Adams, T., & Ellis, C. (2013). *Handbook of autoethnography*. Walnut Creek, CA: Left Coast Press.

hooks, b. (1995). In our glory: Photography and black life. In b. hooks (Ed.), *Art on my mind: Visual politics* (pp. 54–64). New York: New Press.

Hunter, H., Lusardi, P., Zucker, D., Jacelon, C., & Chandler, G. (2002). Making meaning: The creative component in qualitative research. *Qualitative Health Research Journal, 12*(3), 388–398.

Husserl, E. (1963). *Ideas: General introduction to pure phenomenology* (W. R. Boyce Gibson, Trans.). New York: Collier. (Original work published 1913)

Ioannidis, J. P. A. (2005). Contradicted and initially stronger effects in highly cited clinical research. *Journal of the American Medical Association, 294*(2), 218–228.

Iser, W. (1997). The significance of fictionalizing. *Anthropoetics, III*(2), 1–9. Available at *www.anthropoetics.ucla.edu/ap0302/iser_fiction.htm*.

Israel, B., Eng, E., Schultz A., & Parker, E. (2005). *Methods in community-based participatory research for health*. San Francisco: Jossey-Bass.

Jeanty, G. C., & Hibel, J. (2011). Mixed methods research of adult family care home residents and informal caregivers. *Qualitative Report, 6*(3), 635–656. Available at *http://nsuworks.nova.edu/cgi/viewcontent.cgi?article=1081&context=tqr*.

Johnson, R. B., & Onwuegbuzie, A. J. (2004). Mixed methods research: A research paradigm whose time has come. *Educational Researcher, 33*(7), 14–26.

Jones, K. (2003). The turn to a narrative knowing of persons: One method explored. *Narrative Studies, 8*(1), 60–71.

Jones, K. (2006). A biographic researcher in pursuit of an aesthetic: The use of arts-based (re)presentations in "performative" dissemination of life stories. *Qualitative Sociology Review, 2*(1). Available at *www.qualitativesociologyreview.org/ENG/index_eng.php*.

Jones, K. (2010). *Seminar Performative Social Science. What it is. What it isn't* (script). Available at *www.academia.edu/4769877/Performative_SocSci_What_it_is_What_it_isnt_Seminar_script*.

Jones, K. (2013). Infusing biography with the personal: Writing *Rufus Stone. Creative Approaches to Research, 6*(2), 6–23. Available at *www.academia.edu/attachments/31739870/download_file*.

Kahn, K., & Davies, P. (2011). Differentially dangerous?: Phenotypic racial stereotypicality increases implicit bias among ingroup and outgroup members. *Group Processes and Intergroup Relations, 14*(4), 569–580.

Kay, L. (2009). *Art education pedagogy and practice with adolescent students at-risk in alternative high schools*. DeKalb: Northern Illinois University.

King, G. (2011). Ensuring the data-rich future of the social sciences. *Science, 331*, 719–721.

Klein, J. T. (2000). Integration, evaluation, and disciplinarity. In M. A. Somerville & D. J. Rapport (Eds.), *Transdisciplinarity: Recreating integrated knowledge* (pp. 49–59). Oxford, UK: EOLSS Publishers.

Koro-Ljungberg, M. (2008). Validity and validation in the making in the context of qualitative research. *Qualitative Health Research, 18*(7), 983–989.

Krimsky, S. (2000). Transdisciplinarity for problems at the interstices of disciplines. In M. A. Somerville & D. J. Rapport (Eds.), *Transdisciplinarity: Recreating integrated knowledge* (pp. 109–114.). Oxford, UK: EOLSS Publishers.

Kuhn, T. S. (1962). *The structure of scientific revolutions.* Chicago: University of Chicago Press.

Kvale, S., & Brinkmann, S. (2008). *Interviews: Learning the craft of qualitative research interviewing* (2nd ed.). Thousand Oaks, CA: SAGE.

LaJevic, L., & Spriggay, S. (2008). A/r/tography as an ethics of embodiment. *Qualitative Inquiry, 14*(1), 67–89.

Lakkis, J., Ricciardelli, L. A., & Williams, R. J. (1999). Role of sexual orientation and gender-related traits in disordered eating. *Sex Roles: A Journal of Research,41*(1–2), 1–16.

Lancelot, C., & Kaslow, N. J. (1994). Sex role orientation and disordered eating in women: A review. *Clinical Psychology Review, 14,* 139–157.

Langer, S. (1953). *Feeling and form: A theory of art.* New York: Scribner.

Lasker, R. D., Weiss, E. S., & Miller, R. (2001). Partnership synergy: A practical framework for studying and strengthening the collaborative advantage. *The Milbank Quarterly, 79,* 170–205.

Lather, P. (2000, July). *How research can be made to mean: Feminist ethnography out of the limits of representation.* Keynote address at International Drama in Education Research Institute, Ohio State University, Columbus, OH.

Leavy, P. (2009). *Method meets art: Arts-based research practice.* New York: Guilford Press.

Leavy, P. (2010). Poetic bodies: Female body image, sexual identity and arts-based research. *LEARNing Landscapes, 4*(1), 175–188. Available at *www.learninglandscapes.ca/images/documents/ll-no7-v-final-lr.pdf#page=175.*

Leavy, P. (2011a). *Essentials of transdisciplinary research: Using problem-centered methodologies.* Walnut Creek, CA: Left Coast Press/Routledge.

Leavy, P. (2011b). *Oral history: Understanding qualitative research.* New York: Oxford University Press.

Leavy, P. (2013). *Fiction as research practice: Short stories, novellas, and novels.* Walnut Creek, CA: Left Coast Press/Routledge.

Leavy, P. (2014). Introduction. In P. Leavy (Ed.), *The Oxford handbook of qualitative research* (pp. 1–14). New York: Oxford University Press.

Leavy, P. (2015). *Method meets art: Arts-based research practice* (2nd ed.). New York: Guilford Press.

Leavy, P., & Hastings, L. (2010). Body image and sexual identity: An interview study with lesbian, bisexual and heterosexual college age-women. *Electronic Journal of Human Sexuality, 13.* Available at *www.ejhs.org/volume13/bodyimage.htm.*

Leavy, P., & Scotti, V. (2017). *Low-fat love stories.* Rotterdam, The Netherlands: Sense Publishers.

Letiecq, B., & Schmalzbauer, L. (2012). Community-based participatory research with Mexican migrants in a new rural destination. *Action Research, 10*(3), 244–259.

Lincoln, Y. S., & Guba, E. G. (1985). *Naturalistic inquiry.* Beverly Hills, CA: SAGE.

Lincoln, Y., & Guba, E. (1989). *Fourth generation evaluation.* Newbury Park, CA: SAGE.

Lincoln, Y. S., & Guba, E. G. (2000). The only generalization is: There is no generalization. In R. Gomm, M. Hammersley, & P. Foster (Eds.), *Case study method: Key issues, key texts* (pp. 27–44). London: SAGE.

Lincoln, Y. S., Lynham, S. A., & Guba, E. G. (2011). Paradigmatic controversies: Contradictions, and emerging confluences revisited. In N. K. Denzin & Y. S. Lincoln (Eds.), *The SAGE handbook of qualitative research* (4th ed., pp. 97–128). Thousand Oaks, CA: SAGE.

Ling Pan, M. (2008). *Preparing literature reviews: Qualitative and quantitative approaches* (3rd ed.). Glendale, CA: Pyrczak.

Loftin, W. A., Barnett, S. K., Bunn, P. S., & Sullivan, P. (2005). Recruitment and retention of rural African Americans in diabetes research: Lesson learned. *The Diabetes Educator, 31*(2), 251–259.

Lott, J. (2013, October 28). Perspective: In defense of stand your ground laws. Available at *http://articles.chicagotribune.com/2013–10–28/opinion/ct-oped-1029-guns-20131029_1_ground-laws-blacks-ground-defense*.

Lukehart, J. (1997). Collaborative, policy-related research in the area of fair housing and community development. In P. Nyden, A. Figert, M. Shibley, & D. Borrows (Eds.), *Building community: Social science in action* (pp. 47–51). Thousand Oaks, CA: Pine Forge Press.

Makel, M. C. (2014). The empirical march: Making science better at self-correction. *Psychology of Aesthetics, Creativity, and the Arts, 8*, 2–7.

Makel, M. C., & Plucker, J. A. (2014). Facts are more important than novelty: Replication in the education sciences. *Educational Researcher, 43*(6), 304–316.

Makel, M. C., Plucker, J. A., & Hegarty, B. (2012). Replications in psychology research: How often do they really occur? *Perspectives in Psychological Science, 7*, 537–542.

Manders, E., & Chilton, G. (2013). Translating the essence of dance: Rendering meaning in artistic inquiry of the creative arts therapies. *International Journal of Education and the Arts, 14*(16), 1–17.

Manicas, P. T., & Secord, P. E. (1983). Implications for psychology of the new philosophy of science. *American Psychologist, 38*, 399–413.

Masini, E. B. (1991). The household, gender, and age project. In E. Masini & S. Stratigos (Eds.), *Women, households and change* (pp. 3–17). Tokyo, Japan: United Nations University Press.

Masini, E. B. (2000). Transdisciplinarity, Futures Studies, and Empirical Research. In M. A. Somerville & D. J. Rapport (Eds.), *Transdisciplinarity: ReCreating integrated knowledge* (pp. 117–124). Oxford, UK: EOLSS Publishers.

Maxwell, J. A. (1992). Understanding the validity in qualitative research. *Harvard Educational Review, 62*, 279–299.

Maxwell, J. A. (2004, April). *Realism as a stance for mixed methods research.* Paper presented at the annual meeting of the American Educational Research Association conference, Chicago, IL.

Maxwell, J. A. (2012). *Qualitative research design: An interactive approach* (3rd ed.). Thousand Oaks, CA: SAGE.

Maxwell, J. A., Chmiel, M., & Rogers, S. E. (2015). Designing integration in multimethod and mixed methods research. In S. Hesse-Biber & R. B. Johnson (Eds.), *The Oxford handbook of multimethod and mixed methods research inquiry* (pp. 223–239). New York: Oxford University Press.

Mayberry, M., Chenneville, T., & Currie, S. (2013). Changing the sounds of silence: A qualitative study of gay–straight alliances and school reform efforts. *Education and Urban Society, 45*(3), 307–339.

McTeer, M. (2005). Leadership and public policy. *Policy, Politics, and Nursing Practice, 6*(1), 17–19.

Mead, G. H. (1967). *Mind, self, and society from the standpoint of a social behaviorist.* Chicago: University of Chicago Press. (Original work published 1934)

Meade, C. D., Menard, J. M., Luque, J. S., Martinez-Tyson, D., & Gwede, C. K. (2009). Creating community–academic partnerships for cancer disparities research and health promotion. *Health Promotion Practice, 12*(3), 456–462.

Merianos, A. L., Vidourek, R. A., & King, K. A. (2013). Medicalization of female beauty: A content analysis of cosmetic procedures. *The Qualitative Report, 18,* 91–114.

Merleau-Ponty, M. (1962). *Phenomenology of perception* (C. Smith, Trans.). London: Routledge & Kegan Paul.

Merleau-Ponty, M. (1996). *Phenomenology of perception* (C. Smith, Trans.). London & New York: Routledge. (Original work published 1945)

Mertens, D. M. (2005). *Research and evaluation in education and psychology: Integrating diversity with quantitative, qualitative, and mixed methods* (2nd ed.). Thousand Oaks, CA: SAGE.

Mertens, D. M. (2009). *Transformative research and evaluation.* New York: Guilford Press.

Mienczakowski, J., Smith, L., & Morgan, S. (2002). Seeing words—hearing feelings: Ethnodrama and the performance of data. In C. Bagley & M. B. Cancienne (Eds.), *Dancing the data* (pp. 90–104). New York: Peter Lang.

Mills, G. E. (2007). *Action research: A guide for the teacher researcher.* Upper Saddle River, NJ: Pearson.

Minkler, M. (2004). Ethical challenges for the "outside" researcher in community-based participatory action research. *Health Education and Behavior, 31*(6), 684–697.

Mishler, E. G. (1990). Validation in inquiry-guided research: The role of exemplars in narrative studies. *Harvard Educational Review, 60*(4), 415–442.

Mishler, E. G. (2000). Validation in inquiry-guided research: The role of exemplars in narrative studies. In B. M. Brizuela, J. P. Stewart, R. G. Carrillo, & J. G. Berger (Eds.), *Acts of inquiry in qualitative research* (pp. 119–146). Cambridge, MA: Harvard Educational Review.

Montoya, M. J., & Kent, E. E. (2014). Dialogical action: Moving from community-based to community-driven participatory research. *Qualitative Health Research, 21*(7), 1000–1011.

Morgan, D. (1998). Practical strategies for combining qualitative and quantitative methods: Applications to health research. *Qualitative Health Research, 8,* 362–376.

Morgan, D. (2013). *Integrating qualitative and quantitative methods: A pragmatic approach.* Thousand Oaks, CA: SAGE.

Morrison, M. A., Morrison, T. G., & Sager, C. L. (2004). Does body satisfaction differ between gay men and lesbian women and heterosexual men and women?: A meta-analytic review. *Body Image, 1,* 127–138.

Morse, J. M. (1991). Approaches to qualitative–quantitative methodological triangulation. *Nursing Research, 40,* 120–123.

Morse, J. M. (2003). Principles of mixed methods and multimethod research design. In A. Tashakkori & C. Teddlie (Eds.), *SAGE handbook of mixed methods in social and behavioral research* (pp. 189–208). Thousand Oaks, CA: SAGE.

Morse, J. M. (2010). Sampling in grounded theory. In A. Bryant & K. Charmaz (Eds.), *The SAGE handbook of grounded theory* (pp. 229–244). London: SAGE.

Morse, J. M., & Niehaus, L. (2009). *Mixed methods design: Principles and procedures.* Walnut Creek, CA: Left Coast Press.

Motzafi-Haller, P. (1997). Writing birthright: On native anthropologists and the politics of representation. In D. Reed-Danahay (Ed.), *Auto/ethnography: Rewriting the self and the social* (pp. 195–222). Oxford, UK: Berg.

Norris, J. (2011). Towards the use of the "Great Wheel" as a model in determining the quality and merit of arts-based projects (research and instruction). *International Journal of Education and the Arts, 12,* 1–24. Available at *www.ijea.org/v12si1/index.html.*

Parker, R. S. (1990). Nurses stories: The search for a relational ethic of care. *Advances in Nursing Science, 13*(1), 31–40.

Patton, M. Q. (2002). *Qualitative research and evaluation methods.* Thousand Oaks, CA: SAGE.

Patton, M. Q. (2015). *Qualitative research and evaluation methods* (4th ed.). Thousand Oaks, CA: SAGE.

Pelias, R. J. (2004). *A methodology of the heart: Evoking academic and daily life.* Walnut Creek, CA: AltaMira Press.

Pfohl, S. (1992). *Death at the Parasite Café.* New York: St. Martin's Press.

Pfohl, S. (2007). The reality of social constructions. In J. A. Holstein & J. F. Gubrium (Eds.), *The handbook of constructionist research* (pp. 645–668). New York: Guilford Press.

Phillips, D. C., & Burbules, N. C. (2000). *Postpositivism and educational research.* Lanham, MD: Rowman & Littlefied.

Pink, S. (2007). *Doing visual ethnography.* London: SAGE.

Pinto, R. M. (2009). Community perspectives on factors that influence collaboration in public health research. *Health Education and Behavior, 20,* 1–18.

Pitman, G. E. (2000). The influence of race, ethnicity, class, and sexual politics on lesbians body image. *Journal of Homosexuality, 40*(2), 49–64.

Pohl, C., & Hadorn, G. H. (2007). *Principles for designing transdisciplinary research* (A. B. Zimmermann, Trans.). Munich, Germany: Oekom Gesell F. Oekolog.

Polkinghorne, D. E. (2007). Validity issues in narrative research. *Qualitative Inquiry, 13*(4), 471–486.

Rawana, J. S., Norwood, S. J., & Whitley, J. (2011). A mixed method evaluation of a strength-based bullying prevention program. *Canadian Journal of School Psychology, 26*(4), 283–300.

Reason, P., & Bradbury, H. (Eds.). (2008). *The Sage handbook of action reseach: Participative inquiry and practice.* Thousand Oaks CA: SAGE.

Reinharz, S. (1992). *Feminist methods in social research.* New York: Oxford University Press.

Richardson, L. (2001). Alternative ethnographies, alternative criteria. In L. Nelson, A. L. Cole, & J. G. Knowles (Eds), *The art of writing inquiry* (pp. 2502–2552). Halifax, Nova Scotia, Canada: Backalong Books.

Rieger, J. (2011). Rephotography for documenting social change. In E. Margolis & L. Pauwels (Eds.), *The Sage handbook of visual research methods* (pp. 132–149). London: SAGE.

Robson, C. (2011). *Real world research* (3rd ed.). West Sussex, UK: Wiley.

Roller, M. R., & Lavrakas, P. J. (2015). *Applied qualitative research design: a total quality framework approach.* New York: Guilford Press.

Rolling, J. H., Jr. (2013). *Arts-based research primer.* New York: Peter Lang.

Rose, D. (2000). Analysis of moving images. In M. W. Bauer & G. Gaskell (Eds.), *Qualitative researching with text, image and sound* (pp. 246–262). London: SAGE.

Ruel, E., Wagner, W. E., III, & Gilllespie, B. J. (2016). *The practice of survey research: Theory and applications.* Thousand Oaks, CA: SAGE.

Saldaña, J. (1999). Playwriting with data: Ethnographic performance texts. *Youth Theatre Journal, 14,* 60–71.

Saldaña, J. (2003). Dramatizing data: A primer. *Qualitative Inquiry, 9*(2), 218–236.

Saldaña, J. (Ed.). (2005). *Ethnodrama: An anthology of reality theatre.* Walnut Creek, CA: AltaMira Press.

Saldaña, J. (2009). *The coding manual for qualitative researchers.* Thousand Oaks, CA: SAGE.

Saldaña, J. (2010). Exploring the stigmatized child through theatre of the oppressed techniques. In P. Duffy & E. Vettraino (Eds.), *Youth and theatre of the oppressed* (pp. 45–62). New York: Palgrave Macmillan.

Saldaña, J. (2011a). *Ethnotheatre: Research from page to stage.* Walnut Creek, CA: Left Coast Press.

Saldaña, J. (2011b). *The fundamentals of qualitative research: Understanding qualitative research.* New York: Oxford University Press.

Saldaña, J. (2014). Coding and analysis strategies. In P. Leavy (Ed.), *The Oxford handbook of qualitative research* (pp. 581–605). New York: Oxford University Press.

Sandelowski, M., Volis, C. I., & Knafl, G. (2009). On quantizing. *Journal of Mixed Methods Research, 3*(3), 208–222.

Schmidt, S. (2009). Shall we really do it again?: The powerful concept of replication is neglected in the social sciences. *Review of General Psychology, 13,* 90–100.

Schutz, A. (1967). *Phenomenology of the social world.* Chicago: Northwestern University Press.

Scriven, M. (1998). The meaning of bias. In R. Davis (Ed.), *Proceedings of the Stake symposium on educational evaluation* (pp. 13–24). Urbana, IL: Urbana University Press.

Seale, C. (1999). Quality in qualitative research. *Qualitative Inquiry, 5*(4), 465–478.

Shadish, W. R., Cook, T. D., & Campbell, D. T. (2002). *Experimental and quasi-experimental designs.* Boston: Houghton Mifflin.

Share, T. L., & Mintz, L. B. (2002). Differences between lesbians and heterosexual women in disordered eating and related attitudes. *Journal of Homosexuality, 42*(4), 89–106.

Siever, M. D. (1994). Sexual orientation and gender as factors in socioculturally acquired vulnerability to body dissatisfaction and eating disorders. *Journal of Consulting and Clinical Psychology, 6*(2), 252–260.

Silver, C. (2010, April). *CAQDAS tools for visual analysis.* Paper presented at the Mixed Methods Seminar "Using Software Tools In Visual Analyses," Surrey, UK.

Silver, C., & Lewins, A. F. (2014). Computer-assisted analysis of qualitative research. P. In Leavy (Ed.), *The Oxford handbook of qualitative research* (pp. 606–638). New York: Oxford University Press.

Small, M. L. (2011). How to conduct a mixed methods study: Recent trends in a rapidly growing literature. *Annual Review of Sociology, 37,* 57–86.

Snowber, C. (2012). Dancing a curriculum of hope: Cultivating passion as an embodied inquiry. *Journal of Curriculum Theorizing, 28*(2), 118–125.

Spellman, B. A. (2012). Introduction to the special section: Data, data, everywhere . . . especially in my file drawer. *Perspectives on Psychological Science, 7,* 58–59.

Stiman, M., Leavy, P., & Garland, A. (2009). Heterosexual female and male body image and body concept in the context of attraction ideals. *Electronic Journal of Human Sexuality, 12.* Available at *www.ejhs.org/Volume12/BodyImage.htm.*

Stoeker, R. (2008). Challenging institutional barriers to community-based research. *Action Research, 6*(1), 49–67.

Strand, K., Cutforth, N., Stoecker, R., Marullo, S., & Donohue P. (2003). *Community-based research and higher education: principles and practices.* San Francisco: Jossey-Bass.

Strandmark, M., & Rahm, G. (2014). Development, implementation and evaluation of a process to prevent and combat workplace bullying. *Scandinavian Journal of Public Health, 42*(15 Suppl.), 66–73.

Strauss, A. (1987). *Qualitative analysis for social scientists.* Cambridge, UK: Cambridge University Press.

Striegel-Moore, R. H., Tucker, N., & Hsu, J. (1990). Body image dissatisfaction and disordered eating in lesbian college students. *International Journal of Eating Disorders 9,* 493–500.

Tashakkori, A., & Teddlie, C. (1989). *Mixed methodology: Combining qualitative and quantitative approaches.* Thousand Oaks, CA: SAGE.

Teddlie, C., & Tashakkori, A. (2009). *Foundations of mixed methods research: Integrating quantitative and qualitative approaches in the social and behavioral sciences.* Thousand Oaks, CA: SAGE.

Tashakkori, A., & Teddlie, C. (Eds.). (2010). *SAGE handbook of mixed methods in social and behavioral research* (2nd ed.). Thousand Oaks, CA: SAGE.

Tenni, C., Smith, A., & Boucher, C. (2003). The researcher as autobiographer: Analyzing data written about oneself. *The Qualitative Report, 8*(1), 1–12.

Torre, M. E., & Fine, M. (2011). A wrinkle in time: Tracing a legacy of public science through community self-surveys and participatory action research. *Journal of Social Issues, 67*(1), 106–121.

Tourangeau, R., & Yan, T. (2007). Sensitive questions in surveys. *Psychological Bulletin, 133*(5), 859–883.

Trent, A., & Cho, J. (2014). Evaluating qualitative research. In P. Leavy (Ed.), *The Oxford handbook of qualitative research* (pp. 677–696). New York: Oxford University Press.

Umoquit, M., Tso, P., Varga-Atkins, T., O'Brien, M., & Wheeldon, J. (2013). Diagrammatic elicitation: Defining the use of diagrams in data collection. *The Qualitative Report, 18,* 1–12.

Vaughan, K. (2008). Pieced together: Collage as an artist's method for interdisciplinary research. *International Journal of Qualitative Methods, 4*(1), 27–52.

Vogt, P. W., Vogt, E. R., Gardner, D. C., & Haeffele, L. M. (2014). *Selecting the right analyses for your data: Quantitative, qualitative, and mixed methods.* New York: Guilford Press.

Wang, C. (2005). Photovoice: Social change through photography. Available at *www.photovoice.com/method/index.html.*

Warschauer, M., Duncan, G. J., & Eccles, J. S. (2015). Inaugural editorial: What we mean by "open." *AERA Open, 1*(1), 1–2. Available at *http://ero.sagepub.com/content/1/1/2332858415574841.*

Wedel, J. R., Shore, C., Feldman, G., & Lathrop, S. (2005). Toward an anthropology of public policy. *ANNALS of the American Academy of Political and Social Science, 600,* 30–49.

Weiss, R. (1994). *Learning from strangers: The art and method of qualitative interview studies.* New York: Free Press.

Weuve, C., Pitney, W. A., Martin, M., & Mazerolle, S. M. (2014). Athletic trainers in the collegiate setting. *Journal of Athletic Training, 49*(5), 696–705.

Wheeldon, J., & Ahlberg, M. (2012). *Visualizing social science research: Maps, methods, and meaning.* Thousand Oaks, CA: SAGE.

Whitaker, M. (2013, November 22). Stand your ground: Good for defense attorneys, bad for citizens. Available at *www.msnbc.com/politicsnation/stand-your-ground-who-it-helps-and-hurts.*

Whitfield, T. W. A. (2005). Aesthetics as pre-linguistic knowledge: A psychological perspective. *Design Issues, 21*(1), 3–17.

Whitted, K. S., & Dupper, D. R. (2007). Do teachers bully students?: Findings from a survey of students in an alternative education setting. *Education and Urban Society, 40*(3), 329–341.

Whittemore, R., Chase, S. K., & Mandle, C. L. (2001). Validity in qualitative research. *Qualitative Research, 11*(4), 522–532.

Wiebe, S., & Snowber, C. (2011). The visceral imagination: A fertile space for non-textual knowing. *Journal of Curriculum Theorizing, 27*(2), 101–113.

Wilder, J., Bertrand Jones, T., & Osborne-Lampkin, L. (in press). *Writing a literature review*. Rotterdam, The Netherlands: Sense Publishers.

Wolcott, H. (1994). *Transforming qualitative data: Description, analysis, and interpretation*. Thousand Oaks, CA: SAGE.

Wyatt, J. (2006). Psychic distance, consent, and other ethical issues: Reflections on the writing of "a gentle going?" *Qualitative Inquiry, 12*(4), 813–818.

Yin, R. (2006). Mixed methods research: Are the methods genuinely integrated or merely parallel? *Research in the Schools, 13*(1), 41–47.

Zylinksa, J. (2005). *The ethics of cultural studies*. New York: Continuum.

AUTHOR INDEX

SUBJECT INDEX

Note: *f* or *t* following a page number indicates a figure or a table.
Boldface indicates the term's entry in the Glossary.

ABOUT THE AUTHOR

Patricia Leavy, PhD, is an independent sociologist and former Chair of Sociology and Criminology and Founding Director of Gender Studies at Stonehill College in Easton, Massachusetts. She is the author, coauthor, or editor of over 20 books, and the creator and editor of seven book series. Known for her commitment to public scholarship, she is frequently contacted by the U.S. national news media and has regular blogs for *The Huffington Post, The Creativity Post,* and *We Are the Real Deal.* Dr. Leavy has received numerous awards for her work in the field of research methods, including the New England Sociologist of the Year Award from the New England Sociological Association, the Special Achievement Award from the American Creativity Association, the Egon Guba Memorial Keynote Lecture Award from the American Educational Research Association Qualitative Special Interest Group, and the Special Career Award from the International Congress of Qualitative Inquiry. In 2016, Mogul, a global women's empowerment platform, named her an "Influencer." Dr. Leavy delivers invited lectures and keynote addresses at universities and conferences. Her website is *www.patricialeavy.com.*